RADICAL PHILOSOPHY

2.12
Series 2 / Spring 2022

On not becoming Chinese
Jana Cattien — 3

Dismantling the apparatus of domination?
Claudia Aradau and Mercedes Bunz — 10

'Everything can be made better, except man'
Alberto Toscano — 19

Being, becoming, subsumption
Andrés Saenz de Sicilia — 35

What should feminist theory be?
An interview with Amia Srinivasan — 48

Defund culture
Gary Hall — 62

Reviews — 69

    Enzo Traverso, *Revolution: An Intellectual History*
    Hannah Proctor — 69

    Gilbert Simondon, *Individuation in light of notions of form and individuation*
    Gus Hewlett — 76

    Martin Jay, *Genesis and Validity*
    Mimi Howard — 83

    Keti Chukhrov, *Practicing the Good*
    Sascha Freyberg and Lukas Meisner — 86

    Natalia Romé, *For Theory: Althusser and the Politics of Time*
    Till Hahn — 90

    Mattin, *Social Dissonance*
    Mario Aguiriano — 93

    Fredric Jameson, *Allegory and Ideology*
    Stephen Morton — 96

    Anderson, Durkin and Brown, eds., *Raya Dunayevskaya's Intersectional Marxism*
    Senka Anastasova — 99

    Dario Gentili, *The Age of Precarity*
    Francois Zammit — 101

Dan Graham, 1942–2022. Partially reflective mirror-writing
Jeff Wall — 103

Sylvère Lotringer, 1937-2021
David Morris — 109

Response to Renault: The myth of *Aufheben*
Nigel Tubbs — 115

Editorial collective
Claudia Aradau
Brenna Bhandar
Victoria Browne
David Cunningham
Peter Hallward
Stewart Martin
Lucie Mercier
Daniel Nemenyi
Hannah Proctor
Rahul Rao
Martina Tazzioli
Chris Wilbert

Engineers
Daniel Nemenyi
Alex Sassmanshausen

Cover image
Panda Mery, *Looking for a shoe?*, 2020, https://gizmonaut.net/.

Creative Commons BY-NC-ND
Radical Philosophy, Spring 2022

ISSN 0300-211X
ISBN 978-1-914099-01-4

NEW FROM **CRMEP BOOKS**

Centre for Research in Modern European Philosophy

Afterlives
transcendentals, universals, others

Vocations of the political
Mario Tronti & Max Weber

Capitalism: concept, idea, image
Aspects of Marx's *Capital* today

Thinking art
materialisms, labours, forms

Afterlives is edited by Peter Osborne with contributions from Étienne Balibar, Antonia Birnbaum, Howard Caygill, Cooper Francis, Matt Hare, Marie Louise Krogh and Catherine Malabou. Forthcoming October 2022 as ebook direct from CRMEP or pb from your local bookshop.

www.kingston.ac.uk/faculties/kingston-school-of-art/research-and-innovation/crmep/crmep-books

On not becoming Chinese
The racialisation of compliance
Jana Cattien

As philosophy departments in the West come under greater pressure to provincialise themselves, calls to give 'non-Western' philosophical traditions their due have grown louder – and rightly so. But for all that is surely right about 'diversifying the curriculum' as a project driven by the relentless work of anti-racist and decolonial activists, the institutional co-optation of 'diversity' rhetoric continues to locate agency squarely within the 'West': 'we' must diversify what we teach, because 'we' have progressively come to understand the value of a diversified curriculum. This story suppresses an alternative reading, in which Western institutions 'diversify', not because they are progressively becoming better versions of themselves, but because they simply can no longer afford to ignore the economic, cultural and political importance of 'non-Western' nations, China and India in particular. Institutionalised 'diversity' discourse is, in this sense, not 'progress', but the attempt to recuperate as progress what is actually just realpolitik.

This reading might go some way to explaining why 'Orientalism' appears simultaneously as an obsolete and antiquated framework, at least in describing the current relationship between China and the West, and as timely as ever. Indeed, the growing incidence of racist violence against people of East Asian and Southeast Asian descent living in the West might be understood as a violent lashing out in defence of the very entitlement to Orientalism that is perceived as being undermined by China's new superpower status. Similarly, the repeated labelling of East Asians as carriers of the 'Chinese virus' can be read not only as a forceful renewal of 'yellow peril' tropes that associate East Asians with disease and bodily weakness, but also as a defence mechanism allowing Western governments to remain in denial about their own failures in caring for public health during the pandemic.

Ritualistic references to the anti-democratic and authoritarian nature of 'East Asian culture' are, as Shan-Jan Sarah Liu observes, an effective way of discrediting the relative success that East Asian countries have had in controlling the initial outbreak of Covid-19:[1]

> Many people have … said to me that Asia succeeds because Asians are just more collective and more obedient. The discourse is not about how Asians are unselfish; instead, it's about how we obey rules. 'Asian governments can make Asians do anything because they are not democratic', so to speak.[2]

However successful China and other East Asian countries may have been in the initial waves of the pandemic, this success will always be tainted by the 'evilness' of the culture that produced it.

The Covid-19 pandemic has only further intensified the need to emphasise the evil as a means of disavowing East Asia's relatively successful public health record. Alongside being hailed by the WHO as an 'exemplar of public health',[3] China was accused of having fabricated the coronavirus as an act of biological warfare against the West. Even where the spectre of Chinese 'evil' was not explicitly conjured as a threat to pandemic Europe and the United States, libertarian critics of community-based, low-tech public health measures such as lockdowns and universal mask-wearing were able to rely on a well-established association between 'Chineseness' on the one hand, and authoritarianism and compliance on the other. Lockdowns and face masks were not only said to generate an outward appearance of 'unfreedom' within otherwise liberal societies, but were also seen to betray an unfree and uncritical orientation of compliance presumed to eat away at liberal freedom *from the inside*. Where the racialisation of this compliance was not made explicit, as for example by using images of East Asians wearing face masks in pandemic reporting, it could instead be implicit, as in this critique of lockdowns and face masks:

> Sometimes, it can feel as though one's interlocutors live in another world, a place where different rules and standards apply, where different things seem obvious, and where certain facts are not up for debate at all ... When the gulf seems somehow too vast for critical debate to get off the ground, when you are struck by the uncanny feeling of encountering a perspective that is quite alien, maybe that's because they really are from another world.[4]

Here, the authors' opposition to lockdowns and face masks is given rhetorical weight by making the proponents of such measures appear through an already racialised imaginary of compliance as otherness. Those who agree with the measures are portrayed as inhabitants of a 'foreign' place in which authoritarianism rules, not democracy. Compliance is therefore not merely an undesirable trait ascribed to racialised Others, but a racialised threat that somehow lurks *within* the white liberal self as the possibility of its own demise. To comply might not mean to 'be Chinese', but it raises, even for white people, the terrifying possibility of becoming more and more *like* the Chinese.

'Yellow peril' and other diseases

We can find a precedent for this libertarian worry about compliance with Covid-19 measures in John Stuart Mill's classic liberal text *On Liberty*. Mill was worried that Europe was on the way to 'becoming another China' if Europeans did not cease to exhibit a desire for conformity and compliance otherwise found only in the 'East'. Like present-day libertarians, Mill diagnosed his own time with a worrying tendency towards compliance and sameness: 'There is one characteristic of the present direction of public opinion, peculiarly calculated to make it intolerant of any marked demonstration of individuality'.[5] 'These tendencies of the times', Mill went on to say, 'cause the public to be more disposed than at most former periods to prescribe general rules of conduct, and endeavour to make everyone conform to the approved standard'. Although Mill was not writing in the context of a global pandemic that is sometimes alleged to have originated in China, he was preoccupied with an 'Oriental virus' of a different sort: an epidemic of 'despotism' that had allegedly befallen 'the whole East'.[6] Deploying what Mel Y. Chen has called a 'master toxicity narrative' about China,[7] Mill evoked the racialised language of 'toxicity' to draw the contours of this 'Oriental despotism': 'Custom is there, in all things, the final appeal; justice and right mean conformity to custom; the argument of custom no one, unless some tyrant *intoxicated* with power, thinks of resisting'.[8]

The Orientalist image of a Chinese despot who is 'intoxicated with power' served to delineate Western conceptions of legitimate authority from the delirious tyranny that, in Mill's eyes, characterised the 'whole East'. According to David Porter, the rendering of Chineseness as a crazed culture of delirium is the product of a mid-eighteenth-century paradigm shift in European representations of China; a shift whereby China was no longer depicted as the 'home of ancient and universal truths', but instead as a 'site of capriciousness, folly and illusion'. The image of Mill's intoxicated tyrant is already foreshadowed in earlier European representations of Chinese emperors, such as the well-known 'Audience of the Emperor' tapestry from the 'Story of the Emperor of China' series.[9]

Manufactured in France in the early eighteenth century, this tapestry depicts the sumptuous menagerie of the Chinese Emperor, giving the impression not of a legitimate state authority, but of a crazed gathering of all manners of people and animals – including peacocks, dragons, exotic birds and an elephant. Although the 'Emperor seated amidst all this clutter still strikes an impressive pose', the 'overwhelming decadence of the decor ultimately distracts from his own glory'.[10] Just as the various animals and people depicted in the tapestry seem rather unfazed by the Emperor's presence, so too the viewer's gaze is invited to roam around the menagerie. Despite being at the centre, the Emperor can hold neither our gaze, nor the attention of those around him: he is reduced to 'the status of just another curio in the pastiche of exotic splendour that the scene presents'.[11]

Against the background of the tapestry, Mill's image of the 'intoxicated despot' evokes not just an authority that is, metaphorically speaking, 'poisoned' by tyranny, but an authority that is, literally, 'intoxicated' in the sense of delirious. Unlike the notion of 'toxicity' that Chen examines as a label repeatedly ascribed to China in general and Chinese consumer goods in particular – toxicity in the sense of 'contamination' – Mill's idea of 'intoxication' conjures a state of delirium invoked by various kinds of *excess*, both excessive behaviours and excessive states of minds. This association of Chineseness with delirium and excess is well-established: white residents and policy makers alike have long imaged Chinese communities in the West as hotbeds for the contraction and transmission of 'syphilis and leprosy, which was imagined to happen in direct contact with the Chinese, whether this contact was sexual or sensual in nature'.[12] A major cause for concern was the transmission of disease through the 'passing of opium pipes, from "lip to lip"', which was seen as a common pastime for residents of Chinatowns across the West.

The fact that East Asian people with face masks have been seen as *carriers* of Covid-19, rather than as making reasonable efforts to prevent its spread,[13] reflects the persistence of Orientalist associations of Chineseness with compliance and conformity, on the one hand, and disease and bodily weakness, on the other. Indeed, for Mill, the individual can be healthy only if their individuality is allowed to thrive; the Chinese 'tyranny' of uniformity and custom leads 'already energetic characters' to become 'merely traditional',[14] which he equates to weakness: 'Instead of great energies guided by *vigorous* reason, and *strong* feelings *strongly* controlled by a conscientious will, its result is *weak* feelings and *weak* energies, which therefore can be kept in outward conformity to rule without any *strength* either of will or of reason'.[15]

Read in this vein, the term 'yellow peril' emerges as a tautology: as a racialised marker of East Asianness, yellowness is associated with disease even before adding the word 'peril'. For eighteenth-century natural scientist Carl Linnaeus, the colour yellow was already 'more of a sickly yellow than a golden one. In both botany and medicine, his real areas of expertise, it was the colour of disease ...'.[16] As Michael Keevak shows, this semiotic shift in the colour yellow was directly linked to a 'new eighteenth-century Sinophobia that saw the Chinese no longer as white, civilised, morally superior, and capable of Christian conversion, but instead as pale yellow, despotic, stagnant and forever mired in pagan superstition'.[17] If, initially, the association of Chineseness with the colour yellow might have served to emphasise China's cultural proximity to Europe – when China was still, in Mill's words, 'a nation of much talent and, in some respects, even wisdom'[18] – over time 'yellowness' 'was redeployed as a term of complexional distance'.[19] Thus, the emphasis on proximity based on racialised phenotype ('not all Chinese are dark') gave way to a new narrative of racial otherness ('no Chinese is white').

On (not) becoming Chinese

It is somewhat ironic, then, that the very nation that has long been associated with disease and delirium should have garnered so much international praise for the public health measures that it has taken to contain the initial waves of the Covid-19 pandemic. China's 2020 morphing into an 'exemplar' of public health, at least in the eyes of the WHO, presents us with a scenario in which the question of Europe 'becoming another China' has become newly pressing – albeit this time against the backdrop of systematic shifts in the global balance of power from West to East.

For Mill, China was the centrepiece in a dialectics of mirroring in which Europe is propelled forward by encountering a negative mirror image of itself in the Chinese example. The imminent proximity of China's racial and cultural otherness served to underline the urgency of re-asserting our difference from them. As Hagar Kotef puts it, 'the claim that "we" (or some of "us") are (or may become) "like China" is provoked to demonstrate the urgency of change: "we" must remain different, must re-establish our difference, re-draw the proper boundaries, since what "they" do is horrible'.[20] According to Mill, the full extent of the horror that would await Europe if it ignored his warning could be gleaned in the Chinese custom of foot-binding. His worry that Europe might be on the path towards 'becoming another China' was framed as a concern over the increasing resemblance between the character of Europeans and 'a Chinese lady's foot': 'Its ideal of character is to be without any marked character; to maim, by compression, *like a Chinese lady's foot*, every part of human nature which stands out prominently'.[21]

According to Kotef, Mill deploys the image of the bound Chinese foot almost literally – to emphasise the East's *stagnation* as the negative mirror image of Europe's ability to move humanity forward: the bound Chinese feet 'came to signify ... the disfigurement that results from compression, from caging that which should be free to move or to serve as a vehicle of movement'.[22] However, like the contemporary discourse around compliance, the image of the bound Chinese foot not only provides a tangible contrast to European freedom (of movement), but also marks the potential for unfreedom that lies within Europe itself. Rather than situating this unfreedom solely in the 'East', the circulation of the image of the bound Chinese foot in Western political thought allows the spectre of immobility and stagnation to permeate Europe itself. The image takes on a life of its own, reminding Europe of the uncanny possibility that it may become a stranger to itself. As Kotef points out, this means that the very contrast between 'Eastern' stagnation and 'Western' mobility already contains within itself the seeds for a reversal in the balance of power between Europe and the East. To the extent that China, a nation which has stagnated in Mill's eyes, becomes the very motor that drives Europe to keep up with its own movement, the agency of locomotion is displaced from West to East: China is what is 'pushing Europe forward and away in its never-ending attempt to secure its difference'.[23]

China's high rates of economic growth, advanced technological governance and community-oriented public health strategies have not only made this shift in agency more pronounced; they have also transformed its underlying dynamic. To the extent that China has already 'caught up' with Europe, at least in terms of its share of the global economy and technological governance, the prospect of Europe's 'becoming another China' no longer makes sense as a warning about the future in the way that Mill deployed it. Rather than as an ominous prediction about Europe's future, the contemporary articulation of this narrative – that pandemic Europe risks becoming more and more compliant and uncritical (like China) – reads more nostalgically. It is nostalgia for an idealised past in which 'our' horror at the 'alienness' of compliance was still untroubled by the uncomfortable fact of 'our' waning superiority.

Discrediting China's community-oriented approach to public health by labelling it as authoritarian and inhumane is one way of keeping the horror alive. More generally, the ongoing association of Chineseness with compliance, conformity and disease is a way to preserve the predictive force of Mill's eighteenth-century warning, despite the inescapable reality of its growing obsolescence. Pointing at the 'Chinese virus' and at 'Chinese authoritarianism' allows Europe to hold onto the future that Mill once sketched – a future in which Europe progressively becomes a better version of itself, leaving behind both China and the version of itself that threatened to 'become like China'. In this sense, contemporary anti-Chinese racism serves to *defend*, rather than simply continue, the liberal exceptionalist story that Mill's eighteenth-century warning articulates: that the only way to be a flourishing, prosperous and powerful nation is to be like 'us'.

What's in a face?

But the point is not just to say that history has proven Mill wrong. In another sense, perhaps he was right: that no matter how much China and Europe resort to similar kinds of biopolitical and technological governance, 'Europe can never fully become like China'.[24] Europeans may move in dangerous proximity to the compliant Chinese, but they will never be compliant in the same way: 'A people, it appears, may be progressive for a certain length of time [the Chinese], and then stop: when does it stop? When it ceases to possess individuality. *If a similar change should befall the nations of Europe, it will not be in exactly the same shape ...*'.[25] The rhetoric that Mill deployed here is already a kind of insurance policy for the shift in the balance of power that we have seen in recent years. Even if Europe might have adopted compliance-oriented and authoritarian public health measures first adopted by China, there will always be an essential difference that prevents it from becoming as compliant and authoritarian as the Chinese.

Another way, then, to make sense of the proliferation of 'evil' China rhetoric in recent years is as a way of cashing in, as it were, on the insurance policy that Mill offered his readers in *On Liberty*. Ritualistic references to China's authoritarian, anti-democratic and communist evilness reinscribe the idea that the essential difference between China and the West must lie on the 'inside', at some immutable inner core – outward similarities notwithstanding. In Mill, what prevents Europe from moulding into the 'exact same shape' as China is presumably some inner essence that remains unchangeable even as Europe is befallen by a 'similar' change as China. He shows us that it is precisely in those moments where the distance between self and other threatens to disappear that it becomes necessary for the self to turn *inwards* in order to re-establish that distance.

A telling example of this defensive turn to an inner difference is Donald Trump's attitude to the face mask during the Covid-19 pandemic. Having long resisted wearing a face mask in public, even when everyone else was telling him to do so, he finally decided to wear one. But this concession was only possible to the extent that it allowed him to perform a kind of retreat into his quintessential American self: 'I had a mask on. I sort of liked the way I looked. OK. I thought it was OK. It was a dark black mask, and I thought it looked OK. It looked like the Lone Ranger'.[26] Unlike the image of East Asians wearing face masks in public, which were liberally used across Western media news outlets to accompany their pandemic reporting,[27] Trump's face mask symbolises not authoritarianism and a general demise of individual freedoms, but precisely his unwavering allegiance to radical individualism, frontiership and 'American culture'. The difference in this case comes not from the action itself, but from some essential quality presumed to reside *inside* the subject.

Following Vanita Seth's genealogy of the liberal face,[28] it is no coincidence that Trump should look to his face, of all places, for traces of the inner American hero. Long before the pandemic, Islamophobic panics over hijab, niqab and burqa already understood how to mobilise the supposed universal importance of the (visible and exposed) human face for anti-Muslim racism. In 2010, Philip Hollobone, the Conservative MP for Kettering in England went as far as to refuse meeting with constituents who do not want to remove their veil: 'God gave us faces to be expressible. It is not just the words we utter but whether we are smiling, sad, angry, or frustrated. You don't get any of that if your face is covered'.[29]

More recently, but along similar lines, Tucker Carlson informed *Fox News* readers of his disdain for face masks:

> What kind of person covers his face in public? Armed robbers do that sort of thing. So do Klansmen and radical Wahhabis. The rest of us don't do that. In fact, until recently, wearing a mask in public was illegal in many places. The assumption was if you're hiding who you are, you're up to something bad. It made people nervous. By our nature, we want to see each other. We need to see each other. Looking at another person's face is the beginning of connection. Eliminating that connection dehumanises us. That used to be obvious.[30]

In both quotes, the human face is hailed as a privileged site for the expression of an individuality that resides at the inner core of the white liberal subject. Yet, as Seth points out, the face has also become the focus for surveillance and disciplining regimes that seek to classify human faces into different 'types': racial types, criminal types and 'terrorist' types. Aided by the increasing use of facial recognition software, which China is widely criticised for using, the face of typology produces precisely the kind of constrained and schematic subjectivity that the face of individuality eschews.[31] In other words, the face of the criminal 'type' promises transparency and predictability where the face of individuality celebrates the expression of an 'ineffable, intangible, interiorised subject'[32] whose inner truth can only ever be gleaned through, but never reduced to, the face.

Echoing Mill's concern over the imminent loss of European individuality through encroaching ideals of sameness and uniformity, contemporary liberal scholars and activists demand that the increasing presence of facial recognition technologies and physiognomic theories of character 'types' 'must be countered through an assertion of individuality – the socially unencumbered, unique singularity, and complex interiority that is presumed foundational to our "human-ness"'.[33] Despite welcoming the political ethos of these liberal critiques, Seth nevertheless remains critical of the fact that liberal individualism is offered as the only legitimate alternative to typology:

> Such well-intentioned interventions – by journalists, activists and scholars – seeks to confront and challenge the disabling effects of typologies that disempower and stigmatise already marginalised populations. They do so by offering in opposition to typology (identified as immutable, collective, and dehumanising) a defense of individual subjectivity that is singular, agential, fluid, and possessed of a complex and unique interiority that is co-extensive with a universal humanity.[34]

Here too, the idea that there exists at the inner core of the liberal subject some unique essence works as a kind of defence mechanism against the increasing use of facial recognition technologies which posit the existence of 'facial types'. The liberal activists that Seth criticises are drawing on the same escape route that Mill offered to his European readers: even when the West is deploying the same facial recognition technologies that it is labelling China as authoritarian for using, the white liberal subject can always retreat into itself, reassuring itself that it will always remain different at heart no matter the kind of change that might befall it.

Although Mill does not explicitly mention the face as a symbol of individuality, already in *On Liberty* we see the association of Chineseness with homogeneity – the racist idea that the Chinese have succeeded in 'making all people alike'.[35] Unlike the faces of white Europeans, their faces do not suggest the presence of an intangible interiorised individuality, but instead, a homogenising sameness that lives on the surface of their body. For Mill, one outcome of this suffocating sameness, the product of a society in which everyone already 'resemble[s] one another',[36] is the Chinese custom of footbinding.[37] Footbinding represents for him, not only a 'barbaric' cultural practice, but more generally, an undesirable economy of the body in which nothing 'stands out prominently'[38] – *not even the face*. Thus, the 'bound Chinese foot' emerges as the product of a bodily schema in which compliance and conformity are imprinted on to the body in such a way that individuality cannot flourish inside – and thus also cannot manifest 'outside' – the subject. By contrast, the racially unmarked face can house individuality both on its body and, most crucially, inside itself.

Indeed, as Seth puts it, the liberal face of individuality is unique because it is able to transcend its own embodiedness, suggesting, without ever fully exposing, the presence of an 'ineffable, intangible, interiorised subject' – a subject without a body. In other words, the subject's individuality finds its most intimate expression in the face, but it is not reducible to this expression: 'This inner depth that fashions and grounds the individuality we call our own is precisely what the face is presumed to jealously guard, reluctantly betray or openly reveal ... The face secures the fact of our individuality by bearing witness to its expression'.[39] The face both is and is not the body; and that is precisely why it can guard an individuality that is outwardly expressed but ultimately resides at the ineffable inner core of the subject, where it remains protected from whatever threats lie either outside or within.

And so, if a similar change should befall the nations of Europe – increasing authoritarianism through the illiberal use of technological governance, widespread compliance with these increasingly authoritarian governments and a concomitant erosion of liberal individualist rights – still, it will never be exactly in the same shape as China.

Jana Cattien is Assistant Professor in Political and Social Philosophy at the University of Amsterdam. She holds a PhD from SOAS, University of London.

Notes

1. Since first writing this piece, the pandemic situation has changed significantly. Now, in March 2022, the Omicron variant is causing high numbers of infections across China, but the regime is still pursuing its zero-Covid strategy. This worked well at the beginning of the pandemic, but as the virus mutates to become more infectious and less dangerous, zero-Covid becomes harder to justify. Nevertheless, it is worth reflecting on the geopolitical implications of the early days of the pandemic, when China was – even if only for a brief period – widely praised for its public health strategy, and Western nations looked to imitate Chinese public health measures.
2. Nina Fang and Shan-Jan Sarah Liu, 'Critical Conversations: Being Yellow Women in the Time of Covid-19', *International Feminist Journal of Politics* 23:3 (2021), 4.
3. James Meek, 'The Health Transformation Army', *London Review of Books* 42:13 (July 2020).
4. Ian James Kidd and Matthew Ratcliffe, 'Welcome to Covidworld', *The Critic* (November 2020), https://thecritic.co.uk/issues/november-2020/welcome-to-covidworld.
5. John Stuart Mill, 'On Liberty', in *Classics of Moral and Political Theory*, ed. Michael L. Morgan (Indianapolis: Hacket Publishing Company, 1992), 912, 876.
6. Ibid., 876, 911.
7. Mel Y. Chen, 'Racialized Toxins and Sovereign Fantasies', *Discourse* 29:2&3 (2007), 369.
8. Mill, 'On Liberty', 911.
9. David Porter, 'Chinoiserie and the Aesthetics of Illegitimacy', *Studies in Eighteenth-Century Culture* 28 (1999), 33, 36.
10. Ibid., 35.
11. Ibid., 35.
12. Ibid., 371.
13. See for instance the social media campaign 'I Am Not A Virus', which documents and resists the increased incidence of anti-Asian violence in the context of the pandemic. See also Fang and Liu (2021), 5: 'I was worried about wearing masks when I was out because it still wasn't a norm at that time. As an East Asian, I really didn't feel safe wearing a mask when I was out because there had already been incidents where East Asians had been beaten up for carrying the "Chinese virus" or the "Kung flu".'
14. Mill, 'On Liberty', 910.
15. Ibid. (my emphases).
16. Michael Keevak, *Becoming Yellow: A Short History of Racial Thinking* (Princeton: Princeton University Press, 2011), 36.
17. Ibid.
18. Mill, 'On Liberty', 911.
19. Keevak, *Becoming Yellow*, 34.
20. Hagar Kotef, 'Little Chinese Feet Encased in Iron Shoes: Freedom, Movement, Gender, and Empire in Western Political Thought', *Political Theory* 43:3 (2015), 350.
21. Mill, 'On Liberty', 910.
22. Kotef, 'Little Chinese Feet', 349.
23. Ibid., 350.
24. Mill, 'On Liberty', 912.
25. Mill, 'On Liberty', 911 (my emphasis).
26. Amer Madhani and Darlene Superville, 'Trump says he looks like Lone Ranger in a Mask and likes it', *The Washington Post* (July 2020). An enduring presence in mainstream American culture, the Lone Ranger is a fictional Texas Ranger, who fought outlaws in the American Old West to restore law and order.
27. For a good overview of instances of anti-Asian racism in Covid-19 news reporting, see this useful compilation by the Asian-German network *korientation*: https://www.korientation.de/medienkritik/corona-rassismus-medien.
28. Vanita Seth, 'Faces of the Self', *Journal of Race, Ethnicity, and Politics* 5:2 (2020).
29. Hollobone cited in Seth, 'Faces', 250.
30. Tucker Carlson, 'The cult of mask-wearing grows, with no evidence that they work', *Fox News* (October 2020).
31. This is a complex issue in its own right, which I cannot attend to here in the detail that it deserves. See Ruha Benjamin's *Race after Technology* (London: Polity Press, 2019) for an in-depth exploration of how these facial recognition technologies reproduce racist power relations. As she highlights, the face of the non-white other is a crucial site for the production of criminality: white faces are innocent; Black and brown faces signal violent and criminal intentions.
32. Seth, 'Faces of the Self', 257.
33. Ibid., 268-269.
34. Ibid., 270.
35. Mill, 'On Liberty', 912.
36. Ibid.
37. See Dorothy Ko's revisionist history of footbinding for reflections on the question of what it might mean to treat the feet as important sites for the generation of social and political meaning. For instance, Ko cites a woman in Shandong providence who told her interviewer that 'Match-makers were not asked "Is she beautiful?" but "How small are her feet?" A plain face is given by heaven but poorly bound feet are a sign of laziness'. Ko, *Cinderella's Sisters: A Revisionist History of Footbinding* (Berkeley: University of California Press, 2007), 3.
38. Mill, 'On Liberty', 912.
39. Seth, 'Faces of the Self', 257.

Dismantling the apparatus of domination?
Left critiques of AI
Claudia Aradau and Mercedes Bunz

In November 2021, over 140 Artificial Intelligence (AI) researchers signed a letter asking the German government to oppose developments in autonomous weapons systems. With this they attempted to draw distinctions between beneficial and destructive AI: 'Just as most chemists and biologists have no interest in building chemical or biological weapons, most AI researchers have no interest in building AI weapons – and do not want others to tarnish their field'.[1] Yet these distinctions are difficult to maintain, as the lines between productive and destructive, human and machine, science and military have long been blurred. The letter also speaks to a public epistemology of fear, which highlights a particular type of AI or a particular weaponised use as dangerous for humanity, peace or democracy. While many public debates about AI propose to draw (impossible) lines, critiques of AI on the left have focused on disrupting those lines. In this intervention, we discuss how power and labour have informed critiques of AI, which have emerged on the left, before turning to a situation where these critiques format the political practice of working with and upon AI.

Left critiques of AI have shown that public discourses and debates, such as the one above, conceal other lines, which are constitutive of how AI is produced and circulates, and how it deeply infuses our current conjuncture. Clear lines between humans and machines obscure the distinction between what Sylvia Wynter has called 'this or that genre of being human'.[2] The separation between production and destruction obfuscates the lines between what counts as productive, non-productive and unproductive. Finally, the lines between science and the military distract from how labour is mobilised and circulates between the two worlds. Critiques of AI have tried to make these 'other' lines visible and shed light on the many forms of algorithmic injustice and even dehumanisation, uncover labour issues in the production of AI technologies, or reveal the energy consumption of large-scale AI models and their extractive logics. These critiques situate AI at the heart of contemporary capitalism and its violence. But are these critiques a much-needed correction of existing AI, or do they need to resist the ongoing optimisation of AI? Do they amount to an AI abolitionist perspective? Or, conversely, are progressive versions of AI needed or even possible? What aspects need to be considered from a left perspective, when it comes to the politics of AI?

Debating the role of technology as political is a well-known left theoretical problem, of course. While early readings of Marx assumed that the political functioning of technology was a simple question of property rights and that 'dialectics' would purge technology of any class structure, the Frankfurt School explicitly questioned this assumption.[3] Herbert Marcuse, who articulated those scruples about the role of modern technology most clearly, wrote that '[s]pecific purposes and interests of domination are not foisted upon technology "subsequently" and from the outside; they enter the very construction of the technical apparatus'. He argued against a straightforward appropriation, as '[t]echnology is always a historical-social project: in it is projected what a society and its ruling interests intend to do with men and things'.[4] Technology and technological rationality were part of an 'all-embracing apparatus of domination'.[5] Yet if technological rationality was the contemporary form of domination, technics as instruments or techniques could become part of different political projects, of repression as well as liberation. From the 1941 reflections on 'Some Social Implications of Modern Technology' to *One-Dimensional Man*, Marcuse mobilised the ambivalence of technics as an intervention against the technological rationality of domination. 'Technics', he argued, 'as a universe of instrumentalities, may increase the weakness as well as the power of man'.[6] Contemporary critiques of AI have focused on this apparatus of domination, one which is foremost driven by capitalism and colonialism. The language of AI itself is used to signify technological rationality and market value rather than as a definition of a specific range of technics.

In its current form, AI technology is indeed primarily seen as a profit-making machine: the technologies that advanced contemporary AI – machine learning and deep neural networks – have become new means of production as much as phantasmas fuelling speculation.[7] Even though we are a few years into the hype of AI, forecasts still predict a financial growth of irrational dimensions for this technology, which is projected by some in the 'trillions'. Yet the current situation looks a little different. For 2021, the actual economic impact seemed quite low, at least if one wants to believe the McKinsey survey from the same year.[8] Only 27% of the over 1,500 participants they approached in the business world indicated that AI contributes to up to 5% of earnings before interest and taxes, and 5% is not much to begin with.

Despite this, the promise of profit continues to lead to abundant capital for start-ups as well as to a race for AI patents; the corporation that holds the most is currently IBM with over 5,538 patents, followed by Microsoft and Samsung.[9] Alongside these companies, the Chinese Academy of Sciences, Tencent and Baidu also rank high in holding machine learning and AI patents. Thus, in a report on AI by the National Security Commission in the US, patents are translated into the language of an arms race between the US and China. At over 700 pages, the report of the Commission mentions 'China' 604 times. Best known for being chaired by former Google CEO Eric Schmidt, the Commission entangles military and markets under the claim that China's plans, resources and progress should concern all Americans as '[China] is an AI peer in many areas and an AI leader in some applications. We take seriously China's ambition to surpass the United States as the world's AI leader within a decade'.[10] To become a leader in these economic and military markets, however, also means turning a blind eye to the many effects of the production, circulation and consumption of AI technologies, whose most recent hype is based on advances in machine learning.

In the field of machine learning, so-called 'deep neural network architecture' made it possible to classify language, images or other symbols more successfully than in computational attempts that have been made before. Older methods struggled with the ambiguity of symbols – what is said in a sentence or what is depicted in an image. Their meaning could not be made calculable until the computation of AI underwent a paradigm change: with deep neural networks, programmers do not write the rules of an algorithmic model anymore. Instead, they build a computer architecture, a network of nodes based on statistical analysis, through which they run large amounts of data from which an algorithmic model is then inferred. The statistical correlations of data points showed as highly successful: algorithms trained on large amounts of data could make classifications or predictions with a higher success rate than before. The meaning of symbols could now be calculated, but that did not mean that they performed flawlessly. Despite their errors, task-orientated AI programmes have been put into actual use from assisting typing on our phones by suggesting words to London's Metropolitan Police's operational use of live or retrospective facial recognition.[11] AI-powered weapon technologies also rely on image recognition of objects and targets in real-time video streaming from drones and other technologies of surveillance. Moreover, these implementations, often premature applications of programmes that did not undergo independent reviews or testing, amplify and intensify the existing apparatus of domination, as Marcuse would put it. AI may be a new technology, but it emerges from and works upon existing distributions of power. Yet, power has only recently come to feature in critiques of AI, even on the left.

In the history of AI, internal critique has always played a substantial role, ever since Alan Turing asked in 1950 the question 'Can machines think?'[12] These internal critiques, however, have focused less on power and political economy, but have circled around the philosophical question of whether computers, which are executing a programme, have a 'mind' or 'consciousness'. Indeed, these considerations were revived in contemporary AI under a new keyword, that of a much debated 'general AI'. They were also revived through public epistemologies of catastrophe, such as Nick Bostrom's *New York Times* bestseller *Superintelligence* published in 2014. The overall argument – and effect – of this and other publications along those lines is geared towards imagining the future of AI as a catastrophe to come. AI – not just as a potential general AI but even in its supposedly 'weaker' or specific AI form – propels autonomous weapons and leads to loss of human control. Set up in a binary and technophobic way, this discourse of AI catastrophe minimises human agency, downplays the redrawing of lines within humanity and the legacy of struggles that have challenged these lines and recast the very understanding of the human. While warning about AI and implementing a much-needed distrust, these discourses of catastrophe always already have the effect of deterring any engagement in the present.

Therefore, this discourse that bound critical capacities to a catastrophe to come meant that in the meantime the development of real-world AI progressed undisturbed – at least for a while. The so-called 'weak AI' – AI applications that function as long as they target very specific and narrow areas – became a central part of our informational infrastructure so much so that AI has been described as a 'general purpose technology'. Critiques of AI soon started to catch up with this development. Science and technology studies scholar Lucy Suchman has argued that we need to demystify AI and avoid reproducing discourses of AI as a 'thing' or as a 'coherent and novel field of technology development'.[13] Suchman's point can be seen in the discourse of catastrophe, a discourse profoundly based on AI as a 'thing' taking over. While AI is not capable of a generality recognised in human intelligence (some would say 'yet'), the contemporary critique of AI has become strongest in a different field, that of political economy. Suchman offers such a redefinition of AI, which emphasises data and data work. For her, AI is 'a cover term for a range of technologies of data processing and techniques of data analysis based on the iterative adjustment of relevant parameters, according to some combination of internally and externally generated feedback'.[14] The human-machine relation is not a dual one, but one which is formed within capitalist relations of production and reproduction. From the material means of production such as the often-outsourced preparation of the data for the operations of machine learning algorithms, to the societal effects of its application, with bias being programmed into its functioning, critiques of

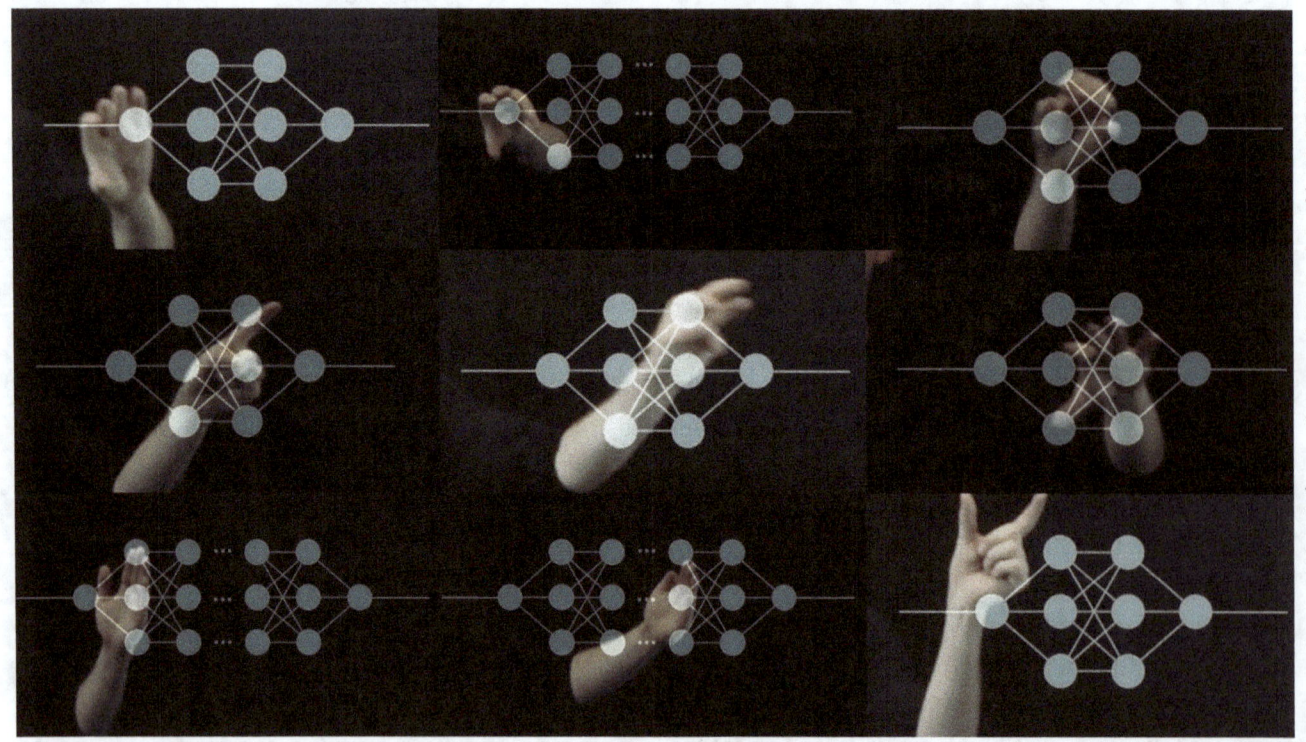

Image: Alexa Steinbrück, 'Better Images of AI', *Explainable AI*, CC-BY 4.0.

AI shed light on contemporary capitalism and its violence. But to what extent is this critique of AI effective? Where are its limits? And to what extent are those critiques pointing beyond capitalism and articulating perspectives from the left?

Power

The critique of power addresses AI as an apparatus of domination and traces the technology through the production of data – data collected by corporations thriving in so-called 'platform capitalism' as well as by the state and its repressive agencies. Power emerges in multiple forms, from the historicity of data, its extraction by corporations and the state, its valorisation and the effects of surveillance and oppression it creates. What statisticians and computer scientists refer to as bias is created by training data reflecting historical or social inequities. When gathering training data, specific groups – such as people of colour, minorities or women – are often underrepresented. They might have been overlooked in the process of data sampling or during the testing of the AI technology. This 'prototypical whiteness' that renders racialised subjects invisible is entwined with surveillance technologies that render them hypervisible, as Simone Browne has shown.[15] For example, a dataset called 'Faces in the Wild', which had long been considered as a benchmark for testing facial recognition software, now comes with the warning that its data is not representative – 70% of the faces are male and 80% white, as digital activist Joy Buolamwini found out.[16] And even if values representing race, gender, sexual orientation or class are removed, AI models, always looking for patterns, turn to proxy discrimination using statistical correlations of postcodes, education or particular expressions to discriminate. As Wendy Chun pointed out in her study *Discriminating Data*: 'These "errors" often come from "ignoring" race – that is, wrongly assuming that race-free equals racism-free'.[17]

To ensure that we are not going to be governed like this, a range of organisations and institutions have been set up: critical work regarding bias is being done at the Data Justice Lab in Cardiff; at Joy Buolamwini's Algorithmic Justice League devoted to the unmasking of AI bias and harms; at the Ida B. Wells Just Data Lab founded by Ruha Benjamin; at NYU's AI Now Institute or the Distributed AI Research Institute (DAIR).[18] DAIR was founded in 2021 by the computer scientist Timnit Gebru, after being fired from her position as Google's co-lead of the Ethical Artificial Intelligence Team for criticising large language models. While these institutions rely on university and funding infrastructures of the Global North, organisations like Coding Rights in Latin America have developed a feminist and decolonial critique of AI.[19] Rather than catastrophist imaginaries of the future, these institutions aim to develop institutional and organisational counter-power to ensure that AI systems are accountable to the communities and contexts in which they are applied.

As power and domination are built into AI technologies through the data that makes algorithmic operations possible, this critique has left activists and theorists puzzling over the systems themselves. For instance, following her firing from Google, Timnit Gebru reflected in a media interview on the dilemmas of addressing bias in a system and the critique of the system itself.[20] Gebru's dilemma emerges from the entanglement of invisibility and hypervisibility of racialised subjects. It is also a dilemma of the many ways in which power operates, where an AI technology that reduces or erases racial bias remains a technology of power, one which renders marginalised and oppressed communities hypervisible and subject to intensified surveillance, policing or other lethal interventions. Here again, AI seems to blur the lines, this time between critiquing the system and the paradoxical effect of supporting the system through that critique.

This paradox can, for example, be seen when it comes to algorithms misidentifying people of colour. In September 2020, in the midst of the Covid-19 pandemic, the case of a professor whose head kept getting removed every time he tried to use a virtual background on Zoom went viral.[21] The issue: the professor was not white. Videochat software relies on facial recognition to determine what parts of the screen should show the background image while leaving the head of the user visible. In this case, the head wasn't detected, because whiteness was used as the software's default for the recognition of a human. This kind of racism in media recognition has a long history. Photographic media have always been 'developed with white people in mind and habitual use and instruction continue in the same vein, so much so that photographing non-white people is typically construed as a problem', as noted by Richard Dyer and others.[22] While many challenged the misrecognition of people of colour, others worried that optimising facial recognition for people of colour also always means to optimise a system of whiteness, one that is quite likely to be turned at some point against people of colour.

Some critics are therefore opposed to this optimisation that discourses of data and algorithmic bias entail. For instance, Ramon Amaro has made the argument that, while such aims 'might widen the scope of machine perception, not to mention the participation of excluded bodies in techno-social ecologies, the solution, as proposed, reinforces the presupposition that coherence and detectability are necessary components of human-techno relations.'[23] Amaro reminds us that an optimisation of algorithms more or less confirms 'what features represent the categories of human, gender, race, sexuality, and so on', but it does not change them, thus pointing to a political dilemma well known within left politics: do progressive demands simply patch the cracks of a system prolonging its existence, or does an engagement with those cracks change the system itself? While the 'ethics washing' of companies (i.e. faking an exaggerated interest in certain issues as a way of getting around regulation) is a real problem, the question remains of what engagement from the left is necessary.

Critiques of power have shown that contemporary technologies of AI, always looking for and multiplying differences, are haunted by a racist-colonialist and classist past, and not only regarding its functioning. Yet these critics are also struggling with the dilemma of AI politics, as the institutes and organisations they lead depend on research funders, donors and universities. The critique of labour, while entwined with the critique of power, has opened different political interventions and ways of not being governed like that. From the statistical focus on bias, the legal language of discrimination and political mobilisation against entrenched inequalities and distributions of humanity, this other critique of AI moved to the 'hidden abodes of production'.[24]

Labour

At an expo dedicated to big data and AI in London, IBM argued that AI 'takes the machine out of the human'.[25] Rather than fears of replacing humans by machines, tech companies reproduce imaginaries of human creativity and authenticity liberated from machinic-like labour. Neda Atanasoski and Kalindi Vora have argued that these imaginaries of machine labour reproduce AI as a 'surrogate' technology, a lesser human.[26] These 'surrogate' technologies do not in fact replace the repetitive labour that some humans are called to do, but they are intensifying the repetitive and machine-like labour which has come to be known as 'microwork'. AI relies on globally dispersed, unpaid or underpaid labour of data cleaning, categorising and featurising. 'But in reality', Phil Jones reminds us, 'the magic of machine learning is the grind of data labelling'.[27] There is no AI without training data, and as training and testing datasets become increasingly massive, they need to be cleaned, curated and improved. This work is done by millions of microworkers, mostly in the Global South. As geographers Mark Graham and Mohamed Amir Anwar have shown, given 'the geographically untethered nature of digital tasks, workers from different parts of the world can potentially compete, thus creating a planetary market for digital labour'.[28] Rather than seeing AI as a high-tech autonomous weapons system that is a killer robot, or an automated facial recognition system – i.e. as a coherent 'thing' Suchman cautioned against – AI is a distributed socio-technical system that is always already produced, circulated, maintained and repaired through dispersed, intensive and underpaid labour.

These microworkers often disappear from analyses of labour, as resistance to AI developments has focused on the mobilisation and unionisation of tech workers. In 2018, over 4,000 Google employees protested against Google's involvement in project Maven, a US Department of Defence project that aimed to automate the analysis of video images from drones.[29] In 2019, Microsoft workers asked the company to cancel a contract with the US army to develop augmented reality technology 'designed to help people kill'.[30] More radically, #NoTechforICE moved beyond resistance to militarisation to expand protest and mobilisation against 'the detention and deportation machinery but also to policing and military operations, endangering the safety and security of communities already vulnerable to criminalisation, from the Bronx to Compton to the southern border'.[31] While the protest focused on labour mobilisation and organisation at the big tech companies in the US, the labour of microworkers remains invisible. The data 'cleaner' becomes the other of the tech worker. Moreover, the dispersed and invisibilised data workers reactivate Marxist fears of the fragmentation of labour. Data cleaning jobs are often part of the gig economy, which has given rise to a new social class forced to live a precarious existence often slipping through the welfare net or finding themselves outside it, and always facing a lack of job security. For Jones, the stakes couldn't be higher: 'that the wretched and the precarious, left disorganised, fall under the thrall of reactionary elements, or else are prone to riot intermittently at the system's edges'.[32] Unlike Jones, Verónica Gago has reclaimed the political potential of the feminist strike to reveal 'the diverse composition of labour in a feminist register, by recognising historically disregarded tasks, by showing its current imbrication with generalised precarious conditions, and by appropriating a traditional tool of struggle to reinvent what it means to strike'.[33] Gago's call for reinventing struggle is also a call for the redefinition of labour in ways that attend to the 'differential of exploitation'.

A recent report by the International Labour Organisation (ILO) highlights these differentials of exploitation when it comes to migrant crowdworkers.[34] While global data is not available, there are estimates that indicate that 17% of workers on online web-based platforms are migrants. For migrant workers who have been excluded from employment or experience discrimination and limitations of access to labour markets, digital work becomes 'simultaneously a site of degradation and one of opportunity for those who have little viable alternatives'. Yet, refugees experience different forms of exploitation to other microworkers, both due to citizenship and global differentials of pay and power. As the ILO report points out, 'freelancers who label data and train algorithms that power AI technology do so mostly without access to a fair wage or basic benefits'.[35] Therefore, beyond concerns about the lack of collective action given the dispersal and isolation of microworkers, research with refugees on digital work has shown that their precarity of digital labour is reinforced through the precarity of their lack of status and multiple exclusions. For instance, refugees often cannot be paid because PayPal, a platform regularly used for payments, does not operate in certain countries. Some are blocked 'due to international sanctions against financial transactions with certain nationalities'.

In Bangladesh, official identification and biometric information are required to buy a SIM card, thus excluding the Rohingya refugees from accessing SIM cards for mobile phones, except through informal markets.[36]

If the move from AI as a 'thing' to data-work sheds light on the differentials of exploitation, another term, widely used now by tech companies, alerts us to how tech companies recast questions of labour. XaaS means 'anything as a service'. XaaS renders the ideology of tech companies, where everything can become a service: platform as a service, software as a service, cloud as a service, and as Jeff Bezos infamously put it, humans as a service. And now: AI as a service. The language of service is not a new one and it belies the claims of unprecedented development and innovation that AI now circulates across private and public realms. Large tech companies with a tendency to monopolise the development of AI such as Google, IBM or Nvidia increasingly tout their technologies as services advantaged by their massive technical infrastructure and high-skilled workers. Nick Srnicek argues that these companies aim to shape AI as a utility in the form of a pre-existing, bookable service or of a tool developed to assist other companies to run AI and build their own for a fee.[37] And at the moment it looks as if their dominance will continue – at least until new research breaks the trend for pretrained models developed on very large neural networks, which currently still deliver better accuracy. 'Mega indexes (are) tracing the outline of capital today', as Leif Weatherby and Brian Justie put it.[38] The language model GPT-3 developed in 2020 by OpenAI/Microsoft has a capacity of 175 billion machine learning parameters and was trained on 500 billion words.[39] Its estimated carbon emissions during training are massive with 552 metric tons of CO_2, a number that has been linked to the greenhouse gas emissions of the average running of 120 US cars over one year, to put it into human perspective.[40] As a reaction, critical research into Green AI tries to find ways to create AI systems that are using fewer resources while being at the same time more inclusive, running again into the same dilemma of AI optimisation.

However, so far the trend of large companies acting as AI providers and offering AI as a service has not shown signs of abating. This has consequences for the labour linked to AI. Describing AI as XaaS blurs the distinctions between productive, unproductive and reproductive labour. The language of 'service' has been rehabilitated in public imaginaries of health and welfare services. Situating AI within the service sector rather than the manufacturing sector not only effaces microworkers and crowdworkers, but also obscures the multiplication of labour statuses and the blurring of boundaries between different forms of labour. As feminist accounts of service work remind us, we need to reflect upon the ways in which the racial division of labour 'protects white male privilege in institutional settings'.[41] Rather than the public value of service unencumbered by exploitation, AI technologies are produced through the unpaid and underpaid labour of workers whose domination is entrenched through the lines of race and gender.

Another politics

The open-source computer vision project VFRAME was developed to assist human rights research. It currently works with an archive of digital information from conflict zones run by the NGO *Mnemonic*.[42] *Mnemonic* is dedicated to the collection and preservation of digital information from conflict zones, so that it can be used in struggles over accountability and justice. Syria is one of the places for which the organisation archives and preserves digital documentation of human rights violations, war atrocities and international crimes.[43] The project with *Mnemonic* started in 2017 and was founded by the artist and digital activist (and/or software developer) Adam Harvey. The VFRAME project includes coder Jules LaPlace and 3D-designer Josh Evans as well as a group of friends and contributors in Berlin with the help of some funding. Emerging out of discussions between researchers, digital activists and investigative journalists, VFRAME was created to assist human rights researchers, for whom the massive scale of the visual data in those archives is a challenge. Finding or paying experts trained to recognise illegal munitions, who can review thousands of hours of footage material, was not possible. Researchers were also aware of the need to avoid the 'vicarious trauma' of going through this massive visual data. This is why the group worked on the development of an AI model that detects and flags up the existence of cluster munitions. The group was interested in showing that 'cluster' munitions – more specifically RBK-250 – were used on civilian populations. The Convention on Cluster Munitions prohibits their use, development, production, acquisition, stockpiling or transfer.[44] Syria, Russia and the US are not signatories to the Convention.

The labour that comes with this is elaborate. It can involve running the AI model through thousands of videos to find example munitions, then going through those manually to find the ones that might be good for testing data and scoop those out. The found images that are of high quality are put onto an annotation platform. Collaborators and friends then do the work to draw exact boxes around them to allow the algorithm to identify and learn what it is supposed to look at – here data cleaning is a collective effort. The newly cleaned data is then folded back into the project benchmarking data to evaluate the models trained on synthetic data. Over many iterations, the AI algorithm learns to detect the munition better and better. Since all of the objects are rare, the use of 3D modelling to create training data has been a gamechanger. The 3D models are placed into environments that simulate conflict zones and then rendered into thousands of photorealist images for use as training data.

VFRAME needs technical teamwork such as that described above to create an AI model which can subvert the intention to keep war atrocities and involvements hidden from view. For this, data needs to be gathered as well as labelled. In areas in which there is no training data, computers remain blind. 'Training datasets are the lifeblood of artificial intelligence', Adam Harvey wrote in his essay on 'Computer Vision'.[45] 'They are so vital to the way computer vision models understand visual input that it may be helpful to reconsider the algorithms as data-driven code …', he went on to explain. The existence of a dataset can make the difference between what can be detected, seen and interpreted and what cannot. It is here where AI models leave room to subvert the capitalist way of seeing. Projects like VFRAME, and also Forensic Architecture's project 'Triple Chaser' to name another example,[46] intervene by creating data.

For us, another politics of AI is at stake in VFRAME, which entwines the critique of power and the critique of labour. While the discourse of evidence and documentation framed in legal terms is also present, as Martina Tazzioli and Daniele Lorenzini have argued about Forensic Architecture, we are particularly interested in the politics of collective organisation and labour.[47] It can be read as a form of counter-power emerging from the motley collective of international activism. At the same time, it also recasts and renders visible the composition of labour. Interfering in the existing data economy that follows capitalist aims, their AI models detect aspects that ruling interests would have preferred to remain hidden. These projects show that in a world administered by algorithms, it does matter what the algorithms can do. And they also show that 'another AI' is possible. Behind the hype about automation through AI models one finds the much more real politics of datasets deciding what can be detected, and what can remain unseen. Or in Adam Harvey's words: 'Becoming training data is political'.

Despite Marcuse's concerns that the ruling interests are projected into the apparatus of technological domination, VFRAME explicitly configures AI as a political intervention. In that sense, Marcuse's distinction between technology and technics is helpful here to render 'another politics of AI' and to differentiate its material-functional aspect (technics) from its ideological framework (technology). As we have seen, unlike technological control and domination, technics are part of technological rationality but they 'can promote authoritarianism as well as liberty, scarcity as well as abundance, the extension as well as the abolition of toil'.[48] Building on the long history of feminist engagement with technology, Helen Hester has more recently cautioned against the work of foreclosure: it is important to reclaim and reposition technical practice as 'one potential sphere of activist intervention'.[49]

Interventions by activists such as VFRAME show that assembling AI as subversive technics and a critical technical practice that moves the field towards another politics of AI is possible. Instead of reiterating futures of AI catastrophe, which reify the power of professionals that can guard the lines between human and machine, military and science, production and destruction, another politics of AI emerges at the interstices of political struggles across borders, efforts at organising and developing common infrastructures away from tech corporations, and collective contribution to data. These AI politics intervene in capitalistic violence by performing a labour of subversion in the present, dismantling forms of contemporary domination.

This labour of subversion that mobilises the ambivalence of technics does not mean that we should stop debating AI-powered weapons. Rather, returning to the letter of the German scientists with which we started, it means that left analyses of AI need to hold together power, labour and domination. AI-powered weapons materialise the destructive productivity of AI. They thrive on the labour of unpaid, underpaid and displaced populations around the world and intensify hierarchies of humanity. Examples like VFRAME show that another AI cutting through the capitalistic ideological framework thriving on misery unfolds in the here and now.

Claudia Aradau is Professor of International Politics at King's College London and a member of the editorial collective of Radical Philosophy. *Mercedes Bunz is Reader in Digital Culture and Society at the Department of Digital Humanities, King's College London, and an editor of the Open Access* meson press. *Her work explores the digital transformation of knowledge, and its effect on power.*

Notes

1. 'AI researchers call upon new German government to back autonomous weapons treaty (2021), https://autonomousweapons.org/ai-researchers-call-upon-new-german-government-to-back-autonomous-weapons-treaty/.
2. Sylvia Wynter, 'Unsettling the Coloniality of Being/Power/Truth/Freedom: Towards the Human, after Man, Its Overrepresentation – an Argument'. *CR: The New Centennial Review* 3:3 (2003), 272.
3. Monika Reinfelder, 'Breaking the Spell of Technicism', in *Outlines of a Critique of Technology*, ed. Phil Slater (London: Ink Links, 1980): 9–37.
4. Herbert Marcuse, *Negations: Essays in Critical Theory* (London: May Fly, 1968), 168.
5. Herbert Marcuse and Douglas Kellner, *Technology, War and Fascism: Collected Papers of Herbert Marcuse, Volume 1* (London: Routledge, 2004), 77.
6. Herbert Marcuse, *One-Dimensional Man* (Boston: Beacon Press, 1964), 165.
7. See Justin Joque, *Revolutionary Mathematics: Artificial Intelligence, Statistics and the Logic of Capitalism* (London: Verso Books, 2022), 200–01.
8. Michael Chui et al, 'The State of AI in 2021 [report]' (New York: McKinsey, 2021), 2, available at: https://www.mckinsey.com/business-functions/mckinsey-analytics/our-insights/global-survey-the-state-of-ai-in-2021.
9. https://www.statista.com/statistics/1032627/worldwide-machine-learning-and-ai-patent-owners-trend/.
10. National Security Commission on Artificial Intelligence (NSCAI), 'Final Report. National Security Commission on Artificial Intelligence' (2021), 2, available at: https://www.nscai.gov/
11. For a discussion of the impossibility of eliminating error in machine learning, see Matteo Pasquinelli, 'How a Machine Learns and Fails: A Grammar of Error for Artificial Intelligence',

Spheres: Journal for Digital Cultures 5 (2019), 1–17; Claudia Aradau and Tobias Blanke, 'Algorithmic Surveillance and the Political Life of Error', *Journal of the History of Knowledge* 2:1 (2021).

12. Alan M. Turing, 'Computing Machinery and Intelligence', *Mind: A Quarterly Review of Psychology and Philosophy*, vol. LIX/236 (1950), 433.

13. Lucy Suchman, 'Six Unexamined Premises Regarding Artificial Intelligence and National Security', AI Now Institute, 2021, https://medium.com/@AINowInstitute/six-unexamined-premises-regarding-artificial-intelligence-and-national-security-eff9f06eea0.

14. Lucy Suchman, 'AI at the Edgelands: Data Analytics in States of In/Security', UC San Diego, The Design Lab, YouTube.

15. Simone Browne, *Dark Matters: On the Surveillance of Blackness* (Durham, NC: Duke University Press, 2015).

16. Priyanka Boghani, 'Artificial Intelligence Can Be Biased. Here's What You Should Know', *PBS*, 2019, https://www.pbs.org/wgbh/frontline/article/artificial-intelligence-algorithmic-bias-what-you-should-know/

17. Wendy Hui Kyong Chun, *Discriminating Data. Correlation, Neighbourhoods, and the Politics of Recognition* (Cambridge, MA: The MIT Press, 2021), 2.

18. See: datajusticelab.org; ajl.org; thejustdatalab.com; ainowinstitute.org; dair-institute.org.

19. Coding Rights, https://linkme.bio/codingrights/.

20. Amanpour and Company, 'Fmr. Google Insider on Whistleblowers, Unions and AI Bias', 16 December 2021, YouTube.com.

21. Colin Madland, 'A faculty member has been asking how to stop Zoom from removing his head when he uses a virtual background. We suggested the usual plain background, good lighting etc, but it didn't work. I was in a meeting with him today when I realised why it was happening', 19 September 2019, Twitter.

22. Richard Dyer, *White: Twentieth Anniversary Edition* (London: Routledge, [1997] 2017), 89.

23. Ramon Amaro, 'As If', eflux (2019), https://www.e-flux.com/architecture/becoming-digital/248073/as-if/

24. Karl Marx, *Capital, Volume One* (London: Lawrence and Wishart, 1986 [1867]).

25. Big Data LDN.2019. "To Intelligence … and Beyond, 13-14 November 2019, accessed 22 July 2021, https://bigdataldn.com/.

26. Neda Atanasoski and Kalindi Vora, *Surrogate Humanity: Race, Robots, and the Politics of Technological Futures* (Durham, NC: Duke University Press, 2019).

27. Phil Jones, *Work without the Worker: Labour in the Age of Platform Capitalism* (London: Verso, 2021).

28. Mark Graham and Mohammad Amir Anwar, 'The Global Gig Economy: Towards a Planetary Labour Market?' *First Monday* 24:4 (2019).

29. Brian Menegus, 'Thousands of Google Employees Protest Company's Involvement in Pentagon AI Drone Program', Gizmodo (4 April 2018), https://gizmodo.com/thousands-of-google-employees-protest-companys-involvem-1824988565.

30. Avie Schneider and Laura Sydell, 'Microsoft Workers Protest Army Contract with Tech "Designed to Help People Kill"', NPR, 22 February 2019.

31. https://notechforice.com/about/.

32. Jones, *Work without the Worker*.

33. Verónica Gago, *Feminist International: How to Change Everything* (London: Verso, 2020), 257.

34. International Labour Organisation, 'Digital Refugee Livelihoods and Decent Work. Towards Inclusion in a Fairer Digital Economy' (Geneva: International Labour Organisation, 2021).

35. Ibid.

36. Ibid.

37. Nick Srnicek, 'Data Compute Labour' in *Digital Work in the Planetary Market*, eds. Mark Graham and Fabian Ferrari (Cambridge, MA: MIT Press, 2022), 241–262.

38. Leif Weatherby and Brian Justie, 'Indexical AI', *Critical Inquiry* 48:2 (2022), 381–415.

39. Emma Strubell, Ananya Ganesh and Andrew McCallum, 'Energy and Policy Considerations for Deep Learning in Nlp', *arXiv preprint arXiv:1906.02243* (2019); David Patterson et al., 'Carbon Emissions and Large Neural Network Training', *arXiv preprint arXiv:2104.10350* (2021).

40. Patterson et al., 'Carbon Emissions and Large Neural Network Training'.

41. Evelyn Nakano Glenn, 'From Servitude to Service Work: Historical Continuities in the Racial Division of Paid Reproductive Labor', *Signs: Journal of Women in Culture and Society* 18:1 (1992), 1–43.

42. VFRAME: https://vframe.io/

43. Mnemonic has also built archives from Yemen and Sudan.

44. United Nations, 'Convention on Cluster Munitions', https://www.un.org/disarmament/convention-on-cluster-munitions.

45. Adam Harvey, 'On Computer Vision', *Umbau* 1 (2022), https://umbau.hfg-karlsruhe.de/posts/on-computer-vision

46. Forensic Architecture, Triple Chaser (2019), forensic-architecture.org/programme/exhibitions/triple-chaser-at-the-whitney-biennial-2019.

47. Martina Tazzioli and Daniele Lorenzini, 'Critique without Ontology. Genealogy, Collective Subjects and the Deadlocks of Evidence', *Radical Philosophy* 2.07 (2020), 27–39.

48. Marcuse and Kellner, *Technology, War and Fascism: Collected Papers of Herbert Marcuse*, 41.

49. Helen Hester, *Xenofeminism* (Cambridge: Polity, 2018).

'Everything can be made better, except man'

On Frédéric Lordon's Communist Realism

Alberto Toscano

Over the past decade or so, Frédéric Lordon has morphed from Spinozist social philosopher and canny heterodox critic of political economy with a formation in Regulation Theory to one of the most prominent intellectual voices of the radical Left on the French scene[1] – a shift crystallised by his protagonism during the Nuit Debout protests that began in 2016 against the El Khomri labour law.[2]

Lordon's activist, even revolutionary turn is evident in his 2019 book *Vivre sans?* (Living Without?). Here, Lordon's critical intelligence is directed squarely at his own side, so to speak, in a patient, sympathetic but also unsparing vivisection of what he diagnoses as the anti-political drift of an autonomist, insurrectionist and 'destituent' camp most strongly identified with his own stablemates at the Paris-based publisher La Fabrique, the Invisible Committee (and their precursor, Tiqqun). This metaphysically-tinged ultra-leftism is articulated theoretically in an epochal challenge to Western biopolitics drawn from the writings of Giorgio Agamben, while its practical counterpart can be located in the inspiring experiments in anti-statist forms of life associated with the Zones à Défendre (ZAD) movement, especially around the occupations at Notre-Dame-des-Landes.[3] Lordon's critical balance sheet also takes in a broader range of theorists and contemporary political experiences (with polemical sallies against Alain Badiou, Jacques Rancière and Deleuzianism, as well as reflections on the uses and abuses of the politics crystallised in the tag All Cops Are Bastards).

A propositional *pars construens* to the critical *pars destruens* developed in *Vivre sans?* is advanced in Lordon's most recent book *Figures du communisme* (2021), which I will turn to in the second part of this article.

Pars destruens: Towards a critique of insurgent reason

Vivre sans? takes the form of a set of numbered and thematically classified reflections on the powers and pitfalls of the anti-institutional imaginary of the contemporary radical and insurrectionary Left, prompted by incisive questions and problematisations from Félix Boggio Éwanjé-Épée (co-author with Stella Magliani-Belkacem of *Les Féministes blanches et l'Empire*, also published by La Fabrique, and editor at *ContreTemps*). As the book's preface avers, this is not a conversation strictly speaking, as the exchanges took place in 2018 and 2019 by electronic correspondence. While it lacks the dialectical brio of a proper interview book like Raymond Williams's *Politics and Letters*, Boggio Éwanjé-Épée's contribution, albeit unobtrusive (a paragraph or sometimes one-page long question-intervention will be followed by 20 or 30 pages of exposition by Lordon), is very significant, not least in obliging Lordon to articulate his position more forthrightly on certain decisive themes (especially the role of race and racialisation in anti-capitalist politics), and in leading him to a looser, more flowing as well as more combative genre of exposition than in previous books like *Willing Slaves of Capital* or *Imperium*.

The guiding question with which Lordon begins – namely, why do movements like the ZAD combine intransigently anti-systemic practices and slogans with a minimalism when it comes to global prospects of eman-

cipation – sets the stage for his exploration of the imaginary of an anti-capitalist Left marked by a kind of post-revolutionary ultra-radicalism. Lordon inquires sympathetically into the lived common sense that sees institutions as an infernal trap for any emancipatory activity – a predicament he approaches in terms of the intimate bond between the division of labour and the division of powers. From the workplace to the university, we witness 'a centripetal, intransitive drift in organisations that only live in view of internal finalities, in the growing forgetting of any external finalities',[4] operating as though governed by a cancerous and fractal law of bureaucratisation that pervades all of our social, economic and political structures of collective action and labour.

Lordon is a fine guide through the phenomenology of our institutional captivity, touching *inter alia* on the lie as a symptom of institutional declension or the perplexing and ubiquitous figure of the spokesperson, understood as the embodiment of institutional pathology, of the imperative to persevere at all costs that defines the being of contemporary institutions. His effort at an immanent critique of an anti-institutional Left imaginary is aided by his frank agreement with its starting point: an '*ethical disgust*' with our time and its forms of life.[5] But it's the philosophical underpinnings of the imaginary of 'living without' that Lordon is concerned with, and which he tackles by juxtaposing its ethical imaginaries of *disidentification* to a Spinozist anthropology articulated around the capacity to *modify oneself* and to *differ*.

The virtue of this Spinozism for Lordon is a kind of *realism* about socially-embedded anthropological tendencies towards belonging, identity, group-formation and an ultimately uncircumventable institutional life – or, as demonstrated at length in his earlier *Imperium*, the impossibility of doing without *power* in human affairs. This lays the groundwork for Lordon's effort to move through the ethical orientation of the contemporary Left to think about the logics of numbers, of force and of material constraints that are the indispensable resources for an anti-capitalist politics. These are in a sense the basic axes of the book: on the one hand, a Spinozist philosophical-anthropological critique of the conception of human life and action that subtends the 'living without' paradigm; on the other, a strategic appraisal of the social dynamics of power that determine any fight against (e.g., the Gilets Jaunes) or flight from (e.g., the ZAD) the grip of capitalism and its state.

Lordon's plea is for an anti-capitalist politics that is intransigent in its opposition and strategic intentions but also doesn't tell itself stories about the collective, psychic and anthropological material it is working with. A powerful leitmotiv in this revolutionary realism, so to speak, is the need (disavowed by the anti-institutional left) to confront the *logic of numbers*, the fact that 'if politics is the business of large numbers, it is not certain that we can really encounter it once we give it an ethic of salvation as its horizon ... The aporia of "politics through ethics" is that one of its terms reserves it for the small number while the other calls on the large'.[6]

Lordon grounds his objections to the anti-institutional imaginary of the contemporary radical Left in a critical and clinical panorama of the anti-political (to wit, anti-realist) tendencies in contemporary European philosophy, presented as the speculative taproots of that imaginary. The four targets of the critique are Deleuze, Rancière, Badiou and Agamben. All, according to Lordon, evade the realist politics of numbers, power and force that are his ultimate horizon – Deleuze by juxtaposing revolutionary becomings to actual revolutionary transition, Rancière by celebrating the rarity of politics, Badiou by presenting a conception of the political subject that makes him into an incarnation of the exceptional Spinozist sage (the one living beyond imagination and ideology), Agamben with his Left-Heideggerian yearning for a catastrophe of forms of life in the context of the *separation* – of beings from being, of actuality from potentiality, of life from itself – that defines Western metaphysics and politics as such.

Lordon presents this 'constellation of antipolitics' with verve, but the price of the polemic is tendentiousness. The conceptual targets of his critique – the distinction between lines of flight/becomings and strata/actuality in Deleuze, or the separation of subjective exceptionality from a degraded everyday in Badiou – are well selected but studiously neglect arguments that might resonate or interfere with Lordon's own. Deleuze, for one, for all his Bergsonism, was also an obsessive thinker of institutions (from his texts of the 1950s on 'Instincts and Institutions' and Hume as a thinker of artifice, institutionality and jurisprudence, all the way to salient dimensions of his work with Guattari), while Badiou's political thinking and practice is signally concerned with a capacity for exceptional political action which is in no way 'aristocratic' or requiring the individualised figure of the 'wise man' (think of the prominent place in his political practice of organising with undocumented workers, of Maoism's refusal of expertise, etc.). That said, Lordon does capture important blindspots and impasses among these thinkers that could be seen to affect their broader political imaginary, for instance by registering both in Deleuze and the ZAD 'the tragic point of the politics of flight: it is entirely likely to reconstitute the very thing it is seeking to withdraw from'.[7]

Lordon is also effective in showing how the very distinction between the rare political subject and the individual as 'interested' human animal that governs, say, Badiou's *Ethics*, is at odds with the insights of Spinoza, for whom the dimension of interest is insurmountable (thus turning Badiou into a Kantian moralist *malgré lui*). Quite rightly, I think, Agamben appears in these pages as the paragon of the speculative-discursive trend that underlies an anti-institutional Left imaginary, especially in terms of his articulation of the guiding notions of *separation, suspension and destitution*, as well as the Italian philosopher's abiding concern with the devastating 'ontological loss' that marks our present condition. Here again, Spinoza (and especially his thinking of *mode* or *manner*) is enlisted to refute the ontology underlying Agamben's thinking of bare life – forcing us to think that 'even in the hell of the camp life is mannered [*maniérée*]'.[8]

Agamben's entire metaphysical perspective is subjected to further Spinozist critique as Lordon tackles the very notion that the power to act could be suspended, that one could appeal to *impotentiality* – since Spinoza teaches us that the effects of any power or capacity follow *necessarily*, such that 'a power suspending itself is a contradiction in terms'.[9] A conception of political action and power drawn from Spinoza is accordingly juxtaposed to a constellation of the antipolitical that evades the urgent challenges of modern political collectivity and conflict via *intransitivity* (Deleuze's becomings without a future), *aesthetics* (Rancière's rare political moments) or *virtuosity* (Badiou's political subject as exceptional sage). *Vivre sans?* also contains some perspicuous comments about how and why *art* plays such a salient role in a thinking of politics as ontologically exceptional, one that ultimately disavows the arena of political struggle as actually constituted by powers, conflict and numbers.

This anti-political anti-realism finds its apotheosis in a thinking of destitution without institution, as advanced by Agamben and the Invisible Committee, which ignores how the multitude exerts power over itself and embodies collectivity in powers and institutions – in an *imperium*, 'the fundamental sovereignty of the whole over the parts'.[10] If we come, Spinozistically, to understand institution as naming 'every effect, every manifestation of the power of the multitude',[11] then the destituent paradigm is sterile. When we understand that the collective is a common power to activate actions, to make its members do something – what Lordon terms *faire faire* – the 'institutional fact' cannot be circumvented (as Lordon will later argue via examples from the ZADs and Chiapas). In the end, 'destroying formal, visible institutions doesn't get away from the institutional fact itself, because it is a fact whose nature is at once ontological, anthropological, and structural'.[12]

To think through how visions of the state haunt the anti-institutional common sense of the radical Left, Lordon explores how the ZAD experiment manifests the way in which norms and institutions pervade even (or especially) those moments and movements that build themselves on an anti-institutional animus and philosophy. In Lordon's Spinozist horizon, there is no exit from institutions and no escape from norms. While we may, indeed *must*, discriminate between norms and institutions, *formally* speaking any form of collective life will not be able to do without either, whether it is a monolithic bureaucratic state or an anarchist commune. The question is not to make oneself ungovernable – a dead end from a Spinozist view – but asking *by whom* one is governed and *how*.

In order to bring this point home, Lordon focuses on some of the sensitive points in current debates across the (French) Left, especially as concerns the *police*. While the latter understood as a specific repressive apparatus can certainly be an object of opposition and abolition (and should be, especially in light of the French repression of the Gilets Jaunes, as Lordon details at some length), a 'formal' concept of the police is unavoidable when approaching any collective whatever. Police is the name here for 'every institutional apparatus of accommodation of differends internal to a collective'.[13] In this sense, we find the police everywhere that a collective interpolates itself into these inescapable internal conflicts – which need not mean that this extremely general police-function will find itself instantiated in someone who looks and acts like a cop.

In this sense, *contra* Rancière, there is no *politics* without *police*, if we understand both as ways of accommodating, mediating and articulating passionate differends *within* collectives. The issue is not to *disavow* but to *control* this function of 'interposition' that defines collective institutions – to disconnect interposition as far as possible from its capture by apparatuses of individual and group *domination*.[14] Lordon explores the way in which (as Pierre Clastres already intimated for so-called primitive societies) the lighter the footprint of official institutions, the more collectives rely on constant internal surveillance of everyone by everyone. This gaze of the collective is among the objects of disavowal in anti-institutional perspectives, and one of the dimensions of experiments in antisystemic life that reveal how 'the "camp of difference" practices similarity [*le semblable*] more than it imagines, even grounding in it the possibility of its experimentations'.[15] What needs to be faced up to instead is the institutional inventiveness of the assemblages (*agencements*) that emerge in flights from and fights against the capitalist state.

When Lordon and Boggio Éwanjé-Épée turn their attention to the limits of a possible state takeover by the Left, it is in order to weigh up with sober realism not just the material but the affective dimensions of the composition of the state personnel (repressive and otherwise). Even its fascist dimensions are understood as 'sadist drives poured into a legitimating institutional mould'.[16] What needs to be confronted then is an alignment of interests between the 'men of State' with their generic passion for *order* and capitalist classes whose priority lies in the *transitive* use of the state *qua* instrument of class reproduction. Here we find 'a generalised bloc of physical and symbolic violence'.[17] If we really confront these material and affective facts then we realise that what the Left needs to confront are '*macroscopic* struggles, gigantomachias. Capital is a titan. To bring it down, we therefore need giants'.[18]

Lordon is emphatic that evading the realistic strictures of this *gigantomachia* and deluding oneself that a *defection* from the state can pose a challenge to the domination of capital, is not an option – notwithstanding the obvious fact that the state is not neutral but is rather (largely, but not totally or ontologically) the state *of capital*. Lordon is particularly biting here on the bad faith of those self-described radical intellectuals who in their phobia of the state sing the praises of the 'huts' (of the exodus from the urban in the ZADs) but who avoid confronting the violence that any secession from the state both involves and requires. Radical innocuousness is here juxtaposed to a *tragic* sense of history.[19]

Lordon embraces a radical critique of the absolute limits of formalistic democracy, and a strategic reckoning with the pitfalls of reformism, while rejecting the idea that only destitution, defection or flight can properly respond to this parlous state of affairs. We are enjoined to reinvent a way of strategically and theoretically reckoning with the fact that capital will go to war with any substantial alternative to its order (this what he calls the 'L point' – L as in Lenin). This obliges us to reimagine and practice anew the horizon of expropriation (not just of capital but of its superstructural scaffolding, above all the media) and the dictatorship of the proletariat as a name for mass democracy in conditions of frontal conflict (though the nature of both that dictatorship and this proletariat remain underdetermined across Lordon's work). Over and over, the conversation returns to the need to ready oneself with a steady pulse and eyes wide open for the seriousness of the confrontation that would follow any real challenge to the neoliberal status quo (as evidenced by the response to the rather modest and strategically immature dress rehearsals witnessed in post-crisis Greece or the Gilets Jaunes mobilisations).

A mass politics, a politics of numbers is here presented as the only corrective to the wielding of colossal class violence against any substantive alternative, while the state reveals itself as a precarious but necessary potential concentration of the energy of the multitude, which in the throes of emergency and transition manifests itself not in its institutional crystallisation but as 'the power of the masses in a state of mobilisation'.[20] Behind this risky but inevitable wager on the question of the state in a horizon of conflict and transformation lies the Spinozist tenet that, *contra* the doxa on the far Left, 'alienation does not come from outside, it is our own production'; the strategic deficit of the Left imaginary is compounded by a philosophical-anthropological error, 'the misunderstanding of the relation of immanence of alienated things to alienated individuals'.[21] This is also the sense in which '[t]he violence of money is *our* violence, the violence of our own acquisitive desire'.[22] As Hegel once

intimated, seeing politics through a tragic lens requires 'consciousness of oneself, but consciousness of oneself as an enemy'.[23]

In one of his interventions, Boggio Ewanjé-Epée rightly notes the way in which the desire for 'living without' is always both a desire for the end of *institutional separation* and for the end of the *division of labour in the economic sense*. For Lordon, we must confront this nexus and do so via a Spinozist philosophical-anthropological definition of the economy as 'the set of social relations in which collective material reproduction is organised'.[24] The division of labour is thus inseparably an economic and political problem. Or rather, it is *the* economic-political problem, and the one that the contemporary anti-statist destituent Left imaginary never properly confronts. Yet, notwithstanding Lordon's genuine sympathy for contemporary experiments in escaping the death-grip of the wage-form, he continues to ask the political question, the revolutionary question, which is that of *scale*, also and especially as concerns the domain of collective material reproduction. But questioning the scale at which capital may be challenged is not separable from matters of affect and anthropology, namely: how can an attack on capitalism be organised that doesn't require the virtuosity and virtues of the ZADists? And how can we confront the fact that these zones and enclaves, however withdrawn, also reproduce themselves *via* the very system they are fighting against, never being fully delinked or autarchic (in energetic, supply or logistical terms)?

Unlike his objections to the theoretical constellation of the anti-political, the critique of the ZAD is a nuanced and sympathetic one, as Lordon also stresses how these enclaves are also experiments and training-grounds in learning how to live beyond the 'gigantic enforced powerlessness, individual and collective' that capital organises, as it deskills multitudes from the most quotidian of activities (though it may be noted that the rediscovery of reproductive skills, from mechanics to baking, is perfectly compatible with 'real subsumption', and can take exquisitely petty-bourgeois or neo-bourgeois forms). For Lordon, there is much to be learned from experiences like the ZAD but, if they're not to be relegated to unthreatening enclaves, they need to be 'scaled up' to the level of the anti-capitalist gigantomachia, and thus incorporated into mixed and transitional forms that cannot depend on the face-to-face gift or the altruistic passions of ethical virtuous. And this strategic, compositional analysis needs to confront the 'conflict of antagonistic affects'[25] that traverses every one of us, when we consider the privations and gains that may be envisaged and desired in terms of an exit from capitalism. Here *Vivre sans?* addresses the crucial role that the 'climate affect' could have in inclining bodies individual and collective towards more radical outcomes – something that Lordon sees as closer to the mixed model of the Lip watch-factory occupation of 1973 than the ZADs: maintaining much of the large-scale division of labour but combining and displacing this with radical efforts at decommodification, emancipation of workers, dis-alienation of tasks – all of this grounded in a drastic transformation of property rights.

By way of conclusion, Lordon returns to a more speculative register in a concerted polemic against the ethico-anthropological dimension of the anti-political imaginary of the contemporary far Left, especially tackling the anti-civilisational notes, the 'Orphic antipolitics' in the writings of the Invisible Committee and Julien Coupat – which bring to a pitch the sterile antinomy, for Lordon, between *institutions-as-death*, on the one hand, and *true-life*, on the other, in their aim of 'living without civilisation' – an antinomy that Spinozist anthropology shows up in all its delusory quality. This confrontation leads Lordon to stress the need to think 'the institutionalisation of destabilisation in the institutions of stability'[26] – a reflection that incidentally bears some affinity with that other, institutional Deleuze (it could be argued that all of *What is Philosophy?*, written with Guattari, is organised in these terms, with *chaos* representing the risk of formlessness, *doxa* the ossification into predictable identity and lifelessness).

Vivre sans? is an invigorating polemical intervention and probably also the best introduction to the overall stakes of Lordon's work – particularly effective in arguing just why Spinozist speculations on philosophical anthropology may be of analytical and strategic moment. It is not uninteresting however to wonder how the argument's scope might have been affected by moving beyond its Franco-centric polemical animus, not least in tackling the practical and theoretical question of 'living without' as it manifests itself in the wealth of contemporary debates and movements that take place today, especially in the US, under the aegis of a renewed *abolitionism*. Arguably, as manifest in a long history of political struggles and experiments, and related theoretical reflections in the Black radical tradition, the question of abolition, pivoting around the prison-industrial-complex and its pervasive juridical and repressive extensions but looking far beyond them, articulates many of the political energies explored in Lordon's work, but shares little if anything with the metaphysical anti-institutionalism that is the principal target of Lordon's criticisms.[27]

Pars construens: For a consequential communism

Figures du communisme (Figures of Communism) consolidates Lordon's increasingly intransigent turn to a revolutionary politics capable of defining the strategic parameters of a break with the capitalist status quo and the institution of a new mode of production, consumption and distribution – which is also to say new regimes of passions and desires. Where previous work, including *Imperium* and *Vivre sans?*, sounded a note of anthropological realism against the 'abolitionist' horizons of a theoretical ultra-left imagining a world without institutions brought about by destituent power, *Figures* can best be described as a protracted plea for *communist realism*, voicing the urgent need for the critique of capitalism to arm itself with strategic and political *consequentiality*. It is a call to recognise that the ravages which capitalism is inflicting on workers and nature alike – potentially putting into question the very viability of human life on the planet – require a move beyond a generic anti-capitalism and the embrace of a systematic and implementable vision of the termination of the profit, wage and finance as structuring principles of our everyday life, ultimately aimed at the transition to a wholly different way of organising collective life, one that can assume, in a new guise, the name of *communism*.

If *Imperium* and *Vivre sans?* contended that the Left should cease telling itself stories about the possibility of doing entirely without the forms of transcendent power and compulsion generated by the multitude itself (state, nation, police, law, etc.), *Figures* shifts register, strenuously arguing that the most pernicious of contemporary political fantasies, especially among self-described progressives, is the notion that the compound violences and catastrophes of capitalism can be addressed through reforms, good intentions, peaceful energetic transitions or parliamentary roads. At the same time, Lordon wants to compensate for what he perceives as the overly speculative-abstract character of recent debates on the idea of communism by advancing a prospect for communism that is also an implementable, desirable, and in some sense a 'quotidian' or everyday (if also utopian and ruptural) 'figure', capable of animating and crystallising social desires otherwise captured by rudderless opposition or anxious reaction.

As the book's prologue intimates, the Covid-19 crisis should not be allowed to go to waste, and the simple if demanding imperative of a wholesale transformation of social life in light of the pathologies further revealed by the pandemic needs to be confronted with sobriety and intransigence. An order of needs wholly other than that imposed by capitalism is on the agenda, beginning with the priority of health and ecology, under the heading of *living well* and *living intelligently*. But neither health nor a virtuous metabolism with nature are possible unless the economic question, the question of livelihood and social reproduction is confronted. This will turn out to be the core of Lordon's communist proposal. Communism is nothing less than the termination of capitalist insecurity, of a precarity that plunges deep into our bodies, psyches, and our very perception of the time of life. As Lordon declares:

> The society which leaves prehistory aims, through collective organisation and at all scales, the greatest possible stabilisation in the material conditions of individuals. No one should have to depend for their life on a versatile intermediary – sovereign and tyrannical – whether it be in the guise of the 'employer' or the 'market'. It is thus up to society as a whole unconditionally to guarantee everyone access to the socially determined means of material tranquillity. ... Private property will no longer have any enjoyment but that of use. Its exploitation for the ends of valorisation belongs to prehistory. Definitively.[28]

This vision of an end to capitalist insecurity and a reorganisation of the priorities of health, life and nature is accompanied not just by the need to reinvent the division of labour but by the recognition that these questions of social reproduction are the premises to 'the development of the creative powers of all'.

As in invocations of *gigantomachia* in *Vivre sans?*, it

is Lordon's unshaken conviction that 'only a phenomenal deployment of political energy can stop capitalism from leading humanity to its demise, a deployment which usually carries the name of "revolution"'.[29] The unprecedented character and urgency of the contemporary situation – especially but not only at the ecological level – requires abandoning all of the inconsequential tales of piecemeal reforms or peaceful transitions voiced by the 'great party of programmes without consequences' and confronting both the magnitude of the task and the formidable obstacles lying in its path, namely the organised force of capital and its institutions. But what must be done also needs to be imagined, made palpable, intelligible, desirable, and this is the task that Lordon sets himself with his plea for *figuration*, one which pivots – in the dialogue he establishes with the Catholic-communist economist Bernard Friot[30] – on the 'wage for life' (Friot's formulation) or the 'general economic guarantee' (Lordon's), understood as the only path through which to free ourselves from the pitiless capitalist domination of the *market* and *employment*.

Only such a general economic guarantee, according to Lordon, can cut through the vicious link between financialised capitalist accumulation, on the one hand, and the twin devastation of workers and nature, on the other – a devastation made even more vicious by the fact that under market and wage conditions any consequential action against ecological catastrophe can often appear to be *against* the immediate interest of workers. The only path to resolve this is the 'disconnection of activity and revenue; collective property of use after the abolition of private property in the means of production; the sovereignty of associated producers; the complete closure of finance; a federal system of funds [*caisses*] that direct the subsidy of investments and the decisions that orient the division of labour'.[31]

The task, the only serious one, is nothing less than the building of a new *mode of production* capable of answering to our material desires, which in turn need to be recalibrated in view of the threat to our life on the planet. Linking back to the polemical survey of the contemporary Left imaginary in *Vivre sans?*, *Figures* rests on the claim that an escape from the economy for the sake of horizontality, enclaves or destituent power is powerless, since, even should we strive to forget it, 'the economy' – namely 'the set of ways in which we collectively face the necessity to persevere materially'[32] – *will never forget us*. Capitalism is destroying us, capitalism must be destroyed – one can sense in this motto the magnitude of the change undergone by Lordon's perspective, not just since his Regulationist beginnings but even from his radical critique of finance and the Euro in the wake of the 2008 crisis.

Part I of *Figures*, 'The Forces of Inconsequentiality (Denials, Avoidances, Delays)', returns us to polemical terrain but this time the critical targets are not on the anti-institutional ultra-Left but share a kind of inconsequential progressivism that refuses to confront the facts of the Capitalocene, choosing instead to levy its criticism at capitalism in its current configuration, rather than capitalism *as such*. Much of the attack here is on a reformist mainstream that proliferates pseudo-solutions which systematically avoid confronting the constitutive link between the structures of capital accumulation and ecological devastation. In passing, Lordon also notes that these bad faith reformisms are also made possible by narrowing down the ecological question to fossil fuels alone while ignoring pollution, extinction, etc. The very notion of ecological crisis as an opportunity for renewing or relaunching a 'Green' capitalism appears as a primary symptom of the incoherence or 'inconsequence' of much liberal and progressive opinion, unable realistically to draw the inescapable conclusions from the very science it supposedly accepts. Capitalist hegemony has reached such an extension and such intensity that the notion of reform or regulation as a solution is simply no longer tenable.

If we define capitalism as 'the acquired (and juridically guaranteed) capacity by private property in the means of production to compel labour-power into a relationship of *hierarchical subordination*',[33] then, according to Lordon, any proposal to democratise the firm as a step towards alleviating or resolving ecological and social reproduction crises is tantamount (if it wishes to be *consequential*) to abolishing capitalism as such. But Lordon is also extremely sceptical about those more philosophical perspectives that bank on transformations in our worldviews or forms-of-life as the prelude to confronting ecological disaster. His Spinozist realism also dictates that *ontological* and *anthropological transitions*, even if they might be possible, require energy and time that is simply not available under current conditions of urgency, which will require mass, ruptural and state-mediated political action (there are many affinities here with Andreas Malm's plea for eco-Leninism in his recent book on the nexus between the pandemic and the climate emergency[34]).

Bad faith reformism applies to the twinned crises of ecology and social reproduction the same delay-and-distract tactics that the notion of a 'democratic and social Europe' did during the crisis of the Eurozone (as he quips, 'abstract Europeanism is the epochal form of a moralism without consequences'[35]). Lordon here repurposes his critique of the critique of the sovereign nation-state from *Imperium* and other texts to skewer climate internationalism as an avoidance of the state's role as the immediate terrain of climate struggles. His proposal is that instead of accepting the reality of a globalised capital while chastising national economies the problem be reversed: 'rather than seeking, with capitalism as given and invariant, a solution to the local-global contradiction – the contradiction of global common goods abandoned to deranged national sovereignties – one needs to tackle the very force which established the externalities of disaster: capitalism'.[36]

Some of the sallies here against the middle-class internationalism of hypocritical jet-setting elites, and of a revolution that will never take place by Zoom, fall a little flat. The negative obsession with travelling and tourism is still a little too internal to the discourses of the contemporary intellectual bourgeoisie (limiting conference travel is not exactly a transitional measure). And while the call for 'slow versions of internationalism' is well taken, the claim that 'internationalism *is not a political form*'[37] is under-argued and unpersuasive, suffering considerably from the lack of engagement with the communist history and theory of the latter, but also with extant forms of struggle against capital and its ecological devastations (Via Campesina, etc.).

Part II, 'Communism as General Economic Guarantee', contains the core of Lordon's contemporary communist prospect – one that combines, on the one hand, the economic-political realism of consequential change (against efforts to rearrange the deck chairs on the Titanic, for which he emphatically faults the likes of Thomas Piketty), and, on the other, the anthropological realism which casts doubt on any communism that would require a thoroughgoing transformation in its human material or would demand from communist the cultivating of exceptional virtues. No communism can demand anthropological engineering, though its transformations, consequential as they must be, will no doubt rewire our needs and desires as they progress.

As things stand, what is the primary obstacle to the communist project? The reign of the economy understood as 'the tyranny of autonomised and fetishised exchange value'.[38] Note that this differs from the transhistorical or 'formal' notion of the economy which Lordon juxtaposes to ultra-leftism in *Vivre sans?*, as well as elsewhere in these pages (as with the 'formal' concept of the police, this is the one that *cannot* be abolished, it's a general function of social life). The key then is how to make collective material reproduction possible outside of the value-form and its associated forms of power. More specifically, it is a matter of destroying capitalist value and employment in tandem, along with their distinctive institutions: the right of private property in the means of production, the labour market and finance.[39]

As in *Vivre sans?*, it is rethinking the *division of labour* at a *macrosocial* level which is the key to any consequential challenge to capital. Without this, marginality, defeat or absorption will be the fate of any anti-capitalism. The macrosocial is not merely cumulative, not just the addition or federation of autonomous communal realities. Autonomies, which are important experiences in themselves and practical schools in which to forge new social and economic habits, will need to be reinscribed into a system-wide division of labour. This will require politically rethinking the division of labour in terms of its ends (for what?) and its means (with whom and with what, in which arrangements, through what forms of power?). The commune-form is not the (only) prism through which to approach this. Any 'transition' that takes these challenges on board will be called upon to confront the fact that the abolition of capitalist social relations will also mean the end or substantial transformation of capitalist lifestyles and material habits. The wager is to make not just politically viable, but politically *desirable*, the passage from quantity to quality, from material acquisitiveness to 'material tranquillity for everyone'.[40] To make people *want* and *will* communism, in other words.

For Lordon, the 'great replacement' (of capitalism with communism) will perforce falter if it makes excess-

ive demands on the not-new men and women who will have to carry out and endure it. In this regard, Lordon seems to be following Brecht's wisdom as voiced in one of his parables of Herr Keuner: 'Everything can be made better ... except man.'[41]

Any transition that fails to deal with basic needs and desires will be immediately devastated by the mortal enemy of revolutionary transitions – the inflationary black market. Sacrifices will no doubt be inevitable, but a material basis must be secured. What Lordon seeks to lay out here then is not a full programme for this communist transition but some substantive and strategic guidelines, what he terms exercises in method and consequence.

A social organisation truly alternative to capitalism and its destructive effects will require holding on to three imperatives: (1) in the unavoidably collective process of material reproduction ('economy' in the non-capitalist sense), individuals participate as equals, without hierarchical subordination; (2) the aim of social organisation is to *guarantee* material tranquillity at the highest possible level; (3) due to the harms it engenders, global production is *a priori* an enemy of nature and must be minimised in scope and intensity at all costs. Failing to answer the question of the mode of production and the forms of social reproduction, anti-capitalism is condemned to remain interstitial, parasitic and in ultimate bad faith in its *de facto* dependence on the mechanisms of accumulation it claims to be opposing. But to pose the question of the macrosocial is also to pose the problem of the state.

Here Lordon seems more sanguine about the local than in *Vivre sans?* He affirms the ethico-political as well as material value of a principle of subsidiarity: 'the more [production] possible at the more local [level] possible'. In dialogue with the work of Bernard Friot, Lordon proposes as a starting point of his communist proposal for social reproduction unmediated by financial markets that the value-added of firms be *entirely* contributed to collective funds that will in turn govern the social redistribution of resources and value. The key requisite of this proposal is the 'euthanasia' of the arbitrary power of bosses and the end of the dependence of individual workers on the power of owners – the 'wage' (Lordon objects to Friot's moniker of 'wage for life', preferring 'economic guarantee' to mark the rupture) reconfigured as a medium of withdrawal from capitalist precarity. Lordon provides a summary sketch of Friot's proposals, focusing on how patterns of consumption are to be guided by citizen deliberation (this is a system dubbed *conventionnement*, the same term used for doctors registered with social security), so that a portion of individual consumption will be channelled towards socially beneficial production.

Lordon notes the significance of the inducement to consume and produce in view of socially agreed goals but especially underscores that political deliberation will take place in assemblies at a territorial level corresponding to the kind of production at hand, weaving together the political and economic. But Lordon's realism rears its head again as he enumerates the immanent reasons of capitalist self-defence, and why Friot's notion that this process could begin *from within the political institutions of capitalism*, from 'democracy as we know it', is misguided (we could add here that Friot seems to underestimate the 'geo-economic' conditions for the *trente glorieuses*, and the place of colonialism and decolonisation within them).

Friot's analogy with postwar social-democratic gains is no longer viable, according to Lordon, who inserts a critical wedge between the quashed or diverted small transitions *within* capitalism and the urgency of the large transition *from* capitalism. This is the premise for his figuration of the 'general economic guarantee', the material bedrock of a communism capable of confronting the intractable challenges of social reproduction. Here Lordon makes another anthropological detour to caution against certain communist temptations – firstly, that of imagining that the abolition of money is a necessary prelude to the abolition of social violence. We are reminded that (acquisitive) violence goes deeper than the capitalist money-form, that the violence is (in) us; but also, that a *macrosocial* division of labour will involve forms of *mediation* that may demand reimagining in a post-capitalist vein the workings of money and markets, now reconfigured so they are no longer tribunals judging over the material survival of individuals. What is called for is nothing less than a 'complete, radical, anticapitalist redefinition of value'.[42]

Lordon advances a mixed system that will incorporate both society-wide planning, socially guided collective projects of production (in the framework of funds whose priorities will be set by political deliberation) and the 'private proposition' (in the sense of initiative, rather than exclusive ownership). Nevertheless, Lordon enjoins us to think seriously about the hardships and potential pitfalls of the transition, to confront the problem of a 'transition within the transition' that will 'freeze' certain aspects of the division of labour in order to secure social reproduction (in the face of inevitable capitalist sabotage and encirclement). Again, certain regulative principles will need to be secured: to *maximise* freedom of economic activity (while recognising an irreducible kernel of subjection and compulsion for the sake of the social good); to work towards the *technical de-division of labour* while being realistic about the needs of specialisation. In the meantime, those assigned *transitionally* to difficult or onerous forms of labour will be differentially remunerated at the highest level.

The passage from the pseudo-freedoms of a capitalist society to the greater freedoms and assumed constraints of a communist one requires developing a communist discursive virtue, namely that of *naming constraints and necessities*, a virtue of 'minimal lucidity' that does not tell itself stories about the spontaneous emergence of social harmony (whether of a neoliberal or *anarchisant* stripe). But the subjections required by communism are offset by its gains: the end of precarity and the stoppage of the planet's destruction; the establishment of the sovereignty of producers and abolition of private property in the means of production (replaced by property of use); the institution of a new macrosocial division of labour, combining planning, collective deliberation and autonomous initiative. For all this to obtain, Lordon argues, *debt* and *finance* must be terminated, with their attendant violence against workers and public services in the name of profitability and austerity. The *normalising, constraining* force of the financial markets, with their impersonal and inflexible limits imposed on any form of emancipatory collective action here appear – lessons of Greece ... – as the number one enemy of any project of social transformation. They are also – along with the principle of money advanced for the sake of higher returns – at the core of the infernal mechanism of ecologically-devastating 'growth'. Finance is to be replaced by *subventions* – non-recoverable funds, no longer indexed to a (greater) return.

Capitalist profitability is accordingly substituted by political deliberation. Any real transition will thus involve an epochal *jubilee* of debts, a destruction of the accumulated capitalist past weighing on any other possible future. But – *réalisme oblige* – this *euthanasia* of the creditor must not translate into an assault on personal savings, lest communism take its usually phobic place in the imaginaries of the middle classes – whence Lordon's reflections on the mechanisms that will set ceilings on these personal savings and their removal from circuits of finance (in other words their transformation into mere funds for personal consumption rather than *capital*).

Having confronted in part questions of need and necessity, Lordon turns to 'luxury' – reimagined not as material abundance (the trap of modernising communisms with their fossil infrastructures of production and feeling), but as 'light', *lux*, the possibility for different expressions of human creative potentials. This will require the abolition *tout court* of the fake creativity that sustains the capitalist circuits of desire, namely advertising (a similar proposal could be found in the writings of Amadeo Bordiga). In a moment perhaps worthy of William Morris, Lordon here talks of the *maximum of beauty for a minimum of objects*, combined with the *decoupling of creativity and remuneration*; he also reminds the reader that an everyday communist aesthetic will emphasise the desires of free producers in very material terms (food, perfume, flower arranging) rather than echo the overly speculative, Platonic aims of certain communist intellectuals.

What will especially reinforce the formation of such a communist aesthetic is *the radical delinking of material survival from creativity* – wholly transforming the status of the artist or the 'creative'. This will not mean ending the (anthropologically inescapable) drive of distinction and recognition (some musicians will find an audience and 'social validation' for their creativity, others won't), but stripping it of monetary and material consequence. From his own perch at the CNRS, Lordon sees some prefiguration of this new regime of creativity in the history of public funding for academic research prior to neoliberal managerial vandalism – a world whose non-monetisable productivity gives the lie to the notion that risk and precarity are spurs to creation.

Having sketched his figure of a communism beyond precarity and capitalist domination, Part III, 'Hegemony, Counter-Hegemony', moves to the political question:

'how do we get there?' The starting point must again be realist: twenty-first-century capital does not negotiate with its opposition; it will not come to any substantive compromises with emancipatory forces, as the social landscape corroborates daily. What we witness (in ways that mirror Dardot et al.'s recent *Le Choix de le guerre civile* [2021]) are both the quotidian blockages to any challenge (via anti-labour legislation, market compulsion, competition, capital flight, rating agencies, etc.) and the exceptional violence that capital will employ to retaliate against any substantive challenge. Any government that tackles the power of finance tackles the very means through which finance disciplines governments and will accordingly be the target of a no-holds barred multi-pronged attack. This, together with the ample apparatus of ideological reproduction in the dominant media, puts an enormous obstacle in the face of the great transition, which must operate in a society always virtually hostage to the whims and imperatives of accumulation.

A chapter on 'Chile 1973' draws the lessons from that capitalist counter-revolution (or counter-reform), and from the plurality of ways in which capital exercised its powers of sabotage – but above all from the tragic fact that Allende's faith in the democratic option ultimately put him in the doomed position of the one who cooperates in a non-cooperative game. Lordon is perhaps too sanguine here about the realism of the 'working class in arms' option in that historical context; it might have been interesting for him to touch on the role the Chilean experience and that of Spain played in the gestation and impasses of Eurocommunism. The ultimate lesson is that there is nothing to be hoped from electoral procedures in capitalism if it is capitalism that is to be challenged. Again, Lordon may be underestimating the power that for some time Unidad Popular managed to leverage precisely from a minority electoral victory, in a dialectic with popular movements across revolutionary, radical and reformist Lefts.

The 'democracy' much feted by the likes of Jürgen Habermas is for Lordon a massively misleading homonym for collective sovereignty, toothless to restrain capital in normal times and easily reversed into exception violence when matters come to a head (here quoting Brecht: 'Fascism is not the opposite of democracy but its evolution in times of crisis'). Communist realism also dictates a question of scale, enjoining us to ask after the level of weight on the international field, but also of complexity and significance in terms of an internal division of labour 'susceptible of being backed by an "us" which is sufficiently important to sustain a macropolitical dynamic towards communism'.[43] This is also the problem of 'communist sovereignty', namely that of the possibility of self-defence for a collective social experiment bent on overcoming capitalism and its forms of value. For Lordon, this is a question that cannot be evaded by pleas for autonomy, marginality and the enclave, or by wishful imaginaries of peaceful transition.

The conditions of possibility of a consequential anticapitalism must perforce be confronted, and here 'the question of the overall scale at which a *complete* communist form of life establishes itself is decisive: for it involves the extension and depth of the division of labour, that is to say the level of development of the productive forces such that it serves both as an antidote to communism as the socialisation of penury and as an instrument of perseverance in a hostile environment'.[44] For, after all, communism in *all* countries will have to begin in *one* of them, or in one part of one of them. Now, while the end of capitalist compromise may indeed by depressing, it must be confronted head on, while paying attention to the growing cracks in hegemony – witness the growing level of social conflict in the face of a take-no-prisoners neoliberalism (here the French example may not be easily generalisable to other jurisdictions). Lordon briefly maps the material, political and affective dimension of this creeping organic crisis in his home country, taking the increasingly 'grotesque' face of mainstream politics as a key symptom (one revealed by the fact that the difference between satire and reality becomes increasingly thin).

Lordon also tackles the nexus of capitalism and antiracism in view of the conditions for a counter hegemonic bloc. This reflection is indicative of the changing debate in France (impelled not least by the Indigènes de la République and its avatars) but also of Lordon's theoretical and political limitations in this domain. In a nutshell, to the notion of a mutual implication of race and capital, or even of the existence of a racial capitalism, he opposes a distinction between capitalist essence and racist contingency quite similar to the one advanced by Ellen Meiksins Wood, among others, and whose proposition that capitalism could in principle function without racialisation seems to strip the *historical* out of the materialism.[45] Here capital appears as merely if violently *instrumentally* racist, grafting its own gradations of inequality onto a racism imagined not just as separate but as in a sense 'anterior' (like patriarchy) – a claim that appears to ignore the ways in which race, racialisation and racism are fundamentally transformed by the capital relation. The notion advanced by Lordon that capitalist domination, crystallised in the wage-form, dominates over other forms of domination[46] is itself problematic, not least because the nexus of race and capital often operates outside of the wage (in extractivism, power over disposable or surplus populations, 'organised abandonment', etc.).

Lordon's passing comments on feminism and social reproduction also suffer from the same analytical limitations – how *contingent* are these forms of domination to the substance of capitalist hierarchy if it could have never established itself without them? The idea of a history of the *relations between relations of domination* is more fecund, and the desire to distinguish among these relations is certainly legitimate, but Lordon is too quick in his desire to demarcate, thereby generating far too ideal-typical an image of capital (reduced to the wage-form and exploitation at the point of production, bypassing entirely questions of land, finance, extraction, etc.), along with some problematic political consequences.

Far too much is made here, to my mind, of the anticapitalist gestures of 'progressive' capitalism in the wake of the Black Lives Matter movement, which shifts the discussion out of the structural and political domain where it should operate, to a more media-ideological terrain. The analytical separation of the wageless from the gendered or the racialised simply does not obtain in the real world of exploitation, so the idea of a *pure* capitalist inequality, an actually independent form of domination does not convince. The very stakes of material reproducibility and survival that for Lordon are the keystone of the capitalist mode of domination are inextricably mediated by racialisation and gender.

Thankfully, Lordon does not take a full-on 'class first' approach, accepting the non-reducible and autonomous character of parallel and interlocking struggles – though at the risk of neglecting the latter's immanently anticapitalist dimensions. Capitalism retains a strategic priority: 'Because it is placed in a superior position in the structural hierarchy [of dominations], a position from which it re-mobilises for its profit all other dominations, the capitalist relation, de facto, organises and practices ... the convergence of dominations.'[47] Lordon also recognises the political role of the affects and tendencies underlying, *inter alia*, the fascist potentials of the psychological wages of whiteness, in what he nicely calls 'penultimate passions', those 'intimate strategies of imaginary reparation' for those one metaphorical rung from the bottom: 'The next-to-last are furnished with the last, who, precisely, allow them to live as the non-last, and from which they will then differentiate themselves all the more violently in that they are objectively the closest'.[48]

Figures is brought to a close by a long letter by Félix Boggio Ewanjé-Epée (the interviewer-interlocutor for *Vivre sans?*), who challenges in an original and engaging way the parameters of Lordon's disarticulation of racial and capitalist domination, principally by reconsidering from both political-economic and more strictly political grounds the intrinsically racialising dimensions of imperialism as a driving logic of capital – and affirming the ongoing relevance of a Marxist archive of debates on race, class and anti-systemic strategies that Lordon largely neglects.

Figures is very much in keeping with the more radical turn taken by Lordon's work of late, and complements in both its polemical and propositional dimensions the critical anatomy of the imaginary of the far Left rehearsed in *Vivre sans?* While brisk and engaging, it is certainly a less systematic book than one might at first imagine; the trace of it having been first drafted in multiple blog posts is tangible (which conversely also accounts for its flow and readability). One also wonders about the decision to begin a nominally propositional book with a critique of progressive bourgeois reason which, while hitting the (easy) target, also surveys positions that a more radical readership may have already dismissed. The book can also be cursory verging on the cavalier in its stated decision to do without any but the most oblique discussion of 'actually-existing communism' – which, whether we're thinking of workers' councils, Cuban experiments with medicine, socialist planning, or what have you, certainly harbours pertinent lessons and materials for present debate. And yet Lordon insists on bypassing any immanent critique of communist historical praxis, all too quickly seeming to accept (namely in the introduction) the idea that between his communism and those historical experiences there isn't much in common. This is comprehensible if limiting as a strategy of persuasion but it takes away from the substance and coherence of Lordon's untested 'figures'.

The classic problems of transition that bedevilled and preoccupied Marxist traditions from the 1870s to the 1970s – concerning the generation of bureaucracies, the ossification of parties and leaderships, violence and power, the management of war economies, etc. – would certainly have been germane to some of the problems of scale, agency and desire articulated by Lordon. Closer to our own moment, while he demarcates himself from some of the 'communisms' voiced by veterans of *les années rouges* like Badiou or Negri, Lordon evades any real reckoning with the mutations in class composition, consciousness and agency that lie in the back of those theoretical developments (the crises of the mass worker and workers' identity, the trajectories of Maoism or *operaismo*), and which led to rich conjunctural and strategic debates in Marxism into the twilight of the 1980s. There is a danger that the sheer starkness of capitalist domination and social inequality in the present is taken as a substitute for the work of inquiry, organisation, recomposition and political reskilling without which communism remains a dead letter, or devolves into another species of radical populism. While the answer won't look the same, the Bolshevik question abides: 'Who, whom?'

The 'figures' of the title make for a compelling sketch, but a sketch nonetheless, not a programme: the exact forms that political deliberation over production will take remain vague, and many questions arise as to whether the 'value' governing this transitional phase retains the features (and the power and the violence) of value in capitalism. In other words, it would have been nice to see Lordon tackle the problems limned by Marx's 'Critique of the Gotha Programme' and related literatures (beginning with Lenin's *State and Revolution*) – problems which, however much they require 'stretching', remain on the agenda of any foreseeable communism. Notwithstanding these issues, and the severe limits in his considerations of the strategic nexus of race, class and gender, Lordon does set out in a compelling way the problems of scale, power, resources and the division of labour which any consequential challenge to capitalism would need to grasp and resolve, while grounding his arguments in the Spinozist political-anthropological realism advanced in other recent works. Here we see, in the leitmotiv of *consequence*, how Lordon's communist realism works simultaneously to challenge an ultra-left ambience that does not fully consider the conditions of possibility for a real exit from capitalism *and* a progressivist bad faith that imagines ecological and egalitarian transitions taking place within the undisturbed confines of capitalism.

Alberto Toscano teaches in the School of Communication at Simon Fraser University and is co-director of the Centre for Philosophy and Critical Thought at Goldsmiths. He recently co-edited The SAGE Handbook of Marxism *(2021), and his previous books include* The Theatre of Production *(2006) and* Fanaticism: The Uses of an Idea *(2010).*

Notes

1. For a bio-bibliographical sketch of Lordon's trajectory, see Alberto Toscano, 'A Structuralism of Feeling?', *New Left Review* 97 (2016), 73–93. For a recent Marxian critique of Lordon, which claims that his work can envisage only the regulation but not the abolition of capital, see Benoît Bohy-Bunel, *Contre Lordon. Anticapitalisme tronqué et spinozisme dans l'oeuvre de Frédéric Lordon* (Albi: Crise & Critique, 2021).
2. For Lordon and Nuit Debout, see this 2016 interview: https://www.versobooks.com/blogs/2833-frederic-lordon-with-nuit-debout-the-fire-didn-t-catch-hold.
3. The convergence between Agamben's writings on the Covid-19 pandemic and the recent anonymous *Manifeste conspirationniste* attributed to Julien Coupat of the Invisible Committee exceeds the remit of this essay, though it could prove an interesting testing ground for some of Lordon's hypotheses about antipolitical radicalism. Incidentally, Lordon has been rather charitable in his interpretations of the popular appeal of conspiracy theories, see his 'Narratives of the Dispossessed', *Le Monde diplomatique*, June 2015, https://mondediplo.com/2015/06/10conspiracist.
4. Frédéric Lordon, *Vivre sans? Institutions, police, travail, argent... Conversation avec Félix Boggio Éwanjé-Épée* (Paris: La Fabrique, 2019), 19.
5. Ibid., 20.
6. Ibid., 37.
7. Ibid., 46.
8. Ibid., 69.
9. Ibid., 83.
10. Ibid., 134. On this dimension of Lordon's thought, see also my 'Foreword – Passions of State', in Frédéric Lordon, *Imperium: Structures and Affects of Political Bodies* (London: Verso, 2022).
11. Ibid., 105.
12. Ibid., 115.
13. Ibid., 139. For Lordon's pointed reflection on the contemporary police in France, see Frédéric Lordon: 'The police force we have is fucked up, racist to the bone and out of control', trans. David Fernbach, *Verso blog*, 29 July 2021, https://www.versobooks.com/blogs/5126-frederic-lordon-the-police-force-we-have-is-fucked-up-racist-to-the-bone-and-out-of-control.
14. Lordon, *Vivre sans?*, 153.
15. Ibid., 156.
16. Ibid., 167.
17. Ibid., 169.
18. Ibid.
19. Ibid., 217.
20. Ibid., 189.
21. Ibid., 195.
22. Ibid., 240.
23. Quoted in Jean Hyppolite, *Genesis and Structure of Hegel's 'Phenomenology of Spirit'*, trans. Samuel Cherniak and John Heckman (Evanston, IL: Northwestern University Press, 1974), 353.
24. Lordon, *Vivre sans?*, 225.
25. Ibid., 250.
26. There is an unexplored resonance here with the account of the fusion and ossification of groups in Sartre's *Critique of Dialectical Reason*.
27. For some reflections on the nexus between communism and abolition, see the last section of my 'Communism', in *Handbook of Marxism*, eds. Beverley Skeggs, Sara Farris, Alberto Toscano and Svenja Bromberg (London: SAGE, 2022).
28. Frédéric Lordon, *Figures du communisme* (Paris: La Fabrique, 2021), 9.
29. Ibid., 15.
30. In 2021, La Dispute published a book-length dialogue between Lordon and Friot: *En travail. Conversations sur le communisme*.
31. Lordon, *Figures du communisme*, 17.
32. Ibid., 18.
33. Ibid., 54.
34. Andreas Malm, *Corona, Climate, Chronic Emergency: War Communism in the Twenty-First Century* (London and New York: Verso, 2020).
35. Lordon, *Figures du communisme*, 71.
36. Ibid., 67.
37. Ibid., 81.
38. Ibid., 81.
39. Ibid., 107.
40. Ibid., 99.
41. This is the parable whose moral is clinched by Mr. Keuner's concluding statement, from which I've taken my title: 'Mr Keuner ran into Mr Muddle, a great fighter against newspapers. "I am a great opponent of newspapers. I don't want any newspapers", said Mr Muddle. Mr Keuner said "I am a greater opponent of newspapers. I want better newspapers." If newspapers are a means to disorder, then they are also a means to achieving order. It is precisely people like Mr Muddle who through their dissatisfaction demonstrate the value of newspapers. Mr Muddle thinks he is concerned with the worthlessness of today's newspapers. In fact he is concerned with their worth tomorrow. Mr Muddle thought highly of man and did not believe that newspapers could

be made better, whereas Mr Keuner did not think very highly of man but did think that newspapers could be made better'. Bertolt Brecht, *Stories of Mr. Keuner*, trans. Martin Chalmers (San Francisco: City Lights, 2001), 64.

42. Lordon, *Figures du communisme*, 126. Lordon's work could be here brought into dialogue with recent efforts in this direction by Nick Dyer-Witheford and Jonathan Beller, among others.

43. Ibid., 196.

44. Ibid., 201.

45. Consider Cedric Robinson's rejoinder to Wood: 'I would argue then that it is quite mistaken to assume – as one Marxist historian, Ellen Wood, put it quite recently, that: "The first point about capitalism is that it is uniquely indifferent to the social identities of the people it exploits. ... Unlike previous modes of production, capitalist exploitation is not inextricably linked with extra-economic, juridical or political identities. ... In fact, there is a positive tendency in capitalism to undermine such differences, and even to dilute identities like gender or race, as capital strives to absorb people into the labour market and to reduce them to interchangeable units of labour abstracted from any specific identity." Just how, one might ask Wood, could she justify the presumption that the human materials of capitalism – capitalists, labourers, managers, and cultural workers – could be "indifferent" to the history, culture, and politics of their formation? For it is precisely in those realms that race consciousness is embedded. The structures of meaning are not the mirrors of production'. Cedric J. Robinson, *On Racial Capitalism, Black Internationalism, and Cultures of Resistance*, ed. H.L.T. Quan (London: Pluto, 2019), 189. The interpolated quotation is from Ellen Meiksins Wood, 'Capitalism and Human Emancipation', *New Left Review* 167 (Jan/Feb 1988).

46. Lordon, *Figures du communisme*, 224.

47. Ibid., 242.

48. Ibid., 247.

independent thinking from polity

Solar Politics
Oxana Timofeeva

"This book is not just a book..., it is THE book we have been waiting for."
Slavoj Žižek

PB 978-1-5095-4965-8 | February 2022 | £9.99

Pleasure Erased
The Clitoris Unthought
Catherine Malabou

An acclaimed philosopher addresses the enigma of the clitoris in culture and philosophical thought.

PB 978-1-5095-4993-1 | June 2022 | £9.99

The Invention of the 'Underclass'
A Study in the Politics of Knowledge
Loïc Wacquant

"It is an essential guide to a more ethical, genuinely reflexive sociology."
Alice O'Connor, author of *Poverty Knowledge*

PB 978-1-5095-5218-4 | February 2022 | £15.99

The Racialized Social System
Critical Race Theory as Social Theory
Ali Meghji

"an important and timely book, especially needed when everyone is talking about Critical Race Theory but few know what it is."
Amanda Lewis, University of Illinois at Chicago

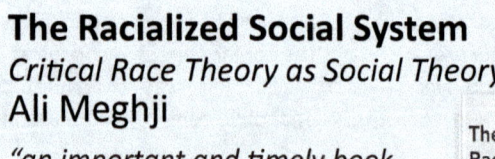

PB 978-1-5095-3995-6 | April 2022 | £15.99

Order your copy now or join our mailing list at **politybooks.com**
@politybooks / facebook.com/politybooks

Being, becoming, subsumption
The Kantian roots of a Marxist problematic
Andrés Saenz de Sicilia

One of the fundamental tensions within Marx's writings arises from the complex relationship between the systematic and historical aspects of his description of capitalist society.[1] A century and a half after the publication of *Capital* – and in light of the historical adventures of communism that must, for the most part, be considered as an accumulation of catastrophic failures – this tension continues to both energise and attenuate the reception of Marx's thought, symptomatically expressing the radically distinctive and still elusory practical-theoretical foundations of his project. On the one hand, capital is depicted by Marx as an ensemble of social relations forming an apparently closed totality capable of reproducing itself purely through its own internal dynamism: capital as self-sufficient system. On the other hand, Marx reminds us that the capitalist mode of production does not fall from the sky but grows out of, or violently breaks free from, the economic structures of feudalism, developing within and in antithesis to past relations and technologies: capital as historical in nature and therefore subject to the turbulent play of conflictual energies shaping and propelling human history. For Marx the capitalist system is a whole, a totality of interlocking relations that presuppose and support one another. Yet at the same time, it is not a whole with a timeless, independent, self-moving existence, an essence suspended in the void. Capital does not develop from nothing but is a historical phenomenon subject to temporal emergence and decay amidst a whole host of 'disturbing influences'.[2]

The 'becoming' of capital as a system is thus dependent on a mode of development that is simultaneously a negation, absorption or negotiation of inherited social relations and forms (of wealth, technology, knowledge, institutions, social roles, practices, etc.) and their subordination to the logic of capital's own 'life-process'. As first and foremost a social relation *of production*, Marx describes, in just a few scattered fragments, how capital subordinates – or 'subsumes' – existing forms of production in order to configure them as capitalist valorisation processes, engines of profit for their owners.[3] As Marx outlines, this can occur 'formally', simply through a transformation of the economic relationships involved in production (underpinned by the introduction of relations of exchange between buyers and sellers of labour-power). But subsumption under capital, Marx notes, can and does also occur in a deeper, 'real' form, which transforms the material composition of production (the techniques and technology of production as well as the products themselves). Both at the economic and material levels, Marx thus identifies the *mechanisms* by which specifically capitalist forms of social domination come into being, transforming existing apparatuses of production and property relations in order to secure the extraction of surplus labour from workers in the form of surplus-value. These 'formal' and 'real' modes of subsumption (along with further, 'hybrid' forms identified by Marx) constitute mechanisms of domination, mechanisms through which the becoming of capital, the augmentation of its exploitative and transformative power over human life, is achieved.[4]

Once a sufficient degree of such subsumption has occurred, once a sufficient mass of social substance has been incorporated and formed in accordance with capital's life process then it might be said that the system is no longer simply *becoming* but has attained *being* and, famously, seems to stand upon its own hind legs independently of the human hands which animate it. Marx describes the 'being' of capital as an organic system, that is, a system capable of reproducing its own conditions of existence, sustaining itself through a cyclical metamorphosis which passes through a necessary sequence of stages or 'forms' regeneratively. Yet in distinction from other organic systems, capital's peculiarity is its need to expand, to accumulate. By definition capital cannot survive by 'simply' reproducing itself, by regenerating itself exactly as it was when its life cycle began. It must, rather, reproduce itself in an expanded form, is driven onwards and outwards to absorb an ever greater wealth of material that it can claim as its own through commodification, exploitation and accumulation. The *being* of capital thus implies no rest or stasis but rather *constant becoming*, constant growth, a spiralling outward of its centripetal energy which runs up against multiple barriers: the resistance of workers, the finitude of nature, even its own destructive drive for insatiable accumulation.

If the becoming of value toward more value, its axiomatic expansion, is systematically presupposed and necessitated by capital, how does this correlate with the other becoming of capital, its historical becoming (and anticipated eventual death) as a finite form of social production? When, how and as an effect of which social forces will capital's reign over human life come to an end?

Revolutionary (im)possibilities

As is well known, for Marx these were first and foremost practical questions, which nonetheless generated prolific theoretical reflection. In the tension which emerges between the being and becoming of capital, its 'organic coherence' yet historical transience, the Marxist problematic of revolution is central. Does revolution follow a progressive arc of necessity, emerging into actuality when capital's 'time has come'? Or does communist revolution rather subsist within and against capital from its beginning, as the ever-present possibility of overcoming that it harbours immanently within itself? The objectivist posture of the former, for which revolution follows a quasi-naturalistic or divine teleology, independent of any individual desires and intentions, is inverted in the subjectivism of the latter, for which revolution emerges as the voluntaristic interruption of capitalist normality: Walter Benjamin's 'emergency brake' on the train of historical progress.[5] In light of communism's multiple defeats and capitalism's monopolistic installation as the sole economic paradigm of the modern world system, neither standpoint would appear to offer a particularly credible horizon of revolutionary anticipation. To the historical objectivist, we may ask: when? To the subjectivist, we may ask: by who? Furthermore, in the absence of any revolutionary challenge to capital's reign, what are we to make of its unchecked development? Might capital's *being-becoming* approach a point of total absorption and saturation of the human life world, not only 'formally', but also 'really'? Might this point have already been crossed, leaving us in a 'post-historical' abyss with no way out?

Because of its implied consequences for the character and organisation of production, and thereby also for the struggles that grow out of production, Marx's tentative and fragmentary conceptualisation of capitalist subsumption has provided an evocative focal point for debates surrounding the transformations (or death) of labour-oriented revolutionary politics. If communism is first and foremost a workers movement, and the experience of work is shaped by the particular forms of domination operative in production, then an analysis of these forms and their evolution would seem to offer at the very least a point of departure, if not a comprehensive blueprint, for engaging critically with the trajectories of struggle that have the overcoming of capitalist social relations as their ultimate horizon.

The theory of capitalist subsumption – if such a theory can be said to exist – compresses synoptically the central significance of the analysis of surplus-value production in *Capital* (the modalities of command and exploitation of labour ranging from the extension of the working day to the introduction of machinery and automation) in an account of capital's tendency to transform not only the directly social and economic aspects of production (with the generalisation of waged work and its corresponding worker-boss power relation) but also the material and technological aspects of production (with the reconfiguration of the labour process and the ascent of the machine/algorithm). In this way, Marx was able to index the experience of specific forms of class-based interpersonal domination and 'objective' alienation (the power of the boss and the machine over workers) to his analysis of the structure and dynamics of capitalist accumulation (the production and realisation of surplus-value, at both a micro and macro level).

For subsequent Marxist thinkers concerned with the historical fate of revolution, subsumption provided a technical vocabulary with which to designate the evolving relation between specific mechanisms of power and the overall dynamics of the capitalist system, between the experience of subjection to the command of capital and the guiding tendencies of accumulation. A putative theory of subsumption was thereby seen to offer the key to grasping not only the 'objective' path of capitalist development but also 'subjective' programs of resistance to it, thus uniting the configuration of conditions from within which revolution must emerge.

This reception of subsumption within Marxist theory has been by turns bombastic and muted, creative and conservative, deployed to diagnose the epochal shifts in capitalist power over society as a whole (as a linear movement through phases of 'formal', 'real' and eventually 'total' subsumption) or to re-affirm the consistency of a basic logic governing every existent and possible instance of capitalist socialisation (as in 'capital-logic' and 'value-form theory'). That is, interpretations of the theory have largely fallen on one side of the tension between history and system with which our discussion began. There is little need to rehearse these debates here, save to note that whilst the latter tendency may claim greater conceptual coherence and fidelity to Marx's texts, it is the former that has been more energising for critical debates, capturing the generalised – if fuzzy – sentiment that capitalist power has evolved and intensified to such a degree that it now invades and interferes with every aspect of our lives, offering no apparent way out. Real subsumption, accordingly, has for many come to stand as a catchword for the imperious enclosure of life by capital, like the map described in Borges' fragment which entirely covers the territory it represents, coinciding with it 'point for point'.[6] No longer restricted in its effects to the 'rationalisation' of discrete labour processes, capital's logic of coercion and technical efficiency would, on this reading, penetrate and transform the entirety of human existence such that, in Negri's formulation, 'society itself has been converted into a factory', or, in Adorno's prognosis, 'the "alteration of the technical composition of capital" is prolonged within those encompassed, and indeed constituted by, the technological demands of the production process'.[7] It is not only the worker's labour – a specific quantum of their time – that becomes 'one of the modes of existence of capital' here, but the worker's (and indeed, the non-worker's) entire life, workers *as such*, individually and collectively, in their inner and outer being. This conception of real (or in some variants 'total') subsumption would thus encompass all that capital has done and continues to do to our world and ourselves, whilst simultaneously circumscribing the evaporating terrain of revolutionary possibilities – their tendential or even consummated impossibilities.

Such interpretations of subsumption imply a theoretical short circuit, whereby the logic of power specific to capitalist production is transposed onto the social totality in an unmediated and absolutised way, sacrificing a nuanced operation of Marx's critical apparatus in favour of a sensational rhetorical diagnosis of the present. Those who have sought to demonstrate the misreading of Marx at stake in these attempts to map formal and real subsumption onto historical phases of capitalist society have, by contrast, toiled to reinsert the theory of subsumption into a systematic account of capital.[8] Yet the difficulty here is that while different forms of subsumption in production do not directly correspond to distinct phases of global capitalist development, those forms – in particular real subsumption – do have profound transformative effects that ripple outward through the broader sphere of life, reshaping the overall context of social action and struggle. The secure theoretical footing offered by a systematic account of capital's being essentially remains silent on the question of capital's historical becoming (and overcoming), other than through an affirmation of the unchanging laws and tendencies of accumulation which supposedly govern its developmental trajectory. The result is a decoupling of the system from its history which 'freezes' it in time.

It thus becomes clear that despite their apparent opposition, both interpretations of subsumption – the systematic and the historicist – reinforce the idea that at an ideological and practical level capital has effectively achieved the suppression of its own subjection to historical finitude. In doing so they sever the critical analysis of capitalism from the constructive problem of its revolutionary overcoming, aborting Marxism's central task. To interpret subsumption from either a purely historical *or* systemic perspective undermines precisely what is theoretically forceful and unique about the category of subsumption with respect to this task.

Subsumption has a privileged status within the Marxist conceptual apparatus because it marks the *interface* between capital as system and capital as history. Whereas categories such as value, commodity and capital are internal to the totality of capitalist form-determinations, subsumption designates the point of articulation between this organic 'system-in-process' and the historical substance through which it lives, which it must absorb and reform in order to exist. As we have seen, it is only through the subsumption of existing social forms of production that capital can emerge into being and establish itself. And even once this has occurred in its 'real' form, Marx insists, it continues to radically remould 'all its social and technological conditions' through a 'constant revolutionising of production'.[9] Subsumption is thus *the* category of mediation relating the capitalist system to its external and internal foundations, which of necessity are subject to the flux of historical time. Whatever is indicated by subsumption is thus that which joins capital as system to the history that it both resides within and acts upon.

What, then, is indicated by subsumption? Here is where the problem resides. Given Marx's rudimentary sketch of subsumption, its tentative appearance in drafts and notes and its failure to be integrated into the final version of *Capital*, the weight it seems to bear as the principle category of mediation between capital's systematic and historical aspects is not supported by a developed conceptual framework. Lacking a robust apparatus of its own, the theory of subsumption has, as a result, been subordinated to two competing schemas of totality which have dominated Marxist thought: a systematic dialectic that totalises synchronically and a philosophy of history that totalises diachronically. Each of these in its own way functions to disarm the revolutionary tension between the form and content of capital, between the system and its history, between the perfect ideal and imperfect materiality of exploitation. In order to re-activate this tension on the plane of theory, so that Marxism can remain operable as a discourse which tracks the movement of

Photo: Panda Mery, 'Prototype for a nonfuctional satellite (2013)' a dynamic and unstable system, of concrete conditions which continually deform their own space of possibilities (to borrow a phrase from Guiseppe Longo), it is necessary to explore what exactly is at stake in the category of subsumption, both in its philosophical pre-history and in its passage to becoming a materialist category adequate to the critique of capitalist domination.[10]

A 'critical' concept of subsumption

The sporadic yet insistent appearance of the term subsumption throughout Marx's writings, from the early critiques of Hegel through to *Capital*, is symptomatic of the complex and ambivalent relation his work has to the German philosophical tradition. Much difficulty around the construction of a coherent Marxist conceptualisation of subsumption stems from a failure to appreciate the depth of this relation and the degree of continuity manifest in Marx's critical orientation, not only with Hegel's dialectic, but with an entire constellation of problems animated at least as early as Kant. Whilst seemingly far removed from the urgency of debates over the fate of revolutionary movements or the deepening of capitalist control over work and everyday life, the aporias within which the discussion of 'real subsumption' now appears confined can perhaps only be resolved through a reassessment of this philosophical inheritance.

Subsumption is broadly understood as a concept of classification or categorisation. In its most abstract and general philosophical form, it designates *a relation of belonging to a class of things*, of *incorporation into a more general category or into a formal unity*, as particulars are related to a universal, or species to a genus. Traditionally, then, subsumption has concerned the problem of ordering or organisation, of establishing a hierarchy between terms, ranging from the most particular to the most general. 'Plato' is subsumed under the genus 'man', which in turn is subsumed under the genus 'animal', and so on. The roots of such a hierarchy lie in Aristotle's taxonomic schema of being, formalised graphically in Medieval thought as 'Porphry's tree'.

This is the meaning which subsumption had in pre-Kantian philosophy. If this was the sense in which Marx used the term when speaking of the 'subsumption of labour under capital' it would not enable him to pose the problem of subsumption in its properly 'critical' form. Which is to say, beyond the problem of logically organising pre-given elements or tracing relations within a given system, he would not be able to develop an interrogation of how those elements come to be constituted in the first place, how they are given form such that they can be made to fit within a systematic totality; how, for example, human activity, which is common to all societies, comes to take the form of a commodity, as 'labour-power', which can be purchased and thus incorporated into capital's accumulation process. This is precisely what Marx must uncover if, in the course of his critical exposition of the system of political economy, he is to show *how* labour becomes one of the 'modes of existence' of capital and to demonstrate that this requires a specific conjunction of historical conditions and forces, rather than expressing a 'natural' relation of belonging. Without the Kantian intervention into the discourse of subsumption, Marx's use of it would express only that labour is incorporated into capital because, tautologically, it pertains to capital within the logic of the system. That is, it would offer no critical leverage on the constitution of the system and its historical impermanence.

Let us turn, then, to Kant's critical reframing of subsumption. At first sight Kant's use of subsumption seems to retain its straightforward and traditionally logical form. Indeed, the 'transcendental logic' which Kant developed and within which his account of subsumption figures was modelled upon the 'general logic' outlined above. But Kant went on to add a new and highly significant dimension to the problem of how a judgement of subsumption can be enacted: that of the heterogeneity between the elements that are to be related in the judgement. He asked not how subsumption is possible in its formally logical sense, as an ordering connection of thought determinations, but rather, in analysing the conditions of possibility for any experience of an object, he asked how sensibility and the understanding – cognitive faculties that are 'entirely unhomogeneous' with one another, and thus generate representations that are different in kind – could be connected subsumptively. This is a problem because 'in all subsumptions of an object under a concept the representations of the former must be *homogeneous* with the latter'.[11] Homogeneity is necessary because subsumption always implies identity: that which is subsumed under a category is said to be a particular instance *of that category*, whilst the subsuming category 'inheres' *in* the particular, which is to say, is embodied *by it*. Whatever is subsumed under some category or form *is* that category or form, in some basic sense specified by the nature of the system ('Socrates' *is* a man and 'man' is embodied *in* Socrates). But whereas logical subsumption deals with universal and particular elements of the same kind (conceptual representations) that only have to be located appropriately within the system according to their generality and specificity ('animal' being higher than 'man' but distinct from 'mineral', etc.) transcendental subsumption deals with non-conceptual elements (sensible representations) that nonetheless are to be subsumed under concepts. How is this identity between unlike elements possible? How can sensations be adapted to concepts, such that they can be presented as 'belonging' under them? This is the basic problem of subsumption in its 'critical' form.

Kant's solution to this problem rests on the identification of a productive act of 'form-determination' by which sensible representations are constituted as particulars for concepts, and so can be presented as subsumed under them. Beyond a relational distribution of homogeneous elements, situated at the appropriate level according to their rank in the systemic hierarchy, Kant exposes a mechanics of cognitive production whereby any particular subsumed under a concept must first have been *produced* as a particular through an act of form-determination (a 'judgement'). The particular element must have been reworked and endowed with conceptual form in order to participate in the system's internal economy.

For Kant, this form-determination occurs through a dissolution of the spontaneous and singular form of unity which the object initially has when received by the senses and its subsequent re-articulation according to a generic schema of conceptual relations. Through this productive process, every object of experience comes to share in the same basic set of organising determinations, a universal form of objectivity common to all subjective experience (both within an individual consciousness over time, and between subjects). Aesthetic representations are subsumed under the 'pure concepts of the understanding' so that something 'unthinkable' becomes 'thinkable', something private becomes communicable. The configuration of an initial 'given' series (sense data) is dissected and its elements are resynthesised according to the logic of a second, dominant series (pure concepts) that determines their unity in a new way. Those elements, in their new interconnected form, now instantiate the universal, abstract 'form' of objectivity in a particular, concrete object (for Kant, the abstract, 'empty' concepts become filled with a sensible 'content'). In this way, the elements of the first series are subsumed under the second series *through a process of synthetic form-determination*. This process forms the object generically, such that it can be related and compared with other objects and so integrated within the system (of self-conscious experience) according to its appropriate place.

Kant thus shows that only through the unifying form-determination of the 'transcendental synthesis' – the division of that which is given to sensation and a subsequent synthesis governed by the concepts of the understanding – can the identity (of particular and universal) implied in subsumption be produced. Rather than solely exploring how *particulars* relate to *universals*, the question of how *individual* or *singular* entities (perhaps even *pre-individuals*) first come to be formed as particular instantiations of a general category thereby also enters into view. The problem of subsumption does not consist in slotting isolated elements into a pregiven structure naturalistically or theistically (that is, assuming their pre-ordained commensurability and belonging to a harmonious order) but of the appropriative reconfiguration of one series or topological distribution according to a second; a forcing achieved by division and recomposition. Kant's model is one of production, a fusion of elements that do not in themselves 'belong' together. More important still, it is not simply that the two types of representation (concepts and sensible intuitions) in the subsumptive relation are heterogeneous *per se*, but that they possess kinds of unity that obey heterogeneous logics of composition (the aesthetic and the discursive). Sensibility generates an entirely different kind of unity (a spontaneous and singular, unrepeatable unity) to that determined on the basis of conceptual relations (which are by definition universal and generic). Kant's account of transcendental synthesis centres on the negation of one kind of unity or organisation that is alien to the dominant logic and its re-formation according to another, thereby enabling the subsumed entity to be absorbed within the framework of a system.

Subsumption and system

This is the deeper, 'critical' problem of subsumption which Kant establishes and within which Marx's use of subsumption is inscribed, a problem which reaches to the foundations of systematicity, asking which processes ground the emergence of a basic, objective set of relations and forms, rather than taking those relations and forms as given by nature. It marks the threshold at which the discourse of subsumption moves from structure to genesis, from taxonomic arrangement to a genetic analysis of the formal homogeneity presupposed by all taxonomy, from a problem of recognition to one of constitution. Acknowledging the distinctive outlines which the problem of subsumption takes on in its properly critical, post-Kantian form is crucial if we are to fully grasp the significance of subsumption in Marx's thought, the status and interconnection of the different forms of subsumption under capital that he outlines, and the political horizons of action implied in the notion of 'real subsumption'.

Considered from the critical standpoint outlined above, subsumption is not simply a procedure which articulates or surveys the internal organisation of a system (understood as an ensemble of forms and their relations) but is rather a category of mediation between such a system and the content or substance which it seeks to form, which it needs in order to live. To speak of forms of subsumption is to speak of modes of *incorporation* into a systematic totality; this is precisely what is at stake in the subsumptive relation, as much for Kant and Hegel as it is for Marx (despite the radically different contexts and evaluations of subsumption in their writings). Subsumption in its critical conception denotes not merely belonging but the process by which such belonging is effected, a process of form-determination which shapes particulars *as* the particulars of that which subsumes them. As we have noted, already with Kant – however obliquely and incompletely posed – subsumption implies moving from the analysis of relations between given things to an analysis of their production, prefiguring the transition Marx makes in *Capital* from the analysis of exchange, as relations between commodities, to the production processes whereby those commodities come to be. Marx is not only interested in the position of the worker within capitalist society or how their labour functions within the cycle of accumulation, but also in how individuals are *formed* as workers, how labour is *formed* as wage-labour, how surplus-labour is *formed* as surplus-value, how the product of labour is *formed* as a commodity, etc. In short, all of those processes of form-determination on which the being and becoming of capital depends and in which capital's life-process are expressed.

However, recognising the theoretical transition from given elements to their production processes does not exhaust the scope of transformation which subsumption undergoes in this critical phase of thought, whose interrogations span from pure reason to political economy. The central question opened up by Kant's intervention is as follows: if subsumption is not merely the recognition and distribution of elements within a system but depends on the *productive process* of synthesis by which each subsumed entity is formed as a *particular* instance of the *universal* which subsumes it, what is the nature of this formative process? What do we speak of when we speak of the form-determination of that which is subsumed? How does the division and synthetic recomposition 'work'?

Kant offers notoriously technical and intricate answers to these questions, all of which ultimately rely on an innovative reworking of classical and early modern conceptions of how the intellect functions (procedures of analysis, comparison, deduction, etc.). In this sense his account of the form-determination of objects of experience is eminently idealist in character: it occurs as a 'judgement', involves multiple procedures of cognition and generates purely subjective effects that make no claim on things as they are in themselves. And yet, however unconsciously it is presented, there is undoubtably a proto-materialist impulse in Kant's account of subsumption insofar as he recognises the resistant 'materiality' and heterogeneity of the sensible 'content' that is to be formed conceptually in order for such objectivity to be engendered. Unlike Hegel, for whom content and form merely *appear* to be exterior to one another but are in truth linked organically as necessary moments of a single encompassing 'idea', Kant recognises that subsumption involves a kind of arbitrary or contingent transition between diverse logics of composition. There is nothing about sensible representations as such that necessitates their discursive re-configuration (there exist beings that feel but do not think). But because the system into which these representations are to be internalised is discursive in character, it demands this re-configuration in order to be able to incorporate them. The system must form the matter that it needs in order to function, and lives more the more it forms (otherwise, Kant says, conceptual form without sensible content remains 'empty', lifeless). This view was the result of Kant's acceptance that there was no metaphysical or logical guarantee underpinning a correspondence between the order of our experience and a 'real' order of things outside of the mind. This proposition meant that the subject could not merely 'intuit' the order of the universe but rather had to generate it in the first place. Unless one adheres to the notion of a 'pure' or absolute order of forms established by a creator god, one is forced to acknowledge that every discrete system depends on the formation of a content or substance that obeys diverse and heterogeneous logics of composition, that is, it depends upon the act of *production*. A system thus lives to the extent that it can successfully form-determine this substance in accordance with its own logic, which is to say, produce it as a moment of its own existence and so *subsume it*.

Metabolic materialism

Marx's great invention, which would establish the foundations for his account of capitalist subsumption, was to take up this insight and repose it in materialist terms. For Marx, the immense power of form-determination that was so central to German idealism was undermined by its limitation to processes of a subjective and ideal character, to theory rather than practice. Marx sought to liberate the force of this synthesis by grounding form-determination not in the dynamics of cognition – processes of conceptual analysis and synthesis, judgement and syllogism – but rather in what he, following Feuerbach, emphatically referred to as the 'real life' of 'real individuals', a notion of life grounded in human flesh and blood instead of rarefied ideas. In this way, Marx's early 'humanism' recoded German idealism's conception of a subjective activity which unfolds in an abstract, ideal domain, transforming it into a conception of objective activity ('*gegenständliche Tätigkeit*') which plays out in the material domain of human-nature interactions. Marx theorised the essential structure of these practical interactions with increasing precision throughout his writings, conceptualising them as *labour* and, more broadly, *production*. The synthesis underpinning capitalist subsumption derives its content from this materialist conception of 'real' human activity as production: a process of form-determination grounded in the transformative and appropriative relationship between social individuals and their material environment.

Developing a materialist account of subsumption thus implied reconstructing (rather than rejecting) the idealist account of form-determination, according to the character and constraints of the human-nature relationship as it plays out on the stage of history, rather than according to the character and constraints of discursive cognition as it plays out within a 'pure' rational subject. Crucially, from the 1850's onwards Marx began to conceptualise productive activity as bound by the conservationist laws of metabolic interchange (the exchange of matter and energy between an organic system and its environment), stipulating that human labour 'can only proceed as nature does ... can only change the form of the materials' it works upon, through 'composition and division' rather than pure 'acts of creation'.[12] Just as with Kant, form-determination here occurs by a dissolution of some previous organisation of the 'content' and its subsequent re-synthesis according to a new schema of objectivity.[13] However, Marx's metabolic reconceptualisation of this process not only establishes material (rather than cognitive) constraints on how it can occur, but founds the objectivity of its resulting product upon an entirely different logic of form, one in which practical *instrumentality* rather than pure rationality is the guiding principle.[14] Accordingly, through labour, as it unfolds in a technically structured production process, human agents are able to appropriate matter and energy in its 'spontaneously' occurring natural forms and rework it in order to produce new, 'synthetic' forms of objectivity that more effectively satisfy their needs and wants. The notion of 'form' at work here does not simply denote some new physical organisation of the material (although this is a necessary condition) but the instrumental end which the material is intended to serve (e.g., the satisfaction of hunger, or the cutting of trees). Labour thus enacts the subsumption of physical material under a practical end, a form-determination of the material which endows it with a novel or enhanced usability.

The objective forms which are thereby produced –

what, in the context of Marx's analysis of the commodity, are designated 'use-values' – are forms whose possibility is conditioned by the inherent properties and limitations of the natural materials from which they are composed. However, this conditioning places only a constraint on what and how humans can produce. Within Marx's materialist framework there is no necessary connection leading from content (natural material) to form (practically useful thing). Instead, as Marx repeatedly affirms, this connection varies contingently across time and place, always being determined by a particular society and its 'mode of production'.[15] Furthermore, as Marx insists, the needs that are to be satisfied through the production of use-values are themselves variable and evolve in relation to the development of production: new forms of production generate new needs in a unceasing creative spiral which describes the becoming of history.

The objective forms that result from the synthetic activity of labour are thus always specific to a certain society and can so be properly thought of as *social forms*. Their production is a process of *social form-determination*: a society practically determining (that is, inventing and actualising) the forms it gives to the natural resources at its disposal so that, through collective effort, collective needs can be satisfied. Modes of production can be thought of as contrasting – and often competing – logics of material organisation or synthesis; instrumental and technical logics which govern the construction of social forms of objectivity. These objective forms are resources for satisfying needs and thereby securing the reproduction of the individuals that make up the society which produces them, as well as all of the material conditions of their existence (that is, the reproduction of the society as a whole). The satisfaction of needs offered by such produced resources can have a greater or lesser temporal and technical immediacy: an animal hunted and cooked satisfies physiological needs directly whereas the cultivation of crops or the formation of complex infrastructure, scientific knowledge, communication networks, etc., satisfy needs in a less direct manner (for example, as 'means of production') or simply satisfy needs that are less 'direct' (in a physiological sense).

There are two basic senses of subsumption operative in this general outline of social reproduction, prior to its specification as capitalist social reproduction: first, the subsumption of some mass of material (encountered in a naturally or historically given configuration) under practical forms of objectivity, which is implied in every act of labour; second, the subsumption of social individuals (those who produce) under a 'mode of production' which regulates their labour activity through a particular conjunction of social relations and technical forces.[16] Both are processes that determine a historically and socially specific form of unity among elements whose prior unity first has to be dissolved (a prior 'objective' unity: *the tree*; a prior mode of production: *feudalism*).

A fundamental reciprocity obtains between these two moments of subsumption in that a 'mode of production' is constituted through human practice (which is form-determining as such) yet comes to shape human practice. It is an objectified result of action that acts back upon the active subjects that bring it into existence and sustain it. Or, to put this in temporal terms, it is a structure produced by past activity that comes to determine future activity (although for much of human history and for many of those subject to them, modes of production have appeared as immutable structures, a matrix of 'second nature' rather than explicitly 'artificial' and impermanent forms of life that can be contested and re-made). Mapping this onto the critical model of subsumption outlined above, it can be said that the metabolic appropriation of natural material that occurs in labour is the mechanism by which the system of collective human existence (as some particular 'society') integrates the 'content' it needs in order to live, endowing it with a practical form appropriate to the society's particular needs. Correspondingly, the subsumption of individuals and their form-determining activity under a 'mode of production' is what guarantees systemic cohesion among all of the discrete acts of labour (and consumption); it unites and determines the overall configuration of all of the discrete forms and their production, aggregating them as a functional totality (just as, for Kant, the transcendental unity of apperception unites every discrete act of subsuming intuitions under concepts, binding them all together in the continuum of a single conscious experience).

Capitalist subsumption

When Marx speaks of capitalist subsumption – more precisely, of the 'formal' and 'real' subsumption of labour under capital – this entire model of metabolic form-determination and social reproduction is presupposed. For Marx, the subsumption of labour under capital is a shorthand which expresses abstractly, as a relation between two elements, what is in fact a relation between two processes: the labour process and the valorisation process. In this relation, the labour process (the metabolic activity of practical form-determination outlined above) is subsumed under the valorisation process (the 'miraculous' increase of capital achieved simply through the cyclical metamorphoses of its forms). Through its subsumption under the valorisation process the labour process acquires a new 'form' or logic of organisation. It has suddenly become 'about' or 'for' something entirely different to that which has historically been its primary purpose. It is no longer oriented towards the satisfaction of needs (however unevenly that satisfaction may have been distributed among social individuals and classes) but now serves the goal of increasing abstract wealth and further, expanded production. In this new form, labour becomes the material engine or 'content' of economic accumulation, a subordinate aspect or moment of capital's life processes:

> *The labour process posited prior to value, as point of departure* – which, owing to its abstractness, its pure materiality, is common to all forms of production – here reappears *again within capital*, as a process which proceeds within its substance and forms its content.[17]

However, as we have seen, in contexts where subsumed and subsuming elements are in some sense 'heterogeneous', we have not adequately grasped subsumption simply by stating what is subsumed under what – we have merely presented it. What is demanded is to explain *how* something comes to be subsumed, to trace the underlying synthesis, the concrete mechanisms of form-determination whose *result* is the subsumptive relation as a *fait accompli*.

Formal and real subsumption describe strategies or mechanisms by which the labour process is adapted or reconfigured (*form-determined*) such that it becomes a valorisation process, and so can be effectively integrated into the system of capitalist accumulation. This primarily involves subordinating the intrinsic goal of labour (the production of use-values) to the goal of valorisation (the production of surplus-value) such that the accumulation of capital rather than the satisfaction of social needs comes to be the principal logic of organisation (the 'form') governing production. Given that surplus-value production is achieved only through the *exploitation* of surplus-labour, what is involved here are mechanisms for ensuring and perfecting the exploitation of labour.

First, with formal subsumption the capitalist uses their 'formal' ownership of the worker's labour time (a contractually agreed duration of work) to appropriate a surplus of product 'containing' surplus-value. In exchange for a wage the capitalist has purchased the right to use the worker's capacities and to appropriate the results. By their legally entitled command over labour, acting as 'capital personified', they are thus able to 'form-determine' this activity as *surplus-value producing* activity, rather than merely use-value producing activity (ensuring, for example, that work is done to a sufficient standard and with a competitive level of productivity).[18] It is only in this way that labour has acted *as* capital – has effectively valorised an initial sum of value, increasing it. The form-determination of the labour process as a valorisation process, achieved through this 'formal' right of ownership and command, is how, in the most basic sense, labour is subsumed under capital, made 'one of its moments', even though the labour process remains essentially unchanged in its technical methods or objective results.[19]

Second, real subsumption designates a second mechanism for form-determining the labour process as a valorisation process. Rather than relying on the capitalist's economic power over labour to ensure its adequate exploitation, real subsumption involves a reconfiguration of the technical structure and material composition of the labour process itself, in order to maximise the production of surplus-value. Here, the metabolic basis of production, which has become the material content of a capitalist social form, is altered in its *materiality* by the capitalist. The labour process is transformed not only socially, in terms of the economic relationships and forms through which it is organised, but at the level of the activity of labour itself and the technologies that enable and orient this activity. The worker is now not only subject to the direct domination of the employer, but also to the indirect domination of the objects that the worker must use in order to realise their metabolism with nature, in order to work at all. Tracing this deeper sense of form-determination through the successive stages of co-operation, manufacture and large-scale industry based on machinery, Marx shows how real subsumption brings about a complete transformation of the modern labour process.

As Patrick Murray has noted, the contrast between formal and real subsumption establishes a distinction between 'social' and 'material' mechanisms of form-determining the labour process (though of course, in a less direct sense, the social is always material and *vice versa*).[20] Maintaining focus on *how* these mechanisms actually operate, it is crucial to stress that this form-determination occurs as a process of *domination and exploitation*, that capitalist subsumption is not an 'automatic' process driven by a logic of natural necessity but an inherently antagonistic and contested social process. In striving to determine the labour process in a new form corresponding to the end of valorisation (an end which is intrinsically contradictory to workers' interests and well-being) capital encounters a resistant materiality, an 'obstinate yet elastic barrier'.[21] This is not simply resistance of a 'passive' materiality as occurs in every act of labour, the inertia of every natural form that seeks to remain as it is against the force of entropy (if nature can be said to be 'passive' in this way), but of the 'active' materiality of workers' subjectivity, a subjectivity capable of posing its own conflicting ends. On the one hand, we can speak of the 'active' resistance of labour to its exploitation by the capitalist, of the rift between the two claims on labour famously dramatised by Marx in his chapter on the working day: the worker's claim over their own body (which bears the capacity for labour) and the capitalist's claim over the commodity they have bought (the use of that capacity).[22] On the other hand, real subsumption clearly expresses a strategy of maximising this exploitation by other means than direct interpersonal command.

Which is to say, rather than relying on managerial discipline and the threat of unemployment to motivate the worker's productivity, the owners of the production process can reconfigure its technical structure in order to make the worker's exploitation an objective feature of that process. Here, the worker must toil not because a capitalist commands it but because the means of production do. The labour process itself is designed to exploit the worker, and so, in order to work at all, the worker must submit to this objective apparatus of domination, becoming a means to *its* end rather than vice versa.

This inversion of the means and ends of production is at the core of the problem of real subsumption, which Marx describes as rendering capitalist power, exploitation and alienation a 'technological fact'.[23] Yet the significance of real subsumption is not limited to the immediate context of exploitation and subjection of the worker in production, it also bears on the wider problem of the historical being and becoming of capital. With the increasing complexity and integrated character of the instrumental forms that have emerged in modernity and whose constant revolutionising is presupposed in capitalist accumulation, the social means of production, taken as a totality, pose the threat of locking humanity into the social logics of the present – which is to say, the destructive logics of class domination and unbound capital accumulation – as they become increasingly 'built in' to the technical apparatuses humanity depends on to live. Driven by competition, capitalists ceaselessly strive to implement ever more effective ways of increasing the productivity and exploitability of labour, but in transforming the labour process, these effects bleed out into the rest of society, which, after all, is composed materially of all of the products that result from these discrete labour processes. Gradually, patterns of consumption, the formation of identities, social institutions, infrastructure and communication, international relations – in short, the entire life-world of humanity – comes to be reshaped by the effects of a process whose driving logic is capital accumulation.

Yet to whatever degree this vast machinery of domination expands and envelops the totality of what we might call life, we have seen that the power of capital is rooted in its effort to control production, in its subsumption of the labour process in which the practical form and instrumental purpose of the means of social existence are decided. This subsumption, however, is riven by tension and conflict, revealing the struggle at the core of the attempt to integrate the resistant materiality of labour into the system of capitalist social forms. In its resistance, labour expresses its being as something other than merely identical with the form and goal it is subsumed under in this system (a system within which it appears as 'variable capital'). It is an element that refuses to submit to the new synthesis imposed upon it, either recalcitrantly or by proposing another synthesis altogether. What is at stake here is not simply a question of worker control and autonomy, but of which ends the human metabolism with nature serves. Capitalist subsumption involves a struggle over the form determination of this metabolism (as a 'labour process') and its product, which by implication is also an indirect struggle over the form-determination of society as a whole. It is in this sense that we can grasp real subsumption as the crucial point of mediation between the abstract being of capital as a system and its concrete historical becoming. By appropriating the human metabolism with nature, capital has highjacked the practical mechanism by which human societies reproduce their life and world, subverting the qualitatively evolving interplay between productive capacities and consumption needs (the basis for all historical becoming). Whilst this metabolism has for much of history served to sustain contexts of exploitation and class domination, the specificity of its capitalist subsumption is its re-orientation toward an abstract, purely quantitative end. This is why Marx claims that, through real subsumption, 'only capital has subjugated historical progress to the service of wealth'.[24]

From Kant to Marx

Was it necessary to take this Kantian detour, through concepts, cognition, synthesis and form-determination, in order to adequately address the relation between capital as system and capital as history? In order to enucleate the problem of real subsumption and its implications for revolutionary struggles? It is not difficult to anticipate the criticisms that such a 'philosophical' framing of these problems might elicit, a framing that may at first sight appear to pull Marx back into the theoretical field from which he sought so intently to escape in the early years of his intellectual formation. Yet paradoxically, it is only by addressing the critical refounding of subsumption which occurs within Kantian philosophy that we can appreciate the full significance of this category for Marx's developed materialism and critique of political economy. It is a case, not of an abstract negation of the philosophical outlook, but one that appropriates its elements whilst transcending its limits.

Two proto-materialist aspects of subsumption in Kant's thought open the possibility for Marx's reworking and redeployment of subsumption: first, the recognition that 'matter' is internally differentiated, or organised according to heterogeneous logics of form (discursive, aesthetic, etc.); second, (and related), the rejection of a 'naturalistic' internalisation of all forms within a single, closed system of being or space of possibilities, a creationist model of the causality of things which would guarantee their co-belonging and harmonious unity in advance. These pre-critical commitments would imply conceptualising subsumption as little more than the hierarchical arrangement of already given entities, a situating of things in their appropriate place within the order of creation. Kant's model, by contrast, is one of production: a synthetic fusion of elements that do not in and of themselves belong together. This enables the problem of subsumption to be posed as two-fold. First, *how* (or by which process) is form determined? Second, *which* forms are to be determined? Both of these aspects of subsumption are relativised according to the specificity of the systemic context within which subsumption occurs.

Appropriating and intensifying these Kantian innovations, the critical elaboration of subsumption as synthetic form-determination is torn by Marx from its idealist context ('cognition') and recoded as a description of the metabolic process of material production ('practice'). Insofar as capital is conceptualised as a system of social forms through which material production is organised and directed (a 'mode of production'), this system possesses historical actuality to the extent that it *subsumes* (and thereby transforms) existing forms of production such that they become capitalist production processes, with all of the social and material repercussions we have seen to result from this. Different forms of capitalist subsumption (formal, real, hybrid) designate the different modalities of this process of reconfiguring production and dominating workers, and thus different articulations of the abstract logic of capitalist accumulation with concrete historical forms of social production and reproduction.

Andrés Saenz de Sicilia is a postdoctoral researcher at the College of Philosophy, National Autonomous University of Mexico (UNAM) and an Associate Lecturer at Central Saint Martins.

Notes

1. The research undertaken for this article was supported by a postdoctoral research grant awarded by the national Autonomous University of Mexico's DGAPA (2020-22) and carried out at the UNAM's Faculty.of Philosophy and Letters under the supervision of Dr. Carlos Oliva Mendoza. This text first appeared in Spanish as 'Ser, Devenir, Subsunción – las raíces Kantianas de una problemática Marxista', *Valenciana Núm 29* (Jan-Jun 2022), 253-279.
2. Karl Marx, *Capital: a Critique of Political Economy, Vol. 1*, trans. Ben Fowkes (London and New York: Penguin, 1976), 90.
3. Marx, 'The Results of the Immediate Production Process', in *Capital, Vol.1*, 1019-1038; Karl Marx and Friedrich Engels, *Marx and Engels Collected Works*, volumes 30-34 (London: Lawrence & Wishart), esp. vol. 30, 54-348; vol. 33, 372-387; vol. 34, 93-121.
4. Marx, *Capital, Vol.1*, 645.
5. Walter Benjamin, 'Paralipomena to "On the Concept of History"', trans. Edmund Jephcott and Howard Eiland, in *Selected Writings Vol. 4: 1938-1940*, eds. Howard Eiland and Michael W. Jennings (Cambridge, MA: Harvard University Press, 2003), 402.
6. Jorge Luis Borges, 'On Exactitude in Science', in *Collected Fictions*, trans. Andrew Hurley (London: Penguin, 2000).
7. Antonio Negri, 'N for Negri: Antonio Negri in Conversation with Carles Guerra', eds. and trans. Jorge Mestre et al., *Grey Room* 11 (Spring 2003), 105; Theodor W. Adorno, *Minima Moralia: Reflections from Damaged Life*, trans., E. F. N. Jephcott (London and New York: Verso, 2005), 229.
8. See, for example, Christopher J. Arthur, *The New Dialectic and Marx's Capital* (Leiden, Boston and Cologne: Brill, 2004), and 'The Possessive Spirit of Capital: Subsumption/Inversion/Contradiction', in *Re-reading Marx: New Perspectives after the Critical Edition*, eds. Riccardo Bellofiore and Roberto Fineschi (New York: Palgrave Macmillan, 2009), 148-62; Patrick Murray, 'The Social and Material Transformation of Production by Capital: Formal and Real Subsumption in Capital, Volume I', in *The Constitution of Capital: Essays on Volume I of Marx's Capital*, eds. Riccardo Bellofiore and Nicola Taylor (Basingstoke and New York: Palgrave Macmillan, 2004), 243-273.
9. Marx and Engels, *Collected Works*, Vol. 34, 30; Marx and Engels, 'Manifesto of the Communist Party', in *Collected Works*, Vol. 6, 487.
10. '... in the analysis of life phenomena, not only biological but also societal phenomena, there is no way to predetermine (mathematically) that space of possible evolutions, the "phase space" of life ... No ecosystem or economic system is in a state of equilibrium, nor approaching equilibrium, with its unique pre-given space of geodesics, unless all its "agents" are dead. Not only is life a process far removed from equilibrium, but it is permanently in "transition", at a critical threshold ... Like the economy, it is always "in crisis", that is, from our perspective, it continually changes space of possibilities and its symmetries.' Giuseppe Longo and Sara Longo, 'Infinity of God and Space of Men in Painting, Conditions of Possibility for the Scientific Revolution', in *Mathematics in the Visual Arts*, eds. Ruth Scheps and Marie Christie Maurel (ISTE-Wiley, 2020).
11. Immanuel Kant, *Critique of Pure Reason*, trans. Paul Guyer and Allan W. Wood (Cambridge: Cambridge University Press, 1998), A137/B176.
12. Marx (citing Pietro Verri), *Capital, Vol.1*, 133.
13. This new schema is that of a 'practical objectivity'. As Bolívar Echeverría elaborates, 'Whichever element of nature ... whichever section of material, of whichever materiality it may be, when it is integrated into a social process of production and consumption, of the reproduction of a social subject, constitutes that which we could call a practical object, or an object that has a socio-natural form'. Bolívar Echeverría, *La contradicción del valor y del valor de uso en El Capital de Karl Marx* (Mexico City: Itaca, 1998), 15 (my translation).
14. In this way, Marx was able to counter idealism without reverting to a mechanistic and deterministic conception of natural objectivity as intentionless process. At the same time, he was able to refine and elaborate the basic notion of human praxis or 'objective activity' which distinguished his materialist outlook, grounding it in the structure of metabolic relationality characterising all organic life. Thus, as Alfred Schmidt notes, 'with the concept of "metabolism," Marx introduced a completely new understanding of man's relation to nature.' *The Concept of Nature in Marx*, trans. Ben Fowkes (London: NLB, 1971), 78-79.
15. 'Every useful thing is a whole composed of many properties; it can therefore be useful in various ways. The discovery of these ways and hence of the manifold uses of things is the work of history.' Marx, *Capital, Vol.1*, 125.
16. Marx, *Grundrisse: Foundations of the Critique of Political Economy (Rough Draft)*, trans. Martin Nicolaus (London and New York: Penguin, 1993), 96.
17. Marx, *Grundrisse*, 304.
18. 'With his money, the money owner has ... bought disposition over labour capacity so that he can use up, consume, this labour capacity as such, i.e. have it operate as actual labour, in short, so that he can have the worker really work.' Karl Marx, *Marx and Engels Collected Works*, Vol. 30, 64.
19. Marx, *Grundrisse*, 298.
20. Patrick Murray, 'The Social and Material Transformation of Production by Capital', 243-273.
21. Marx, *Capital, Vol. 1*, 527.
22. Marx, *Capital, Vol. 1*, 242-3; 989-90.
23. Marx, *Marx and Engels Collected Works*, Vol. 34, 30.
24. Marx, *Grundrisse*, 590.

What should feminist theory be?
An interview with Amia Srinivasan

Amia Srinivasan is the Chichele Professor of Social and Political Theory at All Souls College, University of Oxford, and a contributing editor of the London Review of Books. *Her collection of essays,* The Right to Sex: Feminism in the Twenty-First Century, *was published in 2021. In this interview with* Radical Philosophy *she is in conversation with Victoria Browne, Hannah Proctor and Rahul Rao.*

Radical Philosophy Over the past couple of decades, there has been a significant feminist re-activation of thinkers, ideas and texts of the so-called 'second wave'. Shulamith Firestone, for example, has been given a new lease of life in feminist theory, as has the 'Wages for Housework' movement. Can you comment on this phenomenon in relation to your own work, particularly on the role that Catherine MacKinnon plays in *The Right to Sex*?

Amia Srinivasan In *The Right to Sex* I draw heavily on the work and ideas of earlier generations of feminists, especially from the Anglo-American tradition. Firestone and MacKinnon are important touchstones, as are Angela Davis, Adrienne Rich, bell hooks, the Combahee River Collective and 'Wages for Housework' feminists such as Silvia Federici, Mariarosa Dalla Costa and Selma James. I draw on their work in a way that is intended to be respectful but non-deferential. For example, I find much to admire in MacKinnon's account of heterosexual sex, the ideological function of pornography, and the nature of the state; and yet I am also relentlessly critical of her legalism, her embrace of coercive and carceral state power, and her investment in what I see as symbolic politics that (unintentionally) prioritise the punishing of men over the improvement of the worst-off women's lives. For me – as with Firestone, Davis and Federici – class and capital must be central terms of feminist analysis; unlike MacKinnon, I see gendered domination as grounded most fundamentally in women's assigned role in biological and social reproduction, rather than in heterosexual sex *per se*.

Some of my readers have been taken aback by my willingness to engage with those feminists, particularly MacKinnon and Andrea Dworkin, who have advocated for the growth of the carceral state and targeted sex workers for 'salvation' through restrictions on their ability to work legally, and thus with a modicum of safety. But I want to insist, at the level of method, that everything within (and indeed, outside) the feminist canon should be at our theoretical and political disposal. What would it mean to say that a thinker as powerful and wildly imaginative – not to mention politically consequential – as MacKinnon should not be looked to as a feminist resource? Should we say the same of Firestone? Valerie Solanas? I like this line from Andrea Long Chu's 2018 essay 'On Liking Women', in which Chu insists on reading Solanas with what some feminists would see as undue charity: '[G]enerosity is the only spirit in which a text as hot to the touch as the *SCUM Manifesto* could have ever been received. This is after all a pamphlet advocating mass murder, and what's worse, property damage'.

By saying that all these thinkers and others besides should be seen as at our disposal as feminists is not to say that I'm advocating for a view on which ideas should be sharply distinguished – or assessed in isolation – from their worldly consequences. We should think about what ideas mobilise, produce and sustain. It's important to think about, for example, what anti-pornography and anti-prostitution feminism have brought into the world: not only directly, in making the lives of some of the worst-off women harder, but also indirectly, by providing a carceral cover for the deep social and economic crises produced by capitalism. And yet, anti-pornography and anti-prostitution feminism often says things, at the level of diagnosis rather than prescription, that are deeply insightful about the workings of male power and ideology. I take my lead in part here from Juno Mac and Molly Smith's brilliant defence of sex work decriminalisation, *Revolting Prostitutes* (2018). One of the many extraordinary things the book does is to model how to engage charitably, indeed sympathetically, with one's opponents, even while being relentlessly critical of them. It's a good reminder that 'engaging the other side' doesn't have to be a gateway to a deradicalised or centrist politics – a point that Sophie Smith often makes in the 'Feminism and the Future' graduate class we co-teach.

RP We are interested in the operation of intergenerational dynamics in the book, as you are in dialogue with both older generations of feminist thinkers as well as younger students. For instance, to what extent do you find yourself in productive disagreement with your students? And how would you distinguish your emphasis on the significance of education and pedagogy from the practice of consciousness raising?

AS It's all too easy to portray feminist disagreement as, to invoke Lorna Bracewell, 'a catfight' – or, to invoke Kathi Weeks and Maggie Nelson, an intergenerational drama of mothers and daughters. And yet, as Sophie Lewis recently said when she was visiting my graduate seminar, there is *something* to these intergenerational, matrilineal dynamics within feminism. To be very candid, I detect in many older feminists (though not all – Ann Snitow, who died in 2019, is a blazing counterexample) an intense anxiety about irrelevance and obsolescence. Of course, under patriarchy, women have every reason to be worried about irrelevance and obsolescence as they age. But far too often, older feminists turn their anger on younger women, whom they see as insufficiently deferential or worried about the wrong sorts of things – like gender-fluidity or carceralism, rather than (say) sexual violence or wage gaps. Older feminists too often treat younger generations of feminists as ungrateful daughters trying to kill them off, rather than comrades in a collective struggle, albeit one whose strategies and aims must change with time.

It's an unfortunate dynamic, one that at its extreme leads to a deep, and anti-intellectual, cynicism, in which the work of younger feminists is misrepresented and straw-manned. I take Katha Pollitt's review of my book in *Dissent* to be a depressing and paradigmatic case of this: 'depressing' because one would hope for better from both *Dissent* and from Pollitt herself, given her very important work on abortion. At the end of the review, Pollitt characterises the concerns of my book – which she glibly sums up as 'incels and pornography and professors who sleep with their students' – as 'those of particular interest to the young', meanwhile suggesting that real, adult feminists take on 'the most important issues in the lives of most women'. As examples of the latter, she cites 'semi-fascist nationalist movements around the world' which she claims 'go unmentioned' in the book, and 'the millions of mothers who were forced out of their jobs, some permanently, when the pandemic closed day-care centers and schools'. I'll leave aside the facts that the Covid-19 pandemic was in its infancy when I submitted the manuscript of *The Right to Sex*, that I nonetheless talk about the large number of women who were laid off in its early days (and often flocked to sex work as an alternative), that I devote a great deal of space to talking about the struggle of poor women for decent jobs and socialised childcare, and that I discuss the rise of right-wing authoritarianism in the US, India and elsewhere, and indeed its ideological and material entanglements with the incel phenomenon. The most important question is this: what makes Pollitt think that the central preoccupations of the book – sexual violence, racial domination, the state, the pathologies of capitalism, sex discrimination, the politics of sexual desire, sex work, the family – are only of 'particular interest to the young'? One might just as sensibly ask of Pollitt's own work: is abortion a 'young people's issue' because post-menopausal people can't easily get pregnant?

The absurdity of that question lies in its presupposition that the fates of young women are in no way bound up with the fates of older women, that young women never *become* older women, that the treatment of young women as sexual objects and instruments of biological reproduction has nothing to do with the treatment of older women as surplus to social use. Indeed, the absurdity of the suggestion that racial domination, sexual entitlement or carceralism are 'young person's issues' suggests to me that Pollitt's real complaint isn't that my concerns don't apply to her and other women her age; but more simply that they are not *her* concerns.

Prescinding from this particular skirmish, the deep question here, I think, is: What does it mean to make room in a social movement for younger people? How does one accommodate oneself to the idea that a movement one is used to thinking of as one's own is, in fact, never just one's own, and that its destiny is always beyond one's control? And, indeed, that this is a *good* thing? What does it mean, in other words, to build radical coalition with the future?

To be clear, I'm not saying that this intergenerational dynamic is merely one-way: there's a lot of reductive talk among younger feminists about the 'whiteness' or 'TERFiness' of the second-wave, which flattens out a very complex political formation in order to dismiss it – thereby ignoring, *inter alia*, all the work done by 'second-wave' feminists of colour and trans feminists. Some of this is certainly ignorance, but there is also at work here a sort of chauvinism of the present, and also, I fear, a patriarchal willingness to see older women as irrelevant.

On my students: it is hard to generalise, but I think I tend to be more critical of the nuclear family than they are, more alert to human frailty and fallibility and so less moralising, and more convinced that necessary social transformation will involve genuine loss and sacrifice. But perhaps I'm really describing the difference between my current and former selves. With my undergraduate students, I do often detect a yearning for something akin to consciousness-raising. I wrote about this recently in the *New Yorker*: 'Many of [my students] come to feminism looking for comradery, understanding, community. They want to gather to articulate the unspoken truth of their experience, and to read great feminist texts that will reveal the world to which they should politically aspire.' But, as I wrote, these hopes are inevitably somewhat disappointed – as they were, indeed, for the feminists of the late 1960s and 1970s. In particular, ideological convergence and mutual understanding nearly always give out into difference and disagreement – among the students themselves, and within the texts they read. It is one of my goals to show my students that mapping the contours of feminist disagreement can be intellectually productive, even thrilling, and to show them that a profound kind of personal transformation is possible through the hard, granular work of reading, interpreting, arguing.

Jane Gallop, in *Feminist Accused of Sexual Harassment* (1997), a book I engage with in a different context in *The Right to Sex*, describes what it was like to be a student at the very beginning of academic feminism, when faculty members and students were equally expert, or non-expert, and so were able to see themselves as equals in a collaborative pursuit of knowledge and liberation. That vision – which Gallop calls 'brave if naive' – is no longer possible in the contemporary feminist classroom: 'Students and faculty are no longer discovering feminism together; today, faculty who have been feminists for decades generally teach it to students for whom it is new. We are no longer discovering books together; instead, feminist faculty teach feminist classics we've read half a dozen times to students who are reading them for the first time.' This is, I think, descriptively accurate – and, as such, there is little point in hankering after a lost moment of horizontality in the classroom (as Gallop does), even as we seek to think through ways in which the classroom can be made more, if not perfectly, equal.

RP In the book, you address fears of moralism and a worry that a 'political critique of desire can be too easily mobilised against those who are themselves marginalised'. In response, you draw a distinction between the transformation of desire as a 'disciplinary' project and as an 'emancipatory' project. There is also a memorable moment where you discuss a letter you received from a gay man talking about how he has had to 'work' on his desire for his fat partner, and ask 'is this an act of discipline, or of love?' Could you please say more about the relationship between discipline and emancipation, and between discipline and love? For instance, can an act that begins in discipline become one of love? Or can we understand the discipline as being undertaken because one already loves? Or might it be undertaken because one wants to, but does not yet, love?

AS Yes, all of this. 'Love takes work' is a therapeutic cliché because it is true. I rhetorically counterpose discipline and love – 'is this an act of discipline, or of love?' – but really I mean to trouble the distinction. There can be discipline without love: 'staying together just for the kids'. There is love without discipline: being 'in love' is characterised by, *inter alia*, utter spontaneity, and indeed a will that is not free but incessantly directed towards the object of infatuation. But when we place love in time and extend it, all sorts of things – human fickleness, the obstreperousness of the other, our craving for more, the spectre of lives unlived – make loving difficult. At some point, we all have to put in the work to see our loved ones – friends, lovers, comrades, kin – aright. Love understood as infatuation knows nothing of the challenges of temporal existence, which is why it bristles at the idea that love might ever take work, much less the discipline of the will.

RP Going back to the issue of moralising, how might one talk about ethics without moralising? And is it moralising in general, or moralising about sex in particular, that seems to be the problem? For example, in the book you say of sex that 'there is nothing else so riven with politics and yet so inviolably personal'. Arguably, though, that could also be said of motherhood, and we're interested in pushing the comparison of sex and motherhood further to interrogate why sex is, arguably, a more fiercely protected arena than motherhood or mothering in terms of political critique, and why it seems particularly resistant to being transformed in more socially just directions. For instance, arguments that existing forms of maternal desire and practice must be interrogated and re-made are met, it seems to us, with far less resistance within feminist/queer theory than the same kind of arguments about existing forms of sexual desire and practice. That could be because sex is commonly understood as more of an individual affair compared to mothering/parenting (though of course sex, including with oneself, is thoroughly relational). But is it also down to a sense that there is a kind of inherent 'wrongness' to sex (of the sexy kind), in comparison to mothering/parenting? So whilst childrearing would be collectivised and maternal/parental desire would be redirected or even eliminated in a postrevolutionary feminist society, sex would still require, in some way, the eroticism of unequal power relations. What's your view? Do you think that this kind of assumption is in play in the debates your book has generated, and if so, would you say that this eroticism is something learned, and hence un-learnable?

AS I would deny any sharp distinction between 'sex' and 'motherhood', even though the two can certainly come apart, since one can become a mother without engaging in any sexual activity, and vice versa. What I mean by this denial is that a full political critique of sex must engage a political critique of motherhood, and indeed parenthood; my favourite text that does this – that reveals motherhood as a political institution – is Adrienne Rich's *Of Woman Born*. That said, I of course recognise the asymmetry you describe. Plenty of feminist/queer theory, from Firestone's *Dialectic of Sex* onward, seeks to subject the heteronormative family, mothering and childrearing to not just scrutiny but a transformative agenda. Meanwhile, much contemporary feminism  and queer theory is reluctant to engage in the sort of political critique of sex and sexual desire that was so familiar to radical feminists in the late 1960s and 1970s. What's going on here? As you say, the family, like sex, is also deeply personal and at the same time profoundly political.

I think the answer is complicated, but let me offer one thought. For conservatism of all stripes – from traditional, religiously-inflected social conservatism to neoliberalism – the heteronormative, nuclear family is centrally important. (On the counterintuitive importance of the family for neoliberalism, I cannot recommend Melinda Cooper's 2017 book *Family Values* highly enough.) And, sadly, you see a similar attachment to the heteronormative nuclear family in many corners of the contemporary left. (Richard Seymour has a very good recent piece on this in *Salvage* called 'Abolition: Notes on a Normie Shitstorm', occasioned by leftist outrage at Sophie Lewis's new book on family abolition.) Meanwhile, the socially conservative right is all too delighted to engage in the political critique of sex and sexual desire: consider gay conversion therapy and the hysteria around trans kids. So I wonder if the answer is fundamentally dialectical – namely, that contemporary feminists want to distance themselves (for excellent reasons) from a resurgent right that is both 'pro-family' and 'anti-sex'. The result is a feminism that is 'anti-family' and 'pro-sex'.

I'll add one more observation. You're right that contemporary feminist and queer theory is, on the whole, very open to transformative critiques of motherhood and the family. But, especially within feminism, there is still a presumption that social (and thus biological) reproduction is good. You see this especially in some corners of contemporary social reproduction theory. Now, I'm hardly an anti-natalist or deep ecologist – these are worldviews that always implicitly, and sometimes explicitly, target the 'hyper-fecund' poor women of the Global South. But I don't think of social reproduction as a good *per se* – what 'world' is it, precisely, that we are so keen on reproducing? – and I do want to ask what it might mean if we didn't constantly defer the project of human flourishing to the next generation, both individually and collectively. So I detect an atavistic attachment to the reproductive order even within seeming radical critiques of it.

RP This leads to our next question, which is: if desire is not pre- or a-political, how can we speak of a liberated or liberatory desire 'set free from the binds of injustice'? Does that function as a kind of regulative ideal?

AS Well, just because something is political – that is, shaped by our reigning schemes of social order and cooperation – does not mean that it is destined to be unjust. But one might wonder: *what* exactly is there to be 'set free', if there is very little of desire that can be said to pre-exist the political? It's analogous to the problem of agential freedom once we acknowledge our mutual constitution as subjects. The solution is that we have to rethink our idea of liberation: not the emancipation of transcendent, self-constituting selves, but a more compatibilist understanding that finds room for ideas like autonomy, respect, reflection, criticality and self-understanding against a backdrop of mutual co-constitution. In a sense, one needs to say, with A. J. Ayer, that there is simply a difference between having a gun held to one's head or being the subject of psychological abuse and being formed by one's *Bildung*. But, being feminists, we will also have to distinguish between different kinds of *Bildung*, and notice that many elements of what is understood to be normal enculturation is in fact perverse: that, under patriarchy, girls and women (and indeed many boys and men) are raised with a gun held to their heads. Of course, this is all a promissory note – and more can and has been said. Here, yes, I think a regulative ideal is a useful notion. Liberation – of desire, of agents – is not some final end state, but a process.

RP We're also interested in your engagement with psychoanalytic concepts of desire. For instance, what kind of understanding of the psyche does your discussion of desire rely on or presuppose? Are desires knowable? In relation to this, if individuals' 'bad' desires are understood in relation to the oppressive structures of society (i.e. located in the external world) does this end up with an understanding of desire that is almost like false consciousness? How do psychoanalytic concepts, such as the unconscious, complicate how society is understood to shape/influence desire (which would in turn impact how desire might be 'set free')? These kinds of questions were, of course, points of contestation within the women's liberation movement and engaged with by many of the thinkers you discuss in *The Right to Sex*. How would you respond to the kinds of criticisms Juliet Mitchell made of feminist dismissals of Freud in *Psychoanalysis and Feminism* (1974)? e.g.:

> Feminist criticisms of Freud claim that he was denying what really happens, and that the women he analysed were simply responding to really oppressive conditions. But there is no such thing as a simple response to reality. External reality has to be 'acquired'. To deny that there is anything other than external reality gets us back to the same proposition: it is a denial of the unconscious.

AS Desires are sometimes knowable, and sometimes not, or not immediately to the subject herself. Psychoanalysis, beginning with Freud, has an extraordinary amount to offer feminism. It cautions against simplistic accounts of the psyche that would reduce the subject to a coherent and knowable set of desires, beliefs and goals. It reminds us that things are often not as they appear to be: that loathing can be love, that a fantasy can be a remedy, that shows of strength can be confessions of weakness. The question is how to bring together the Freudian account of the psyche – which, in its universalism, and notwithstanding Freud's own prejudices, is in a sense deeply egalitarian – with the deeply inegalitarian political reality of which psychoanalysis has long been embarrassed. What does it mean, in other words, to see all human persons as playing out universal dramas of repression – as all, in an important sense, lost and thwarted children – while at the same time seeing that, in the immanent world of social 'reality', some of these same people are enormously, almost untouchably powerful, and others devastatingly unfree.

The person who I think does this most beautifully and powerfully is, unsurprisingly, Jacqueline Rose. She insists on holding together what are often thought of as contradictory impulses – between condemning male violence and recognising the psychic fragility out of which it is born, between seeking legal redress for sexual violence and recognising the essential ungovernability of sex, and between registering the ubiquity of male sexual entitlement and leaving open the possibility that individual men might distinguish themselves from the script of masculinity. Rose refuses both an orthodox radical feminism that would see male power as a perfect, totalising achievement; and also an orthodox psychoanalysis that prefers to de-emphasise if not totally deny the 'real' differences in power and material means that divide us.

You can see the important political work done by Rose's psychoanalytic frame in her discussion of trans identities. She writes: 'The bar of sexual difference is ruthless but that does not mean that those who believe they subscribe to its law have the slightest idea of what is going on beneath the surface, any more than the one who submits less willingly. … The "cis"—i.e. non-trans—woman or man is a decoy, the outcome of multiple repressions whose unlived stories surface nightly in our dreams'. Rose is reminding us that alternative ways of being sexed and being gendered – different possible ways of responding to the 'bar of sexual difference' – literally haunt us, all of us, at night. No one, trans or cis, has a perfectly reconciled relationship to the socially-constructed script of sex/gender: the human psyche is far too complex and interesting for that. This suggests that trans-exclusionary politics is, at least in part, driven by an anxiety on the part of 'cis' people to reassert their own fidelity to a social order that, in fact, does not even serve them. This is just one way in which the uncertainty, instability and ambivalence thematised by psychoanalysis can be politically productive for feminism.

RP In your book, a primary concern is that the 'consent' standard shields existing desires and practices of sex from political critique, but there is another worry too – also articulated by Katherine Angel – which is that it precludes sexual exploration and the cultivation of desire because it assumes we know what we want in sex in advance of actually doing it, and can thus seem at a remove from the intimacy and immediacy of sexual encounters as experiences that unfold in the present tense. In Angel's work, this emerges as a point about the temporality of desire, i.e. that desire doesn't exist in advance of sex but rather is activated and emerges in process through mutual exploration. Could you say a bit more about that, and about current practices and promotion of 'consent training' – in universities for example. Is there an alternative way for institutions to combat rape myths and masculine entitlement?

AS The consent model, as Linda Martín Alcoff has argued, is fundamentally juridical – and so we should not be surprised that it has rather serious limits as a non-juridical criterion for ethical sex. In a courtroom, we need a criterion that distinguishes criminal sexual assault from non-criminal sex that has some hope of being operationalised – and non-consent is not bad for that, and certainly an improvement on historically prior criteria, like 'presence of violence'. But why should we expect consent to be that which distinguishes ethical from non-ethical sex? Two considerations show why this is a mistake. First of all, there is a great deal of ethically ugly sex that, as feminists, we should not seek to make illegal, lest we want to further strengthen the hand of the carceral state. Second – and this is a point MacKinnon makes so well, though she and I draw different lessons from it – the presence of consent is compatible with ethically-vexed sex, given that women often (because of their cultural training) consent to sex they don't want to have. In this regard, the shift to an 'affirmative consent' standard isn't a great help: now we have the phenomenon of women saying yes to sex (as they are culturally trained to do) they don't want to have. When, we want to know, will women feel emboldened to assert what they want, and men no longer be turned on by 'getting' what women don't want to give? (By this I'm not saying that consent-training is pointless. One of my recent graduate students has argued that, while consent might not be the mark of ethically OK sex, *consent-training* might well have the indirect effect of strengthening those things that centrally matter for ethical sex, like respect of other and self.)

The problem with what I've just suggested so far – that ethical sex involves people feeling free to assert what they want while being tuned into what others want – is that it can appear to presuppose a naïve conception of desire. People, all people, find themselves wanting conflicting things: for example, to act out a rape fantasy, and to not be the sort of person who is turned on by a rape fantasy. And, as I said earlier, what we want is very often opaque to us, and does not necessarily pre-exist in a stable form the sexual encounter itself. There is an issue of temporality here, as Angel says, and there is also the ever-thorny issue of the unconscious. So we've got to place our regulative ideal of ethical sex in time, and introduce all the complexities of the ambivalently desirous subject. To do this we have to turn our attention to the relationality of sex: to the process whereby people engage in a mutual exploration – and indeed sexual co-constitution – grounded in something like recognition of the other. And we've got to do so in a way that doesn't reinforce a reactionary ideal of the long-term, loving, monogamous couple. Any ideal of ethical sex worth having must be able to see anonymous, one-off sex as paradigms.

RP To follow up on this, a central focus of 'consent training' seems to be making consent and the withdrawal of consent intelligible. Yet your review of Joanna Bourke's *Loving Animals* in the *London Review of Books* ends on a note of scepticism about whether the consent of human as much as non-human animals can ever be completely intelligible given the will to power that seems to animate the sex drive. We may be more certain of our inability to trust ourselves to know what an animal wants, but given your thoroughgoing problematisation of consent, can we ever trust ourselves to fully know what a human wants?

AS Yes, I think we can, sometimes: it's an 'I know it when I see it' situation, though of course certainly people are mistakenly all-too-confident about what others want. One key, I think, is not to get epistemically lazy about other people, especially those one 'knows well'.

RP You are clearly wary of calling on the state to do things that feminism might want, whether this be the 'redistribution' of desire, the regulation of pornography or the more stringent punishment of sexual violence. Where does this place you in relation to socialist feminism and socialism more generally, which has sought to take control of the state even if only to hasten its demise? How, for example, should we read Angela Davis running for Vice President of the United States?

AS Angela Davis gets my vote any day, obviously. But to understand the state, and feminism's particular relationship to it, I turn to MacKinnon. In *Toward a Feminist Theory of the State* (1989) she writes: 'feminism has been left with these tacit alternatives: either the state is a primary tool of women's betterment and status transformation, without analysis (hence strategy) of it as male; or women are left to civil society, which for women has more closely resembled a state of nature. The state, and with it the law, have been either omnipotent or impotent: everything or nothing.' I think this is fundamentally right. Feminism must reject both a left politics that counsels a simple rejection of and retreat from state power, and a liberal politics that turns incessantly to the state. Neither will serve women as a class. (A similar thing can be said of Black communities in the US, who often see themselves as suffering from both over-policing and *under*-policing.) The state must be itself a terrain of feminist struggle; as MacKinnon says, this involves understanding the state as male (and we might add: white, straight and capitalist) in order to know how to engage it strategically, and in particular how to advocate for reforms that carry within them the seeds of transformative change. I don't generally agree with MacKinnon's specific strategic prescriptions – they involve, I think, an undue optimism about the law, an optimism that doesn't carry through her own insight about the state as ideologically male. But her diagnosis of the problem, for feminism and the state, remains perennially apt.

RP We understand your background and training have been in analytic philosophy and we're interested in your relationship to analytic philosophy today, and how you would identify your philosophical allegiances and positioning. For example, in a recent issue of *Radical Philosophy* (RP 2.02), Alice Crary argued that analytic feminist philosophy takes for granted that 'ethical neutrality is a regulative ideal for all world-directed thought' which is 'fatal to feminist politics'; and elsewhere you have spoken about philosophy needing to be more world-oriented or world-directed. Can you elaborate on what you mean by that? Would you agree with Crary's diagnosis, i.e. that the primary problem is the analytic conception of reason? And do you think that disciplinarity is also part of the problem here?

AS I'm a huge admirer of Alice Crary's work, and share much in common with her philosophically. One point of difference is that I am not particularly invested in the question of how we should think about reason. Instead, I am much more engaged by questions of how we should think about knowledge. But we agree that taking up ethically-loaded perspectives is a precondition of seeing the world aright – for reasoning well or coming to know – and that we should reject aspirations for an ethically-neutral account of the social and political world, including the world of non-human animals. I think the difference in our focuses – rationality vs. knowledge – has to do with differences in our philosophical formations, and perhaps doesn't amount to much.

It's important to say here, and I know Alice would agree, that the ideal of ethical neutrality doesn't characterise all analytic philosophy, even if it characterises some of it. (It also characterises, perhaps surprisingly, some contemporary Critical Theory.) Figures like Elizabeth Anscombe, John McDowell (Alice's doctoral supervisor), Cora Diamond and my brilliant Oxford colleague A.W. Moore all share, in one way or another, the thought that human subjectivity has an essential role to play in the acquisition of objective reality. It is perhaps worth noting that all these philosophers are in one way or another indebted to Wittgenstein.

When I've talked about analytic philosophy needing to be more world-directed, I've meant to be picking up on the ways in which a certain common (and dominant) mode of analytic moral and political philosophy seems to be animated by an intense anxiety about social and political reality – as if the world of other people (and indeed non-human animals) cannot be faced until a theory can be found to mediate between the self and that world. In a sense, this just *is* the philosophical impulse: philosophy is born out of an alienation from the world. So much analytic moral and political philosophy appears to begin from the thought that the world itself contains no ethical answers: that one cannot learn about how things should or should not be by closely observing the world. Thus such philosophy has little use for sociology or history, except as a storehouse of examples.

RP In relation to this, do you think there is something inherent to analytic philosophy that has made it a major vector of transphobia in the UK? In other words, is it only coincidental that the transphobic feminist philosophy emerging in the UK is analytic? And what about the Britishness of it? For example, Alyosxa Tudor speaks of 'TERFism' as 'white distraction', but can you comment on the specifically British context we're situated in at the moment and the form of academic transphobia that presents itself as 'sound thinking' and 'common sense'?

AS This is a big question to which I don't have anything like a satisfying answer. To begin with one obvious point: analytic philosophy is the 'question everything' discipline *par excellence*. So if any discipline is going to take up a politically vexed (or indeed culturally settled) question for apparently neutral inquiry – Is torture permissible? Should disabled infants be euthanised? Should wild carnivores be exterminated? Are trans women indeed women? – it is going to be analytic philosophy. That is not to say that analytic philosophy's self-image as the discipline that questions everything is wholly accurate. Some questions are beyond the pale, even for analytic philosophers: I *think* that a moral philosopher making an argument for chattel slavery would get some pushback. (Though perhaps they would be welcomed to publish in the *Journal of Controversial Ideas*, two of whose editors have argued for, *inter alia*, the permissibility of torture, infanticide for disabled infants and the forced extinction of wild carnivores.) For my part, I am a firm defender of academic freedom – not to be confused with free speech (this is something I've written about with Robert Mark Simpson) – and worry about the tendency, in some quarters of the left, especially the student left, to look to authorities, especially university administrations, to regulate and punish speech. At the same time, I think there is something worrying – I want to say *ailing* – with a discipline that finds itself pulled again and again to these questions and these methods of investigating them.

Take, for example, Peter Singer's discussions of people who are cognitively disabled. Why leverage such people's rights to be treated with respect – rights, at best, precariously and hardly universally recognised – in an argument for the improved treatment of (certain) non-human animals? I find it difficult not to think that there is more than just a concern for animals motivating arguments like these – and this impression is deepened when I see repeated uses of the slur 'retarded' in the literature, and a reluctance to take disabled people's testimony about their lives (especially that they are 'worth living') seriously. Is this just neutral inquiry into a philosophically interesting question?

I think a similar question can be asked of other interventions within analytic moral and political philosophy, including about trans-inclusion. Kathleen Stock, for example, is very invested in portraying herself as a reasonable, judicious philosopher, carefully making her way through the arguments and following them where they lead her. But anyone who has watched her on social media over the years knows there is also a good deal of vitriol there, a certain populist spirit that takes clear pleasure in riling people up, and a lack of intellectual generosity and rigour. It is these habits of mind and communication – habits that Stock is very good at suppressing when she needs to, as for example in her extraordinarily effective performance on BBC *Woman's Hour* after she resigned from Sussex – that irk many of her critics within philosophy. There *are* interesting philosophical questions about gender, gender identity and sex raised by the experiences of trans people, just as there are interesting philosophical questions raised by the phenomena of abortion, rape, sex work and racial domination. I don't hold with the view that we shouldn't 'philosophise about people's lives' – where would the work of Simone de Beauvoir or Angela Davis be if that principle were applied? – but I do think that such philosophising demands a special quality of ethical attention and intellectual care that is too often lacking in certain (though by no means all) quarters of analytic moral philosophy.

I wonder too, when it comes to the 'trans debate' specifically, whether the fact that analytic philosophy has been so historically male-dominated has some explanatory role to play. There is a lot of justified anger among women in philosophy; as Michèle Le Dœuff writes, 'When you are a woman and a philosopher, it is useful to be a feminist in order to understand what is happening to you'. Perhaps for some cis women philosophers, who have had to fight so hard for a place in the discipline, the spectre of the 'trans woman infiltrator' becomes a convenient and psychically potent scapegoat. This relates to what I've found to be the most illuminating account of the Britishness of the trans-exclusionary phenomenon, put forward by the feminist journalist Katie J. M. Baker in a great piece called 'The Road to Terfdom' in *Lux* magazine (a socialist feminist glossy to which everyone should subscribe). Baker points to the importance of the parenting website Mumsnet as a site of anti-trans radicalisation; here, women who are justifiably aggrieved by the difficulties of child-rearing in a neoliberalised social sphere are taught to direct their anger at the so-called 'trans lobby'. In the UK, I think this phenomenon – that of trans people (especially trans women) being scapegoated for

real grievances – generalises beyond Mumsnet, though I think it's hard to overstate just how important social media has been in creating and sustaining this phenomenon, not least because of its tremendous influence on the mainstream British press.

There is also the fact that in the US the enemies of trans people are so clearly also the enemies of cis women, lesbian women and gay men; just look at recent developments in Texas, where a raft of legislation has simultaneously attacked abortion rights, trans rights and the rights of lesbians and gay people. So perhaps, in the US context, it's more obvious who your political bedfellows are when you, as a feminist, engage in trans-exclusionary politics. In the UK it's less obvious that trans-exclusionary feminists are giving succour to the right, though of course they are: not least by encouraging the mainstream press to obsess over 'the trans issue' while the Conservative Party orchestrates a project to drain the public sphere – the NHS, arts institutions, universities, the BBC – of all life, while increasing the privatised misery of ordinary Britons.

RP In 'How to Do Things with Philosophy' (2018) you write: 'it's not enough to take our familiar philosophical tools and turn them toward new topics ... We need instead to re-examine our tools, to ask ourselves what we are doing with them, and why'. How has this insight informed your own approach to writing *The Right to Sex*? In connection to this, would it be possible to say something reflecting on the fragmentary and aphoristic form of the Coda to the chapter 'The Right to Sex', which is written in a very different style to the book's main chapters? And how do you understand the role of a philosopher in relation to the role of the public intellectual? If, as you say in the opening paragraph of *The Right to Sex*, feminism is 'a political movement to transform the world beyond recognition', how do you understand the role of the feminist philosopher?

AS I think of *The Right to Sex* primarily as a work of feminist theory rather than feminist philosophy, since that latter term (at least in the world of analytic philosophy) is associated with a form of feminist theorising that attempts to use the proprietary tools of analytic philosophy (e.g. conceptual analysis, semantics and pragmatics, epistemology, metaphysics, etc.) to establish the truth or plausibility of claims that are relevant (in principle) to the lives and fates of women. It's not a method that particularly appeals to me when it comes to writing about feminism. My favourite texts of feminist theory are more formally innovative than what you typically find within analytic feminism. These texts don't just say things but also try to *do* things: create new desires and forms of political subjectivity, disclose new imaginative possibilities, encourage new kinds of political reflectivity and consciousness. You can't read something like Silvia Federici's 'Wages Against Housework' as just a set of propositions about household labour. The rhetoric of the text alone – 'They say it is love. We say it is unwaged work. They call it frigidity. We call it absenteeism. Every miscarriage is a work accident' – should make it clear that Federici, and her fellow WFH feminists like Mariarosa Dalla Costa and Selma James, are attempting to do more than give a conceptual analysis of 'work', or offer an argument for the waging of women's labour in the home. As Federici says, the demand for housework wages isn't a demand for a 'thing' but for a new 'political perspective'; Federici is trying to bring into existence a new form of political consciousness, and create a new political constituency.

It is to this tradition of radical, utopian feminist theory that I see my book as a small contribution. In it I try to say true things about the political formation of sexual desire, about the workings of patriarchal ideology, about the dangers of invoking coercive state power, about the often sorry state of contemporary Anglo-American feminism. But I am moreover interested in contributing to that feminist tradition that incites women, and indeed men, to desire and demand more: that refuses to accept narrow reformism of the status quo as the best for which we can hope, and that not only sees but *feels* unfreedom in all its guises – class, race, caste – as bound up with the unfreedoms of sexual domination. I am interested in reinvigorating the feminist imagination, while at the same time making clear the material conditions, especially economic exploitation and immiseration, that are inimical to the workings of that imagination.

I think that for some philosophers, including some feminist philosophers, this sort of work is unrecognisable as theory (let alone philosophy). For example, in a review of my book in *The Raven*, Sally Haslanger accused me of lacking a social theory – that is, a theory of how a society works and how it changes, especially in progressive ways. Indeed, she declares that, whatever it is that I am doing in the book, I am 'not doing theory'. Now, I'm a fan of Sally's, both personally and philosophically; it's hard to overstate her importance for the development of contemporary analytic feminism, especially feminist metaphysics. But I think her reading of my book reveals a fundamentally limited understanding of what feminist theory is and can do, one that is too much in the grip of the analytic worldview and too detached from the actual history of feminist praxis. By 'feminist theory' Haslanger seems to have in a mind an overt and systematic account of how society works under conditions of patriarchal domination. It is true that I offer no such account in *The Right to Sex* – as Haslanger notes, that is not the point of the book, nor (this is not noted by Haslanger) the point of many canonical works of what is generally taken to be feminist theory.

But anyone coming from the broad tradition of Marxist and socialist feminism would recognise the social theory that underpins my work. It is this theoretical tradition and orientation that explains my focus on biological and social reproduction as central to women's oppression; my insistence on the primacy of class as an analytic category for feminism; my specifically anti-capitalist critique of carceral feminism; my understanding of the heteronormative nuclear family as a central mechanism of capitalist production; my interest in forms of radical coalition across axes of identity; my conviction that poor women, especially poor women of colour, are agents of historical change; my anxiety about state power and bourgeois moralism; my embrace of certain psychoanalytic framings of sexual domination; and, above all, my insistence on a utopian spirit that Haslanger disparages as 'wishful thinking'. (For what it is worth, I find the dismissal as 'wishful' of demands – like socialised childcare and on-demand abortion – that feminists of the 1970s thought would be quickly met, nothing less than a capitulation to a neoliberal common-sense that opposes itself in every way to women's liberation. It also, I think, betrays a misapprehension of the role that demands can play in radical politics, as if the whole point of them was to be 'reasonable'. Kathi Weeks' *The Problem With Work: Feminism, Marxism, Antiwork Politics, and Postwork Imaginaries* is excellent on the function of the feminist 'demand'.)

Haslanger takes special aim at, as you aptly call it, the 'aphoristic and fragmentary' fourth chapter of the book, which serves as a coda to the book's title essay. 'Does feminism need theory?', Haslanger asks rhetorically. 'Or can we make do with a scattered set of insights and questions, some of them numbered, that don't obviously cohere?' Again, what I think Haslanger is missing is the basic Marxist insight that social and political life contains contradictions – not in the sense of logical contradictions (I'm still an analytic philosopher!), but in the sense that a single political formation can contain within it tendencies that pull against each other. For example: does the family offer a refuge from capitalism or is it a site of its reproduction? The answer is: both. Is male sexual violence the expression of men's power or their vulnerability? Both. Is the criminal law a potential tool for feminist justice or is it a weapon of the capitalist state? Again: both. The point of the 'Coda' is to explore these and other contradictions – or, in a more psychoanalytic register, to embrace the ambivalences of political and social life. For example, I write, analysing the incel phenomenon: 'On one hand, there is the pathology of what is sometimes called neoliberalism: an assimilation of an ever-increasing number of domains of life to the logic of the market. On the other, there is the pathology of patriarchy, which has, in capitalist societies, tended to see women and the home as refuges from the market, as sources of freely given care and love ... That these two tendencies are in tension does not mean they do not serve each other, or that they do not form an organic unity.'

One thing I think Haslanger gets very *right* about my book is that I am trying to both perform and instil what she calls a 'critical feminist consciousness'. But she insists that this is not yet to do 'theory', because her idea of theory comes, ultimately, from philosophy: a theory is a total model of the world, or it is nothing. I wonder which other feminists would turn out not to be doing theory on this view of things: would Elizabeth Spelman? bell hooks? Andrea Dworkin? Cherríe Moraga? Alexandra Kollontai? Would Maggie Nelson, Sara Ahmed, Andrea Long Chu, Sophie Lewis, Lola Olufemi? What precisely is gained by saying that the work of such feminist intellectuals isn't something called 'theory'? And what might be lost?

One small irony here is that I often think that Haslanger, in advancing her project of 'ameliorative metaphysics' – in which philosophers offer analyses of concepts that they think best serve our political needs – has an impoverished social theory, one that gives the philosopher, as conceptual technocrat, an oddly privileged role in shaping social and political reality by way of pragmatist fiat. On this view, the philosopher will explain to their folk audience which understandings of concepts it would best serve justice for them to take up. The problem is not only that this approach ignores Gramsci's reminder that theory is something that is not done just by intellectual elites, but encoded in and revealed through everyday action. It is moreover that it ignores what was supposed to be innovative about *feminist* theory. In a 1979 essay titled 'Feminist Theory and the Development of Revolutionary Strategy', the great Marxist feminist Nancy Hartsock counterposed the feminist understanding of 'theory' to that traditional left perspective that 'held that the working class was incapable of working out its own future and those who would lead the working class to freedom would be those who ... were equipped with an *all-inclusive theory that would help them organize the world*' (my emphasis). By contrast, Hartsock says, 'Feminism as a mode of analysis, especially when consciousness-raising is understood as basic to that method, requires a redefinition of the concept of intellectual or theoriser, a recasting of this social role in terms of everyday life.' Feminist theory, Hartsock is suggesting, is not about building models of the world that will serve as a map for the masses, but rather engaging in and encouraging a sustained critical analysis in conversation with those one sees as equal comrades in struggle. (My thinking about what is distinctive about feminist 'theory' – and its relegation to 'non-theory' by the disciplines of philosophy and political theory – is much influenced by Sophie Smith).

An interesting test case is Haslanger's ameliorative analysis of 'woman' in her 2000 paper 'Gender and Race: (What) Are They? (What) Do We Want Them To Be?', a paper I regularly teach to undergraduates. With great analytic clarity, Haslanger arrives at an analysis of 'woman' that will be strikingly familiar to those acquainted with the history of feminist thought, especially the work of Simone de Beauvoir, Shulamith Firestone and Adrienne Rich. What, we might ask, is gained by using the tools of analytic metaphysics to arrive at this familiar place, especially given that few people not trained in analytic philosophy can make their way through a metaphysics article? I don't mean this as a rhetorical question. I think this sort of work is really useful for *analytic philosophers* who are struggling for a feminist consciousness – which, in large part thanks to Sally's work, increasingly many are. It's just that most people aren't analytic philosophers, and most feminists get on just fine without analytic philosophy. If you're an analytic philosopher, it makes sense for you to demand a full 'theory' (i.e. model) of the world before acting, to want specific action-guiding prescriptions, and to feel unsatisfied with a feminist intervention that fundamentally throws you back on yourself, trying to enliven you as a political subject rather than tell you precisely what to do. On my view of things – call it a 'theory' or not – intellectuals don't best serve radical politics by telling people what to do. I want more for feminist theory, and I want to invite others to want more for it alongside me: I want it to be, as bell hooks said, itself a liberatory practice.

Defund culture

Gary Hall

Following the spread of the Omicron variant this winter there have been renewed calls for the UK Government to fund the arts and culture through the Sars-CoV-2 pandemic and beyond. 'We are in crisis mode', Nicolas Hytner, former artistic director of the National Theatre, told the BBC's Newsnight programme. 'We need to see short-term finance, we need to see loans, we need to see VAT looked at again, we need to see business rates looked at again'.[1] Meanwhile, both the BBC and *Guardian* are running major series, titled *Rethink* and *Reconstruction After Covid*, respectively, to explore how society should change in the wake of the coronavirus outbreak.[2] In the first part of what follows I explore how the 'culture wars' can help to explain the lack of enthusiasm on the part of the current Conservative administration when it comes to supporting the arts during a time of mass contagion. In part 2 I then argue that, if we really want to rethink the future of society post-pandemic, instead of defending existing models of state funding of the arts, we should respond to the latest crisis in the creative industries by *defunding* culture and many of its major institutions.

The culture war and attack on the arts

For more than a decade the British Conservative Party, supported by the country's right-wing media, has relied heavily on a hostility to the European Union to help win elections and remain in power. Since Britain's January 2020 withdrawal from the EU, however, Brussels can no longer be blamed so convincingly for the UK's problems. What we are seeing now is the Conservative Party endeavouring to move on from Brexit by devoting more of its attention to the wider 'culture war' it began during the Vote Leave campaign of 2016. Such a 'war' is portrayed as necessary because of purported attacks on national history and identity. Research reveals that the total number of articles published in the UK press each year concentrating on the 'existence or nature' of the culture war increased from a mere 21 in 2015 to 534 in 2020.[3] Yet this conflict is far from confined to the pages of newspapers and magazines. It is also being conducted on the battlefield of the country's elite institutions. Witness the reaction to the National Trust heritage charity acknowledging in 2020 that almost a third of the stately homes it owns, including Winston Churchill's country estate Chartwell, have links to slavery and colonialism. Sir John Hayes, a former minister and the founder and chair of the Common Sense Group of Conservative MPs, went so far as to tell the House of Commons that 'defending our history and heritage is our era's Battle of Britain'. In another example, this time from 2021, Oliver Dowden, then UK culture secretary, intervened to veto Dr Aminul Hoque, a lecturer at Goldsmiths College, University of London, from being reappointed to serve a second term as a member of the board of trustees of the Royal Museums Greenwich because of his backing for decolonisation.

Declaring war on the 'wokeism' that is held as leading to the removal of statues (such as that commemorating Bristol slaver Edward Colston) or to the renaming of buildings (including Edinburgh University's David Hume Tower because of the philosopher's writings on race), has several other advantages besides forging electoral coalitions. It has distracted from the UK Government's disastrous handling of the coronavirus contagion, as well as Afghanistan, the Ukrainian refugee crisis, Brexit and the economy: the rising energy prices, petrol, food and labour shortages, along with the revelations of cronyism, corruption and partying during the pandemic. But the culture war also helps to create an environment in which it is acceptable for the Government to reduce the amount of support it provides to those sectors that are liable

Photo: Panda Mery, 'Weapons of mass creation', 2020.

to be most critical of its socially conservative politics, including on asylum, the right to protest, secrecy laws, and so forth. (Which isn't to say that the Conservatives can't still get things badly wrong in this regard: a 2020 Government-backed advertising campaign encouraging ballerinas to retrain for jobs in cybersecurity had to be quickly withdrawn after it generated a barrage of protests.) Public, local government and business investment all having fallen since 2008, many arts organisations have indeed been left struggling to survive during the pandemic due to a lack of a public funding package.[4] Nor has the antagonism toward those areas of society perceived as fostering critical thought and dissent been confined to the arts, heritage or media sectors. It is now a decade since Michael Gove, as education secretary, excluded the creative arts from the core school curriculum. A lot of institutions have subsequently scrapped their art, music and theatre programmes. At the same time, well-off private schools have been able to invest in substantial arts centres so their alumni can continue to lead the field.

Yet if the Tories are not committed to protecting the creative industries under Boris Johnson, they *are* apparently in favour of introducing the teaching of Latin. In 2021 the Department of Education announced a £4m Scheme to do just that, with plans to roll it out across 40 schools as part of a four-year pilot programme for 11- to 16-year-olds, beginning in September 2022. At the heart of this is the prospect of a return to an era when, as Richard Beard shows in *Sad Little Men*, his book about the institutions that shaped both Conservative prime ministers David Cameron and Boris Johnson, Britain's private schools were quite explicit in placing greater emphasis on the 'development of character' than on the 'acquisition of knowledge'.[5] Traditionally, such schools taught very little history, geography or even science, focusing more on sport to exhaust and distract their pupils so they wouldn't be tempted to have sex with one another.[6] 'Compliance was more important than critical thinking', writes Beard. When it came to academic subjects these schools concentrated mainly on the classics and religion. Along with their nostalgic instinct to 'hide in a glorified' – and often fictitious – past, evident right down to their 'almost accurate historical costumes', and associated aversion to new ideas and to difficulty and complexity, this goes a long way toward explaining why so much culture in England, in particular, has tended to be, as Beard notes, safe, homogenous and anti-intellectual.[7]

The withdrawal of support from creative subjects by successive Conservative governments is also having an impact on universities, and specifically on what courses are available for students to take at which institutions.

Again, arts and humanities education – including media studies, philosophy, history of art, music, dance and performing arts – can continue (in some form at least) at the kind of wealthy 'global-brand' institution that admits a lot of private school pupils in a manner it cannot so easily at others. The result? Between 2009-10 and 2019-20 the number of university students enrolled in humanities courses in the UK declined by 18 percent.[8]

In fact, universities are an explicit target in this culture war for their supposed left-wing campus politics, 'no platforming' and 'cancel culture'. (What's more they're a target despite research showing that 'there's not a great deal of awareness or particular focus among the UK public about universities being in the front line' of the culture wars, or even of being particularly left-wing.[9]) There has been open Government hostility toward the arts and humanities especially, due to their supposed teaching of 'cultural Marxism' and 'critical race theory', as well as their 'low value' and 'dead end' degree courses. Consequently, just as many cultural and arts organisations and venues have suffered from a lack of financial aid during the pandemic, we now have the arts and humanities in education being deliberately defunded because they are not considered 'strategic priorities'. According to the University and College Union, the cuts 'halve the amount of money available for creative and arts subjects' from the beginning of the current 2021/22 academic year. 'The reforms are part of Government plans to prioritise funding for "high-value" courses like STEM and medicine.'[10]

Culture must be ~~defended~~ defunded

Understandably, the response of many liberals, as well as of those on the left, has been to argue, by contrast, that culture *should* be publicly funded, and to an increasing extent, not least because Britain's creative industries are such a success economically and in terms of soft power. The Government's own data shows they contribute £111bn to the economy and are second in this respect only to the country's financial services. This has led to initiatives such as The Public Campaign for the Arts. Established in 2020 'to protect UK culture from the impacts of the coronavirus pandemic', and now the nation's biggest arts advocacy organisation, their stated 'mission is to champion the value of the arts and creativity in the UK'.[11]

However, much as one may wish to dispute the Government's depiction of arts and culture, or of universities, as being unworthy of substantial financial support, this left-liberal argument also takes aim, I want to argue, at the wrong target. Part of the point of universities, and of the arts and humanities especially, is to provide spaces where society's accepted, taken-for-granted beliefs can be examined and interrogated. Keeping this in mind, I want to argue that perhaps we can see the defunding of culture – somewhat counter-intuitively – not just as threat but also as an *opportunity*: one that gives us a chance to argue for transformative change by asking *whose*, or indeed *what*, culture it is exactly that we want to be funded?

In my recent book *A Stubborn Fury*, I wrote about how 39% of the UK's 'leading people' are privately educated (that's more than five times as many as in the general population), with nearly a quarter graduating from Oxford or Cambridge. It is these predominantly upper- and middle-class individuals who receive most of the financial assistance for education in the UK. Approximately £3 is spent on students in private schools for every £1 that is spent on pupils in the state system.[12] The majority of this money is channelled to London and the south-east of England, where there are 3.8 and 3.6 private schools per 10,000 pupils respectively, compared to just 1.2 in the north-east.[13]

The upper and middle class also receive the largest proportion of the available support when it comes to the creative arts. It was found in 2017 that half of the country's poets and novelists attended private school and 44% were educated at Oxbridge.[14] Yet just 7% of the UK population go to private school and approximately 1% graduate from Oxford or Cambridge.[15] Clearly, not everybody has the same opportunity to contribute to the arts and culture. If you want to be a published literary author, for example, best be in that 1%. Ideally, that means coming from the south-east of England, because then you have a 35% chance of gaining a place at Cambridge if you apply, compared to just 26% if you live in Wales. (This figure drops to 19% for Welsh students who apply to Oxford.) It also means being upper class economically: in 2017 it was revealed that more than four-fifths of offers to Oxbridge were to the 'sons and daughters of people in the two top socio-economic classes', and that the situation is steadily growing worse.[16]

All of which raises the question: should we simply call for culture to be publicly funded as it has been, and thus continue to bestow opportunities and resources primarily on those who have long received the bulk of these? The evidence is clear that the current institutions and structures are far from working for everyone – especially not working-class, Black and Global Majority people, whose parents largely *do not* belong to the top two socio-economic classes. (Over 50% of Black children in the UK are growing up in poverty, according to analysis of Government statistics released by the Labour Party in 2022.[17]) Given the injustice of this situation, should a certain amount of those opportunities and resources not in fact be *disinvested* from the cultural sphere as it currently exists – and strategically transferred to other areas of society instead?[18]

My title, 'Defund Culture', as well as referring to the Government's own withdrawal of public backing for the arts, is of course a homage to the contemporary demand for the defunding of the institution of the police. This is a demand with a long history connected to struggles over class and racial injustice.[19] In the US, Angela Davis and other activists were already calling for the defunding of the police in the 1960s. Davis herself traces the history of this demand back to at least 1935: the year when W. E. B. Du Bois published *Black Reconstruction in America*, in which he pushed for the abolition of institutions such as prisons and police forces that he saw as being entrenched in racist beliefs.[20] It was, however, the resurgence of the Black Lives Matter movement in the summer of 2020, following the deaths of George Floyd, Breonna Taylor, Tony McDade and many others, that brought the call to defund the police to renewed prominence. In the UK, this demand was then given further impetus by a number of events that took place in 2021, including the conviction of Wayne Couzens – a serving officer nicknamed 'the rapist' by some of his colleagues in the force 'as a joke' – for luring Sarah Everard into his car using his police credentials, and then kidnapping, raping and killing her, as well as the arrest and eventual jailing of Jamie Lewis and Deniz Jaffer, a pair of police constables who took 'inappropriate photographs' of murdered sisters Bibaa Henry and Nicole Smallman, and then shared them in two WhatsApp groups.

As has often been noted, #DefundThePolice does not necessarily mean abolishing all law enforcement *per se* – although it's sometimes interpreted in that way, by its opponents especially, among whom are that powerful minority for whom the role of police is to protect their land, property and interests. Instead, what such a demand is perhaps most commonly taken to mean is that if forces are not serving their communities, and are instead harming large sections of them, including women, working-class people and people of colour, then at least some of the public money the police receive should be transferred to other sections of society – local residents, voluntary organisations, citizens groups, and so forth – to provide community help and resources in different ways. There's a recognition, too, that the police today are required to deal with a great number of problems they are not properly trained for and that are better handled by others. So, Defund the Police can also mean debundling a lot of their responsibilities and redistributing them to the likes of educators, drug clinicians and mental health specialists, instead of requiring officers to act as everything from social workers and peace negotiators to ambulance crew. Of course, for some radical scholars and activists, Ruth Wilson Gilmore and Mariame Kaba among them, defunding the police *is* undoubtedly about working toward a police-free future. It's about forces being fully disinvested and disbanded and cities being without police or even policing (which is not the same as their being without help, public safety or first responders).[21] Whichever way it's interpreted, though, Defund the Police is concerned with taking a new, different, decriminalising approach to law enforcement, rather than privatising it or reforming it by punishing a few individuals. The idea is to present a radical vision of the future in which the structural and systemic issues that lead to crime, such as social and economic inequality, poverty and homelessness, are addressed in a fashion that offers life-giving alternatives to the carceral logic of the prison industrial complex.

The call to Defund the Police is frequently rejected as unrealistic, as well as threatening. Indeed, the association with #DefundThePolice is one of the reasons that Black Lives Matter is itself often condemned as 'Marxist' and extremist. (Most obviously, in the UK, as far as culture is concerned, it is this association that has led the Government and some fans to criticise football players for taking the knee, insofar as this anti-racist gesture is perceived as having politically radical overtones.) Yet Defund the Police is a philosophy that is backed up by the available research[22] – to the extent that, as Howard Henderson and Ben Yisrael point out, at least 13 cities in the United States have more or less successfully engaged in policies designed to defund the police.[23] Similarly, in an article about how it was Elinor Ostrom's research into defunding the police that led to her celebrated work on the commons – that is, on how people can manage and share resources in their own community – Aaron Vansintjan notes how 'Indigenous Peoples continue to practice safety without the police, such as [in] a community in Whitehorse, Canada. Indigenous citizens of Chéran, Mexico "threw out" the police and took safety into their own hands. There is now little crime that was otherwise common in this part of Mexico.'[24]

Can a similarly radical vision of the future be presented regarding the funding and administration of culture in the UK? As with the call to defund the police, until culture is *by* and *for* all of society, and not primarily private school and Oxbridge-educated white people from the south-east of England, should we demand that it, too, be defunded – with some public institutions even abolished – and the responsibilities for participating in, managing and sharing culture redistributed to others? I'm thinking particularly of those who are already exploring antiracist, anticlassist and antiheteropatriarchal models for doing so.

The changes I'm pointing to would go rather further, in this respect, than merely giving more people from a wider range of backgrounds the kind of opportunities that might enable them to contribute to art and culture. That is to say: it's not just a matter of devising a fairer means of distributing places at private schools and Oxbridge – say, by using a system of quotas, vouchers or even a lottery to be more inclusive of diversity. After the 2020 resurgence of Black Lives Matter protests, the journalist Reni Eddo-Lodge became the first Black Briton ever to top both the non-fiction paperback and overall UK book charts, while novelist Bernadine Evaristo became the first woman of colour to top that for paperback fiction.[25] In the text of her Goldsmiths Prize Lecture that same year, Evaristo emphasises 'novels need to be generated by and speak to a variety of demographics'. And, of course, it *is* extremely important to 'talk about who is writing the novel and what they are choosing to write about', as Evaristo says, and to start including those whose histories have long been invalidated and excluded: 'areas such as women's fiction, world literature or the lesbian novel'.[26] I'm aware that all this is situated in a particular context. But – and this is a critical aspect of the issue that too often goes unrecognised – there remains a risk that, without a more radical commitment to defunding and reconfiguring the creative industries as they currently are, the dominant culture of privilege will continue to thrive. As I put it in *A Stubborn Fury*, paraphrasing Eddo-Lodge, there will just be more women, northerners and people of colour involved in creating and disseminating it.[27]

This article is intended more as a speculative provocation than as an actual economic plan. However, there are a number of ways of funding a more radical redistribution of opportunities and resources that it might be worth exploring as a starting point. These include:

- Defunding London and the south-east: for example, by ensuring a disproportionate share of financial support – whether it comes directly from the Department for Culture, Media and Sport or via Arts Council England (ACE) – no longer continues to go to London and the likes of the Tate, National Gallery and V&A (all of which benefited historically from slavery). In spite of repeated calls for a change to this policy, an analysis of data for 2018-19 shows that London still attracts around a third of ACE investment. This works out as £24 per person, with other areas of the country receiving only £8.[28]
- Defunding private education by taking away the public subsidies and charitable status of private schools and reallocating their endowments, investments and properties with a view to gradually abolishing these establishments.
- Defunding Oxbridge, since it, too, is hardly working for all of society.[29] Money could then be redirected to encourage projects such as the attempt of Cambridge PhD student Melz Owusu to set up The Free Black University in the wake of the Black Lives Matter protests. Owusu wants to decolonise higher education by redistributing knowledge and funding, and putting Black students and staff at its centre, along with a radically reconceived university structure, curriculum, teaching, learning and assessment system. As Owusu recounts: 'I was like, hmm, this idea of transforming the university from the inside and having a decolonised curriculum isn't going to happen with the way the structures of the university are.'

Many universities are 'built on colonisation – the money, buildings, architecture – everything is colonial'.[30]

It is so apparent as to have become almost a cliché, but the impacts of Sars-CoV-2 have offered us a chance to present a radically different vision of what the future of society can look like and how we can make it happen. Such a transformative change will be disruptive of the status quo. Yet with respect to culture (and much else besides) the coronavirus has already been disruptive of the status quo – albeit in ways that have sometimes served the interests of the Government and their allies in business and the media. Moreover, as the Conservative Party's response to the Covid-19 crisis shows, we *can* make transformations in our priorities today that previously would have been considered unreasonable. Ideas about big state intervention in social life that might once have been dismissed as Marxist or socialist were suddenly the only thing that could save us. Between February 2020 and July 2021 the UK Government devoted a total of £370 billion to dealing with the pandemic and its economic impact. Not to introduce profound changes in the financing of arts and culture is therefore clearly a political decision, not a pragmatic one.

In arguing for the defunding of culture I appreciate that there's a danger of building a case that could quite easily appear to lead to a further stifling of critique of the Government, Brexit, authoritarian nationalism or the free market by undermining liberal institutions such as the National Theatre and National Trust. However, the likes of #DefundtheBBC, and the plan of Dowden's successor, Nadine Dorries, to axe the corporation's licence fee, which issue from the right, are not the only alternative to advocating for financial assistance to be given to those social and cultural elites who have long received the lion's share of it.[31] The creative industries can be taken in a very different direction to either of these options. While it may seem a strange thing to say at a time when liberal democracy is under violent attack in many parts of the world, in fact the *undermining* of certain liberal institutions is precisely what is required if we want to reconstruct a better world after the coronavirus crisis – a world in which it is *not* private school and Oxbridge-educated straight white cis people from London and the south-east who receive the vast majority of support, while others in society continue to be marginalised, overlooked or otherwise silenced.

Gary Hall is Professor of Media and Director of the Centre for Postdigital Cultures at Coventry University. His books include A Stubborn Fury: How Writing Works In Elitist Britain *(2021),* Pirate Philosophy *(2016) and* The Uberfication of the University *(2016).*

Notes

1. John Dunne, 'Sir Nicholas Hytner: Venues Struggling with Omicron Need Fresh Financial Support', *Evening Standard*, 16 December 2021.
2. BBC, 'Global Voices Come to BBC Radio to "Rethink" the World After Coronavirus', *Media Centre,* 15 June 2020, https://www.bbc.co.uk/mediacentre/latestnews/2020/rethink; GNM Press Office, 'The Guardian Launches Reconstruction After Covid, A Major New Long Read Series By World-Leading Authors and Experts', *Guardian*, 16 November 2021.
3. Bobby Duffy, Kirstie Hewlett, George Murkin, Rebecca Benson, Rachel Hesketh, Ben Page, Gideon Skinner and Glenn Gottfried, *'Culture Wars' in the UK*, The Policy Institute, King's College London, June 2021, 4, https://www.kcl.ac.uk/policy-institute/assets/culture-wars-in-the-uk.pdf.
4. The National Campaign for the Arts, *Arts Index: England 2007-2018*, June 2020, https://forthearts.org.uk/wp-content/uploads/2020/06/NCA-Index-07-18_-1.pdf.
5. G. A. Walters, Headmaster of Pinewood School, in its 1975 prospectus, quoted in Richard Beard, *Sad Little Men: Private Schools and the Ruin of England* (London: Vintage, 2021), e-book.
6. This point is made by Robert Verkaik in *Posh Boys: How English Public Schools Ruin Britain* (London: Oneworld, 2018), 36. However, Beard provides another reason for the concern these schools have with diverting their pupils away from sex: 'Postcolonial historians look at "sublimating" as an animating force behind Empire-building, so that public school Englishmen, less distracted by sex than other Europeans, repurposed their frustration by conquering foreign lands'.
7. Beard, *Sad Little Men*.
8. Gabriel Roberts, *The Humanities In Modern Britain: Challenges and Opportunities*, Higher Education Policy Institute, Report 141, 2021, https://www.hepi.ac.uk/wp-content/uploads/2021/09/The-Humanities-in-Modern-Britain-Challenges-and-Opportunities.pdf.
9. Bobby Duffy, co-author of *'Culture Wars' in the UK*, quoted in John Morgan, 'UK Public "Don't See Universities As A Front Line In Culture Wars"', *Times Higher Education*, 5 August 2021.
10. UCU, 'UCU Condemns 'Biggest Attack on Arts in Living Memory' Announced By Office for Students', *UCU: Universities and College Union*, 20 July 2021.
11. Public Campaign for the Arts, 'People-Powered Campaigns for Art, Culture and Creativity', accessed 3 January 2022, https://www.campaignforthearts.org/about/.
12. Francis Green and David Kynaston, 'Engines of Privilege: Britain's Private School Problem', *LSE Events*,

11 February 2019, accessed 3 January 2022, https://www.lse.ac.uk/Events/Events-Assets/PDF/2019/01-LT/20190211-Engines-of-Privilege-presentation.pdf.

13. Department for Education, 'Schools, Pupils, and Their Characteristics: January 2018', 28 June 2018, London, https://www.gov.uk/government/statistics/schools-pupils-and-their-characteristics-january-2018; Golo Henseke, Jake Anders, Francis Green and Morag Henderson, 'Income, Housing Wealth, and Private School Access in Britain', accessed 3 January 2022, https://francisgreenspersonalwebpage.files.wordpress.com/2021/02/henseke_et_al_ed_econ_2021.pdf.

14. Gary Hall, *A Stubborn Fury: How Writing Works in Elitist Britain* (Open Humanities Press, 2021), 11. These figures are for those appearing in *Who's Who* and are taken from Nicola Solomon, 'The Profits from Publishing: Authors' Perspective', *The Bookseller*, 2 March 2018, https://www.thebookseller.com/blogs/profits-publishing-authors-perspective-743226; and Aaron Reeves and Sam Friedman, 'The Decline and Persistence of the Old Boy: Private Schools and Elite Recruitment 1897-2016', *American Sociological Review* 82:6 (2017), 1139-1166.

15. Hall, *A Stubborn Fury*, 24. The figures are taken from Sutton Trust, *Elitist Britain: The Educational Backgrounds of Britain's Leading People*, Sutton Trust and Social Mobility Commission, 25 June 2019, https://www.suttontrust.com/our-research/elitist-britain-2019.

16. David Lammy, 'Oxbridge Access Data' (2017), cited in Hall, *A Stubborn Fury*, 10. Further evidence to this effect is provided by Francis Green and David Kynaston. They, too, show that attendance at private school is 'concentrated at the very top of the income distribution'. See Green and Kynaston, 'Engines of Privilege', https://www.lse.ac.uk/Events/Events-Assets/PDF/2019/01-LT/20190211-Engines-of-Privilege-presentation.pdf.

17. Jemma Crew, 'More Than Half of Black Children Growing Up in Poverty – Labour', *Independent*, 3 January 2022.

18. Even in those areas where things are a little better, such as the publishing industry, in which women are now taking up 92% of publicity, 88% of rights and 78% of editorial roles, these still tend to be '"white, middle-class, cis-gendered, heteronormative women"'. Sharmaine Lovegrove, founder of Hachette imprint Dialogue Books, quoted in Johanna Thomas-Corr, 'How Women Conquered the World of Fiction', *Observer*, 16 May 2021. The above figures are taken from *UK Publishing Workforce 2020: Diversity, Inclusion and Belonging*, Publishers Association, 2021, 10: https://www.publishers.org.uk/wp-content/uploads/2021/01/The-UK-Publishing-Workforce-Diversity-Inclusion-and-Belonging-in-2020.pdf.

19. A first version of 'Defund Culture' was presented at the Radical Open Access: Experiments in (Post-)Publishing Symposium, organised by Mark Amerika and Janneke Adema, and held at the University of Colorado at Boulder, 1 October 2021. The first of October was also the beginning of the 2021 Black History Month in the UK.

20. Angela Davis, interviewed in Amy Goodman, 'Freedom Struggle: Angela Davis on Calls to Defund Police, Racism & Capitalism, and the 2020 Election', *Democracy Now!*, 7 September 2020, https://www.democracynow.org/2020/6/12/angela_davis_on_abolition_calls_to.

21. See Ruth Wilson Gilmore, *Golden Gulag: Prisons, Surplus, Crisis, and Opposition in Globalizing California* (Berkeley: University of California Press, 2007); Mariame Kaba, in conversation with Maya Schenwar and Victoria Law, 'Abolish Policing, Not Just the Police', 2 July 2020, https://www.haymarketbooks.org/blogs/184-abolish-policing-not-just-the-police.

22. See Alex S. Vitale, *The End of Policing* (London: Verso, 2017).

23. Howard Henderson and Ben Yisrael, '7 Myths About "Defunding the Police" Debunked', *Brookings: How We Rise*, 19 May 2021, https://www.brookings.edu/blog/how-we-rise/2021/05/19/7-myths-about-defunding-the-police-debunked/.

24. Aaron Vansintjan, 'What Elinor Ostrom's Work Tells us About Defunding The Police', *Grassroots Economic Organizing*, 18 June 2020, https://geo.coop/articles/what-elinor-ostroms-work-tells-us-about-defunding-police.

25. Reni Eddo-Lodge, *Why I'm No Longer Talking to White People About Race* (London: Bloomsbury, 2017); Bernadine Evaristo, *Girl, Woman, Other* (London: Hamish Hamilton, 2019).

26. Bernadine Evaristo, 'The Longform Patriarchs, and their Accomplices', *New Statesman*, 1 October 2020.

27. Hall, *A Stubborn Fury*, 106, n.8.

28. 'London Receives a Third of All ACE Funding', *Arts Professional*, 12 July, 2019, https://www.artsprofessional.co.uk/news/london-receives-third-all-ace-funding.

29. I am not advocating abolishing Oxbridge, or universities, or indeed all liberal cultural institutions, here. I prefer to go beyond modernist-left liberal discourses to advocate a radically pluralised politics that is capable of including the modernist-left, the liberal and the pluriversal at the same time. For more, see my 'Pluriversal Socialism - The Very Idea', *Media Theory* 5:1 (2021), http://journalcontent.mediatheoryjournal.org/index.php/mt/article/view/126. However, I'm aware there are those who do advocate abolishing the university as well as the police and prisons. Harney and Moten, for example, write that the left slogan '"universities, not jails," marks a choice that may not be possible. ... Perhaps it is necessary finally to see that the university produces incarceration as the product of its negligence. Perhaps there is another relation between the University and the Prison – beyond simple opposition or family resemblance – that ... of another abolitionism'. Stefano Harney and Fred Moten, *The Undercommons: Fugitive Planning and Black Study* (Brooklyn: Minor Compositions, 2013), 41.

30. Melz Owusu, in Harriet Swain, 'Payback Time: Academic's Plan to Launch Free Black University in UK', *Guardian*, 27 June 2020. For more on the vision of The Free Black University, see https://www.freeblackuni.com/vision.

31. For a discussion of #DefundtheBBC, see Steven Barnett and Doug Specht, '#DefundtheBBC: The Anatomy of a Social Media Campaign', *The Conversation*, 10 June 2020, https://theconversation.com/defundthebbc-the-anatomy-of-a-social-media-campaign-140391.

Reviews

Lost at sea

Enzo Traverso, *Revolution: An Intellectual History* (London: Verso, 2021). 480 pp., £25.00 hb., 978 1 83976 333 5

The second volume of Peter Weiss's epic historical novel *The Aesthetics of Resistance* opens in Paris in 1938. Recently defeated international brigade fighters in the Spanish Civil War, the unnamed narrator and his dejected comrades have taken up temporary residence in a grand building made available by its owner to the members of the peace movement and Popular Front. Unable to sleep, the narrator stumbles upon a book by two survivors of the infamous shipwreck of the Medusa. The recent catastrophes he has just lived through recede and he finds himself absorbed by tragic events that unfolded over a century before.

In 1816, the Medusa set sail from France for Senegal to repossess the colony for the recently restored French crown. Led by an incompetent royalist captain, the ship diverged from its convoy, drifted off-course and ran aground on a sandbank. The Medusa's passengers began to escape in small boats but these couldn't accommodate everyone on board so 147 people were placed on a hastily constructed raft with few provisions, no mast and no oars. By the time the Argus, a ship from the Medusa's original convoy, discovered the raft by chance thirteen days later, only fifteen of the raft's original passengers remained alive. Stories of the horrors endured on the raft told by the survivors – of suicide, delirium, murder, starvation, cannibalism – soon circulated in France and caused a huge public scandal. The avoidable tragedy of the shipwreck became a symbol of the callousness of the recently restored monarchy, a kind of early nineteenth-century Grenfell Tower fire.

Weiss's narrator leaves the bookshelves at dawn to walk through the deserted city towards the Louvre, where he seeks out Théodore Géricault's 1819 painting *The Raft of the Medusa*. The book's long opening paragraphs intersperse visceral descriptions of the shipwreck with discussions of the 'agonizing restlessness' that characterised Géricault's attempts to convey the 'distress and desperation' of the events on canvas. This chance encounter with a historical disaster has a paradoxical effect on Weiss's protagonist: 'It was as if, reading of the bygone events described here, everything that lay torn open within me could be brought to a reconciliation.'

Enzo Traverso's *Revolution: An Intellectual History* also begins with an encounter with Géricault's painting in the Louvre, though he makes no mention of Weiss's novel. Traverso proposes reading the artwork as 'one of the most powerful allegories of the shipwreck of revolution.' He claims the painting, in whose corner the rescuing Argus can be glimpsed, not only represents a disaster but also anticipates future struggles. He views the black man on the raft as 'the premonition of anti-colonialism and black liberation' and interprets the red flag being waved, which in the early nineteenth century did not yet have an association with left-wing struggle, as a harbinger of communism. He sees in the conflict and tumult on Géricault's canvas a tension between resignation and hope, 'between capitulation and the obstinate search for an alternative, between abandonment and rebirth, between impotence and despair before a landscape of defeats and the desperate effort to resist.' By contrast, when Weiss's narrator first lays eyes on the painting he is unable to focus on the rescuing ship but instead experiences 'anxiety, a feeling of hopelessness. Only pain and desolation.' He encounters the painting in a moment of political defeat, in which the solidarity and common purpose that had united him with his comrades have suddenly evaporated. He understands that Géricault intended to show that the last survivors had clung to a desire to live in spite of everything they had endured, but in the faded colours of the painting's 'scabbing' sur-

Théodore Géricault, Sailboat on a Raging Sea (c. 1818-19), 86.GG.679, The J. Paul Getty Museum, Los Angeles.

face he sees only the unresolved inner turmoil of the artist, in whom the 'revolution had been inscribed ... like a scar', a subjective rupture he also recognises in himself and his peers. Traverso emphasises the painting's hopeful aspect, but beginning his book with an image of catastrophe and suffering, of dead and dying people in a moment of restoration rather than revolution, sets a sombre tone and lacks the immediacy, intensity and emotional resonance conveyed in Weiss's engagement with the artwork. If this is what hope looks like then it's incredibly murky. The survivors are few; the possibility of rescue uncertain.

So, what is a revolution for Traverso? He begins with the image of a shipwreck, but elsewhere describes revolution as an earthquake and a volcano. Revolutions interrupt and erupt; they break the continuum of history (I'm paraphrasing Traverso who is fond of paraphrasing Walter Benjamin's theses 'On the Concept of History' (1940)). A revolution, he says, is 'a collective act through which human beings liberate themselves from centuries of oppression and domination'; it is 'a singular amalgam of innovation and chaos' that displays 'a spectacular iconoclastic charge'. Revolutions 'are precisely the moments in which the excluded are no longer voiceless and clamour to be heard'. They are, less precisely, 'concepts converted into action', which 'follow an autonomous dynamic, as uncontrolled spirals that aim at obliterating the past and inventing the future from a *tabula rasa*.' Violence, he declares, using an unfortunate biological metaphor, 'is inscribed into their genes.' Yet for all that Traverso's prose proliferates declaratives, definitions and metaphors, there remains something curiously slippery about his object.

Is this book about ideal or actual revolutions? Is it about revolution as such or an assortment of particular revolutions Traverso happens to find interesting? Is it about revolutions, revolutionaries or the revolutionary? Is it just about political revolutions or also about other kinds of revolution (sexual, industrial, intellectual)? Is it, rather, about communism or perhaps capitalist modernity? Is it about theories of temporality and liberation or is it about insurrectionary practices? That the book is about all of these things at various points is not necessarily a weakness. As Leon Trotsky asks in the 1930 Preface to his *History of the Russian Revolution*, one of Traverso's key sources: 'How can you take as a whole a thing whose essence consists in a split?' Traverso grapples engagingly with tensions between ideas and realities, theories and practices, dreams and nightmares. His subtitle 'an intellectual history' is perhaps a little too modest, given *Revolution* addresses a phenomenon both thought and lived. But what, ultimately, is to be gained from reading about past revolutions in the calamitous present, when the book itself refuses to make a strong case for doing so?

Revolution is structured thematically and conceptually, rather than as a chronological series of case studies focused on particular historical revolutions. Though confined mostly to a 1789-1989 timeframe, the book's examples are eclectic, jumping around historically and geographically to discuss revolutionary temporalities, subjects, bodies, symbols and concepts. Traverso is explicit that he has no interest in separating 'good' from 'bad' revolutions but instead contemplates both the utopian and the catastrophic: 'The happiness of insurgent Havana on the first January 1959 and the terror of the Cambodian killing fields'. Interested neither in valorisation nor condemnation, Traverso is not concerned with extracting strategic lessons from historic victories and defeats but offers instead a 'critical *elaboration* of the past', a past that he believes, the contemporary left is at risk of forgetting. His opening chapter is typical in its methodological approach, considering the locomotive as a symbol of revolution, while examining the significance of actual trains in past revolutionary struggles. Traverso begins the chapter with Marx's declaration that 'revolutions are the locomotives of history' and ends with Walter Benjamin's riposte: 'Perhaps revolutions are an attempt by the passengers on this train – namely, the human race – to activate the emergency brake.' If the train had been an image of the inevitable forward-moving progressive trajectory of history for Marx, Benjamin, writing at the beginning of the Second World War, saw teleology leading only to catastrophe. Traverso's chapter closes abruptly with an image of the ramp at Auschwitz.

Though vividly written, full of sparkling details and sharp theoretical insights, the individual chapters – unwieldy, sprawling, bloated – often feel like they're sinking under their own length. A chapter on revolutionary intellectuals, for example, piles example upon example until any overarching argument is buried beneath biographical subtleties and anecdotal niceties. The closing pages include a list-like typology of the revolutionary intellectual and charts of individual intellectuals of various generations, indicating key biographical experiences that united them. This offers a summary of the historical terrain just charted but struck me as a curious quantitative exercise that produced no obvious qualitative insights. Indeed, it seems methodologically closer to the 'universal history' Benjamin attacked than to the historical materialism he extolled: 'Its method is additive; it musters a mass of data'. If the experience of reading the book is anything like sitting on a train, it is nothing like speeding along tracks towards a glowing horizon, nor does it slam on the brakes. It's more like when you think you're getting an express train on the subway in New York only to find you're on a local train that stops at every single station on the line and then gets stuck at one for ages with no explanatory announcement from the driver. It's fine, you get somewhere in the end and maybe there's something interesting to look at through the window in the meantime, but it's hard not to feel impatient and fidgety. *Revolution* is bursting with ideas, images and examples, but for something so full, when I finished it I felt strangely empty.

At various moments, Traverso evokes the intensity of feeling unleashed by revolutions, celebrates the new forms of relationship that develop within them, and insists on the centrality of their corporeal dimension. Revolution, he proclaims, 'is a moment in which politics is suddenly flooded with feelings and emotions.' But if revolutions can be visceral, 'ecstatic, euphoric' experiences in which people 'display a quantity of energies, passions, affects and feelings much higher than the spiritual standard of ordinary life', this does not necessarily distinguish them from other forms of collective political action. Uprisings, rebellions, riots, occupations, picket lines or demonstrations could be characterised in a similar way, as his own description of insurrections makes clear:

> Insurrections are moments of collective effervescence in which ordinary people feel an irrepressible desire to invade the streets, occupy the sites of power, exhibit their own strength, if necessary take up arms, and celebrate liberation through manifestations of fraternity and happiness.

Equally, none of these events necessarily feel uplifting. In the book's introduction he acknowledges that revolutions can be tragic and often sink into despair. Indeed, revolutions can even be boring, disappointing, deflating. *Revolution* constantly foregrounds such contradictions but because it is, however ambivalently, an attempt to transmit something positive from the revolutionary past to the present, it also gets tangled up in them.

Traverso's general pronouncements are haunted by spectres of their exceptions and often literally followed by non-ghostly clusters of caveats and counter-examples. In attempting to distil pure essences from the mess of history, Traverso keeps crashing into a contradiction between the universal and the particular, the ideal and the actual. His insistence on wanting to avoid romanticising the past and his refusal to sort 'good' events from 'bad' is paired awkwardly with constant general programmatic statements about revolutions, statements that do not say what revolutions should or could be, nor what they have sometimes been, but proclaim what they *are*. He doesn't want to celebrate any particular revolutions but he does want to celebrate revolution (except, unless, despite...). Thankfully Traverso does not spend time constructing pedantic taxonomies, policing terminological borders or dismissing political events for not being proper revolutions, even noting the '*structural symmetries* between revolution and counterrevolution' at one point. But although he may not explicitly label some historical moments revolutions, while disqualifying others – like Alain Badiou's designation of some things as 'events' according to his own idiosyncratic definition – he nonetheless constantly says what revolutions *should* ideally involve and therefore implicitly expresses criteria for judging them. Why else bother writing such a book in the first place?

Even though Traverso may not claim that collective emotional intensity is unique to revolution, an attachment to a distinction between the conscious and the spontaneous persists in his account, albeit in a fairly muffled taken-for-granted kind of way. Revolutions, he suggests, are distinguished from other kinds of event by the consciousness of the people who make them. Beneath his rejection of an orthodox Marxist faith in teleological historical progression lurks a continued attachment to an understanding of the conscious subject coupled with a mild disdain for the 'spontaneous' event that belonged to that tradition: 'Revolutions are usually conscious accomplishments by collective subjects.' What becomes of the conscious baby, once the bath water of historical progression has been thrown out? Do the historical examples he discusses bear out this understanding of human subjectivity, agency and volition? Doesn't the consciously acting revolutionary subject also have an intellectual history? Can revolutions happen without such subjects at their helm? What would it take for such subjects to emerge again?

The aftermath of revolutions also sets them apart from other kinds of disruptive political event, which only temporarily ruffle the status quo without overturning it. Traverso is clear that revolution is both event and process, though he makes fewer pronouncements about the emotional qualities associated with the latter. He admonishes the radical left for celebrating liberation while neglecting 'the political and juridical norms required for establishing freedom as a durable order', but acknowledges that experiencing such transitions can be subjectively damaging. *Revolution* remains alert to the contradiction between rupture and consolidation, fleeting experience and lasting tradition, a theme central to the book's third chapter, 'Concepts, Symbols, Realms of Memory'. Traverso discusses how revolutionary iconoclasm precedes the creation of new symbols and rituals, wrestling with the contradictions inherent in attempting to memorialise something that is ephemeral by definition: 'The revolutionary spirit cannot be bottled and displayed in museums'. He contemplates distortions that occur when revolutions are institutionalised, domesticated or folded into national narratives and explores forms of 'counter-memory' that persist when revolutions end in defeat. For Traverso, the impulse to preserve and catalogue is anathema to the ruptural force of revolution; like pinning a butterfly to a board. He argues that revolutionary meaning 'lies in the void left by the destructive force of the revolution itself.' And how to build monuments to a void? These discussions of memory and memorialisation also raise meta questions about the project of the book itself and the counter pantheons, archives and chronologies it seeks to construct, questions which are geographical as well as historical.

In a chapter discussing conceptual distinctions between freedom and liberation, Traverso attacks Hannah Arendt for her dismissals of anti-colonial struggle and lambasts her for acknowledging the French and American Revolutions, while ignoring the Haitian Revolution. Specifically, he takes aim at her essay *On Violence* (1970), in which she argued that the violence of the colonised outstripped that of their oppressors because it remained 'pre-political': 'To write this in 1970 was neither simply inaccurate nor distastefully contemptuous; it was the expression of an astonishing intellectual blindness, not to say a clearly Eurocentric and Orientalist prejudice.' Traverso is careful not to repeat the kinds of prejudices displayed by Arendt. His long chapter on revolutionary intellectuals, for instance, includes discussions of figures such as Ho Chi Minh, Manabendra Nath Roy and Che Guevara, alongside a parade of Europeans. *Revolution*'s conceptual structure enables geographically disparate events to be discussed side-by-side, while his final chapter 'Historicizing Communism' includes a section considering historical connections between communism and anti-colonialism.

Yet, just as Traverso quietly clings to the figure of the conscious revolutionary subject, with the notable exception of the Mexican Revolution, his chapters are structured such that anti-colonial struggles and non-European revolutions, though acknowledged and discussed, remain peripheral to his account and their inclusion does not seem to alter how he interprets events that took place in Europe. His approach is like adding a new wing to an existing museum in which the objects in the main building remain in their original places; he extends rather than rearranging, reconfiguring or rebuilding. Paris (1789, 1848, 1871) and Petrograd (1917) are the two revolutionary metropoles at the centre of *Revolution*. Traverso invokes the Haitian Revolution and CLR James's *The Black Jacobins* plenty of times, for example, but never discusses either the event or the book at any length. In the introduction he lists a series of revolutionary moments that promise a book of global breadth: 'France in 1789, Haiti in 1804, continental Europe in 1848, Paris in 1871, Russia in 1917, Germany and Hungary in 1919, Barcelona in 1936, China in 1949, Cuba in 1959, Vietnam in 1975, and Nicaragua in 1979.' But the book's index lists 66 page references under 'French Revolution', while the Nicaraguan Revolution isn't listed at all and neither are the 1975 revolutions in Angola or Mozambique, which he mentions in passing in another synoptic paragraph in the concluding chapter. Towards the end of the book, Traverso declares that 'Bolshevik literature was full of references to the French Revolution, 1848 and the Paris Commune, but it never mentioned the Haitian Revolution or the Mexican Revolution.' Rather than chastising

Théodore Géricault, detail, *Raft of Medusa* (1818-19). Photo: Steven Zucker, CC BY-NC-SA 2.0.

historical actors for failing to acknowledge the Haitian Revolution without discussing it in any detail himself, a more fruitful methodological approach could have taken a cue from Kristin Ross's *Communal Luxury* (2015), which draws out the internationalism and anti-colonial aspects of the history of the Paris Commune in order to unsettle its established historiography and so avoids the 'additive' approach Benjamin criticised. Sergei Eisenstein may not have been a Bolshevik leader but the fact that he planned to make films about both the Haitian Revolution and the Mexican Revolution indicates that these events were not completely absent from Soviet discourse.

In the aftermath of the collapse of state socialism, the meaning of events like the Paris Commune changed. Ross describes this shift as liberating, as an opportunity to return to history unbound by 'official communist historiography'. Traverso is not so sure. Though *Revolution* is not pervaded by the gloomy tone of his previous monograph *Left-wing Melancholia* (2017), it shares with that work the apparent conviction that history really did end in 1989. For someone so apparently enamoured with Walter Benjamin's understanding of 'messianic time' and so keen to expand established canons of revolutionary history, it seems strange that Traverso nonetheless demonstrates a melancholic attachment not to state socialist history itself but to the particular vision of historical progress propounded by state socialist textbooks. Of course, he knows that telos is dead and that it would be absurd to claim otherwise, but he nonetheless seems to see its death as fatal for the left (even if its existence was only ever imaginary) and equates it with the death of left-wing historical consciousness as such. Traverso invokes historian Eric Hobsbawm who by 1989 no longer believed in the teleological vision of history as a 'succession of emancipatory waves' moving towards freedom that had informed the structure of his five volume 'Age of...' account of the nineteenth and twentieth centuries. The moments of liberation punctuating his narrative had happened but he could no interpret them as arrows pointing inevitably in one direction. I thought instead of the revisions CLR James made to *The Black Jacobins* between its original publication in 1938 and reissue in 1963. The preface to the first edition explicitly situated it in relation to the 'booming of Franco's heavy artillery, the rattle of Stalin's firing squads' and was informed by the recent US occupation of Haiti and James's anti-colonial organising with the International African Friends of Abyssinia, while the revised book, in which he rejected vanguardism, was informed by political struggles and historical events that took place in the intervening years, particularly the Cuban Revolution. Both editions responded to the present and looked to the future.

In his theses 'On the Concept of History' (1940), Benjamin rejected historicism, 'universal history' and social democratic understandings of progress in favour of a historical materialism that 'grasps the constellation which his own era has formed with a definite earlier one'. His phrase 'blasting open the continuum of history' is quoted so often – both generally and in Traverso's book specifically – that it has lost something of its force, but crucially for Benjamin the historical materialist is situated in a present they wish to transform: 'it is our task to bring about a real state of emergency, and this will improve our position in the struggle against Fascism'. Traverso borrows from Freud the notion of 'working through' the past but his implied patient, the contemporary left, is left out of his (case) history. Indeed, the present, including any discussion of twenty-first-century revolutions, is conspicuous by its almost complete absence. Traverso attaches great significance to the collapse of state socialism, understood primarily as the collapse of a meta-narrative, but has virtually nothing to say about revolutions that have occurred in actually existing post-Soviet states. In a recent interview in *New Left Review*, Voldomyr Ishchenko describes Euromaidan, various 'colour' revolutions in former Soviet republics and the Arab Spring as 'deficient revolutions'. Given Traverso's proclaimed intention to discuss revolutions irrespective of their deficiencies it is frustrating that he does not offer any analysis of such events. But the occasional passages in which he deigns to address contemporary struggles offer clues to understanding why *Revolution* seems so confused about its own existence.

Traverso claims his book is both 'a work of mourning but also a training for new battles', but like his claim that *The Raft of Medusa* represents both resignation and hope these scales are not balanced. In the introduction Traverso writes that:

> The new anti-capitalist movements of recent years do not resonate with any of the left traditions of the past. They lack a genealogy. They reveal greater affinities – not so much doctrinal but rather cultural and symbolic – with

Théodore Géricault, detail, *Raft of Medusa* (1818-19). Photo: Steven Zucker, CC BY-NC-SA 2.0.

anarchism: they are egalitarian, anti-authoritarian, anti-colonial and mostly indifferent to a teleological view of history… Being orphans they must reinvent themselves.

Though he concedes this is partially freeing, he argues that an absence of historical memory makes current movements vulnerable: 'for they do not possess the strength of the movements that, conscious of having a history and committed to inscribing their action in a powerful historical tendency, embodied a political tradition.' Similarly in his conclusion he lists various post-89 social and political movements – from Occupy to Syriza, 'alter-globalisation' to Black Lives Matter – claiming they are cut off from history and 'deprived of a useable legacy.' What about when students in Cape Town demanded 'Rhodes Must Fall', when a statue of Edward Colston was tossed into the river in Bristol, when student activists clashed with cops in 'book blocs' of insurrectionary classics in 2011, or when Chilean millennials sang songs from the early 1970s in 2019 demonstrations? I'm under no illusions about the parlous state of the contemporary left and share Traverso's commitment to 'working through' experiences of twentieth-century communism, but if this book really was intended to provide people in on-going movements with historical resources to inform their struggles – 'training for new battles' – Traverso might have made an effort to engage with them less dismissively.

Weiss's engagement with the faded greens and greys of *The Raft of Medusa* is far more despairing than Traverso's but, like Géricault piling corpses from a morgue into his studio in an attempt to enter into the suffering of others, Weiss folds the past into the present. In describing the fate of the people on the raft, the pronouns shift from 'them' to 'we'. Historical devastation and hope merge with the experiences of the current moment:

> Those gathered together on the raft still did not want to believe they had been abandoned. The coast was visible … But night fell, and they still had not received help. Powerful swells swept over us. Hurled back and forth, struggling for every breath, hearing the cries of those washed overboard, we longed for the break of day.

Hannah Proctor

About time

Gilbert Simondon, *Individuation in light of notions of form and individuation* (Minneapolis: University of Minnesota Press, 2020). 440pp., £88.00 hb., £20.99 pb., 978 0 81668 001 6 hb., 978 0 81668 002 3 pb.

Gilbert Simondon, *Individuation in light of notions of form and individuation, Volume II: Supplemental Texts* (Minneapolis: University of Minnesota Press, 2020). 336pp., £88.00 hb., £20.99 pb., 978 1 51790 951 2 hb., 978 1 51790 952 9 pb.

Simondon's longest and most philosophically ambitious text has finally arrived in English, in a fine translation by Taylor Adkins. *Individuation in light of notions of form and information* was originally submitted in 1958 as Simondon's *thèse principale*, alongside his *thèse secondaire*, *On the mode of existence of technical objects* (supervised by Jean Hyppolite and Georges Canguilhem, respectively). But whilst the latter was published in French in the same year, *Individuation* was not published until 1964, when it appeared in an abridged format, including only parts one and two. Part three was eventually published as a stand-alone volume in 1989 and parts one and two were re-published in 1995. It was only in 2005 that the first complete French edition of the text appeared. Perhaps to make up for slow and partial publication, the 2005 edition was released as a kind of bumper-pack, including both Simondon's unabridged thesis and a selection of other texts written around the same period. This English edition faithfully reproduces the contents of the French but offers the same collection of 'supplemental texts' in a second volume, whilst Adkins accurately renders Simondon's dry and dense prose in English, complete with extraordinarily long sentences punctuated by copious semi-colons.

The primary thesis of *Individuation* is that philosophy has mistakenly tried to grasp the genesis of individuals on the basis of static beings. In focussing undue attention on the individuated rather than the individuating, for Simondon, philosophy has hitherto failed to think individuation proper. The potential significance of this mistake is made clear by Simondon's ontological hypothesis that many (if not all) beings are never fully individuated, but instead continue to individuate so long as they exist. In order to think the genesis of individuals, then, it is no good thinking of them as eventually individuated, or their individuation as a temporally discrete teleological process. Instead, we must invert the normal sequence and think individuals according to their individuation, or better, think individuals *as* individuations.

The two major proponents of this misunderstanding are hylomorphism and atomism, according to Simondon, and it is these that his own 'transductive' conception of individuation attempts to replace. The mistake that hylomorphism makes is to begin with an individuated being, using a conception of individuation to explain how it came to be this way. Not only does this presume that individuations terminate with substantial and static individuated beings, but it also presents only the 'extreme terms' of the process – matter and form – leaving their mediation and its duration an 'obscure zone'. Thus, whilst hylomorphism conceives individuation as a generative mediation of matter and form, it fails to properly think both becoming and relation. The medieval recourse to a 'principle of individuation', and the debate as to whether it is in the matter or the form, further emphasises this failure, according to Simondon, as it amounts to the proposition that the individual somehow pre-exists its own genesis, either in the matter or the form before individuation. One might respond that principles of individuation in any such Aristotelean argument require instantiation: whichever gives the general and whichever the singular, matter must in any case meet form to generate an individual. Simondon's contention, however, is that such hylomorphic conceptions of individuation ignore the meeting of matter and form; whilst this duration and mediation is seemingly at the heart of hylomorphic individuation, it is left obscure. It is this durational relation, then, that ought to be the starting point for thinking individuation. Thus, he writes both that 'The veritable principle of individuation is mediation' and that 'The veritable principle of individuation is genesis itself'. Ultimately, this results in a position whereby individuals cannot be said to be individuated, rather they continue individuating, and they do so relative to a milieu.

The atomistic error is rather simpler: it entirely ignores the genesis of individuals, or at least atoms, those fundamental beings which make up all others. If atoms are eternal, then they have no genesis to speak of, and if they are unchangeable, then they are merely substantial seats for accidental relations and geneses. Thus conceived, atoms are an abject failure to think a relational genesis.

Those expecting careful and sustained discussion of key texts which formulate and defend hylomorphism and atomism will be disappointed. There is little close or extended engagement with any philosophical texts or thinkers throughout *Individuation*, and these two -isms are no exception. Whilst the text opens with the claim that hylomorphism and atomism are the only two approaches to individuation, hence acknowledging their predominance and longevity, there is little exploration of the reasons for their success. Combined with the apparently wholesale rejection of atomism and hylomorphism presented in the introduction, this leads to the feeling that either Simondon is keeping the detail and sophistication of his criticism of these vast and complex philosophical tendencies to himself, or that he has underestimated much of what is convincing about them.

For example, Aristotle conceived of two kinds of generation: substantial and accidental. Individuation might be a substantial genesis – Socrates is born – but that individual may continue becoming accidentally – Socrates dyes his hair. It is thus wrong to impute that what results from hylomorphic genesis is simply static and unchanging. This misses what is powerful about Aristotle's position, including his criticism of Plato. Whilst Simondon mentions this in his 'History of the notion of the individual' (included in Volume II), he does not develop the sense in which his own transductive position differs, or discuss it in *Individuation*. Equally, Simondon's own conception of continued individuation seems to inform his grasp of hylomorphism: he never fully reckons with the sense in which the problem of principles of individuation has more to do with differentiating beings considered by ontologies built on the back of genera and species. If the principle is in the matter this tends to equate numerical individuation (no two lumps of matter can be the same); if it is in the form this requires that forms can be singular (when the Socrates-form meets matter, for example, the former is made actual whilst the latter is made individual). The resort to principles of this sort may seem unimportant (other than for scholastics), but crucially it points to the fact that thinking according to genera and species implicitly demands an explanation of the relation or abyss between the general and the singular, or between *infima species* and individual. Thinking that he has adequately dealt with hylomorphism leads Simondon to claim that genera and species are irrelevant for his conception of individuation, which is both misleading and unconvincing, as we will see in a moment.

Similarly, whilst the existence of atoms might be presupposed by atomisms, Simondon's critique relies on an etymological elision whereby 'atom' equates to 'individual'. His reasoning rests on the translation of the Greek *atomos* into the Latin *individuus,* both sharing the sense of un-cuttable or in-divisible. But this does not justify equating 'atoms', considered the fundamental elements which make up any and every being, and 'individuals', considered as *both* fundamental elements *and* relatively autonomous unifications of those elements. Indeed, Simondon's point is not that we cannot presuppose the existence of anything whatsoever without offering an explanation of its genesis – he presupposes energy / matter in this way, for example – but instead that if something is an individual, we ought to supply an explanation of its genesis or individuation. Whilst he argues, with help from Einstein and Louis de Broglie, that subatomic particles change substantially with their genesis (as their mass varies according to their velocity) and relative to a milieu, he does not discuss their absolute or substantial genesis, and thus their existence is in fact presupposed.

Certainly, Simondon's transductive conception of individuation does not rely on an unchanging substantial seat for accidental change, as Aristotle's does, and his criticism of atomism might be justified by his contention that atoms change, but neither are made plain in the text, and both are open to objections.

In spite of these reservations, the image Simondon offers of atomism and hylomorphism is clear and affords a highly lucid contradistinction with his own position. The critique of hylomorphism offers an opportunity to present the continuous genetic aspect of transductive individuation and to point out the extent to which mediation between matter and form is at once crucial and obscure in the hylomorphic picture. The critique of atomism serves primarily as a negative expression of relation. Unlike atoms, transductive individuations are not substantial terms for which relations are merely accidental. Instead, individuations *are* a relation to a milieu.

Transductive individuation is thus both genetic and relational, individuals are individuations relative to a milieu, and transductive relation is not accidental, optional or merely possible, but substantial and necessary. Simondon has recourse to other significant concepts, like homeostasis, preindividuality, potential energy and autonomy (and less significantly, in my opinion, metastability and information), but this individual genetic substantial relation is the axis around which much of his discussion turns.

Before we turn to the rest of this long and complex text, we might note here that Simondon's meagre discussion of other philosophical texts and scant citation begs the question as to where all of this came from. Discussion of texts and thinkers tends to pertain only to minor aspects of Simondon's wider position. Whilst Freud, Goldstein, Jung, Kant, Rabaud, Weismann and Wiener all appear briefly, these reflections offer little clue as to what philosophical inspirations or disagreements might have driven or structured Simondon's broad position as laid out above.

This absence might be explained to some extent by the fact that he wrote 'History of the notion of the individual' during the same period, which deals exclusively with other philosophical conceptions of the individual, and is, with classical form, structured chronologically according to periods and thinkers, beginning with 'The Ionian physiologists'. But any help it might provide for reading *Individuation* is far from straightforward. There is little mention of the problems dealt with in the latter, whilst many key sections are either highly orthodox (those on Plato and Aristotle, for example) or bizarrely heterodox (Kant gets three pages, concerned primarily with energy and electromagnetism). To top it off, the text ends with 'Novalis, Holderlin, Henrik Steffens', and thus excludes thinkers such as Bergson, Heidegger and Sartre, who Simondon studied and whose traces are palpable in his work. Attributing inspiration thus remains highly speculative, and the work of comparative criticism must be borne almost entirely by the reader.

The final, major aspect of Simondon's argumentative approach in *Individuation,* which takes up much of the text, is to defend and develop his basic position through recourse to theories and examples, primarily taken from the natural sciences. In this way, he analyses an extraordinary range of exemplary and problematic geneses, from crystallisations and subatomic particles to Sacullina barnacles, termites and mammalian reproduction. These examples do not serve only as evidence for his claims (or as content subsumed by transductive form); rather, each example serves to develop and complicate Simondon's conception of continuously genetic and relative individuality.

Discussing examples and their theoretical conditions of possibility, Simondon's analysis is at its most refined, offering subtle reflections on unorthodox scientific theories and their contrast with the mainstream, and acknowledging geneses which do not comfortably fit his description of individuation. In these sections Simondon's writing is at its most dense and unwieldy, with long descriptive passages (reminiscent of many in *On the mode*), sometimes almost entirely untethered from the line of enquiry from which they started out (and sometimes also the broader thesis of *Individuation*) and crucial argumentative moments which are highly compressed.

One is amply rewarded for struggling through these sections, though. Simondon offers novel approaches to ancient problems with recourse to new scientific theory and example. Particularly significant are various reflections on the one and the many, and on autonomy and dependence. These are characteristically offered through various examples in which individuals are unified multiplicities of atoms, cells or inter-dependent or colonial beings, such as termites or the Portuguese man o' war. These serve both to clarify the sense in which individuations are both relationally dependent on a milieu (which includes other beings) but also independent from the milieu, insofar as they are discontinuous with it. In many such discussions Simondon is admirably frank in acknowledging limitations, both regarding the extent of particular areas of scientific research, and in his own capacity to provide final and all-encompassing resolutions to these problems.

Living beings, he suggests at one moment, might be said to exist on a scale of individuation, from partially individuated beings to those which are able to individuate (if they happen to break away from an initial group), to those which are more straightforwardly, and in some cases necessarily, autonomous from an initial group. This contrasts with more straightforward descrip-

tions of transduction and assertions of its application to any individuation, and serves to demonstrate Simondon's willingness to bend the simplified conception of individuation that he lays out in the introduction and conclusion in light of scientific examples.

Above all, these discussions clearly formulate the problematic sense in which individuations, for Simondon, are both necessarily dependent upon one another in a milieu, but also to some extent unified, distinct and independent from one another. This distinguishes his position from Bergson's, for which each generation is always open and continuous with others, and from Deleuze's, for which unity is an expression of creative genesis rather than a condition and constraint. (Whilst this problem sounds like that of transindividuality, it is worth noting that Simondon argues that vital individuation amounts only to inter-individuality, which does not require a new individuation, like that of the transindividual or collective, serving to drive a wedge between the vital and the transindividual, and giving credence to the criticism that the latter is like spirit overlaid on purely vital multiplicity.)

If discontinuity and autonomy are left somewhat indeterminate in the transductive image by the incompleteness of science or the un-unifiability of its ontic descriptions, the science of energy offers a means for generality. Simondon thus convincingly defends his claim that transductive relational ontogenesis applies to many, if not any, sort of physical, vital and psychic being insofar as these relations are energetic. Indeed, a transducer, though he does not mention it, is generally understood as an electrical device which transforms energy from one form to another, such as a microphone or a solar panel. And in this way, transductive beings relate to a milieu from which they receive energy which is transformed, in terms of sustenance or nourishment – such as through photosynthesis – but also the sensations of life, through energetic transformations which make possible light, colours, sounds and smells, for example. Any being which exists through its energetic relations to a milieu thus strongly suggests inclusion in Simondon's transductive description. This functions extremely well for all sorts of living beings – from amoeba and chantarelles, to grass and humans – though it is worth noting that it would seem, by the same stroke, to severely restrict Simondon's ontology to crystallisations and living beings. Things like stones or crystals (as opposed to crystallisations), though ultimately reducible to energy/matter, do not depend on an energetic source or relation. Simondon never explains how beings like stones (or technical objects), which seem, in his terms, to be individuated rather than individuating, should be incorporated into his conception of transductive individuation.

Energy is not Simondon's primary means for generalising transduction, however. Indeed, there is a tension in *Individuation* between the numerous examples and their apparently identically transductive nature *qua* individuations (which amounts to a mirror of the problematic distinction of the general and the individual, science and singularity). Examples are not occasional means to embellish the text, but are instead crucial to Simondon's argument. He thus proposes a 'paradigmatic method' for marshalling the many examples in the text, which entails making analogies between different examples, using his concept of transduction as a common term. Whilst this might seem a logical way to accommodate many different beings, especially since he is seeking a term which can apply to 'any' individuation, it also highlights the irony (present in any *concept* of individuality) that transductive individuation is a term with general, if not universal applicability. Simondon's analogical reason forces him into a contradictory position whereby individuations are identical: both absolutely singular and identically transductive. Deleuze attempts to avoid this contradiction from the start by contending that only difference is shared, whilst any other identities are mere surface effects of a prior differential energy. This means that any self-identical concept, like living being, which would appear to subsume differences, is inadequate to the true differential materiality of being.

The danger for Simondon is that if all beings are identical *qua* transductive individuations, whilst recourse to genera and species is disallowed on the grounds of being 'hylomorphic', then his ontology would be distinctly flat. As it is, Simondon's close and consistent use of scientific examples and his determining of differences according to domain – physical, vital, psychic, collective – avoids such levelling, but only at the cost of reintroducing categories into his ontology. *Individuation* is structured according to categories of individuation (whether there is a transductive continuity amongst them or not), whilst it is also replete with species in the guise of examples.

One of the lessons of Bergson's and Deleuze's philosophies is that however much one might want rid of categories, they are here to stay. Recognising that they are immovable, in order to get around them Bergson and Deleuze argue that they are immaterial. In this regard, what Simondon fails to properly address is whether his exemplary species are material or natural, or otherwise immaterial, functions of intellect, language or scientific technique, for example. Bergson opts for the latter, regarding species as intellectual divisions of the continuity of duration. Species of life never go all the way, for Bergson. Whilst the *élan vital* is forced to divide into species as a result of its necessary relationship to matter and matter's own necessity, individual living beings and species thereof are never entirely divided from or are ultimately always continuous with the *élan vital*. Deleuze largely follows suit, holding that kinds cannot be said to be natural or material. Bergson and Deleuze attempt to explain away categorial self-identities as functions of intelligence or mere expressions of something deeper (the virtual). They are at pains to do so precisely because they recognise the enormous significance of categories. Simondon, by contrast, makes surprisingly little attempt to explain this relationship, and never sufficiently confronts the question as to the relationship between science and singularity or universality and individuality.

Simondon relies on science to make his argument in *Individuation*, and more particularly, he relies on scientific examples or specific categories. That he deploys species is unsurprising – Bergson and Deleuze have taught us as much. What is crucial is whether these species are material or immaterial; that is, natural or material limits on the indeterminacy of generations in advance, or otherwise intellectual and practical categories used in science and everyday life. For Bergson and Deleuze, categories are not material constraints on generation, but merely expressions or appearances of a deeper material-energetic source. Simondon does not offer a straightforward answer as to whether species are material or immaterial, as he does not formulate the problem as such. He argues at once that we should not think individuation according to genera and species, but he goes on to think individuation *using* specific categories. Are any of these categories material, or are they rather the only means to access the undivided or non-specific real?

Most straightforward, perhaps, is Simondon's affirmation of homeostasis as a real or material operation, required for the life (or the avoidance of death) of living beings, and also for their distinction from other beings. Regulation of temperature, for example, through behaviours such as sweating, produce negative feedback loops which serve to maintain temperature within a specific range, relative to changing conditions of a milieu. Each repetition might be different, but this does not mean that the discontinuous and specific target range differs. Rather, differential repetitions are constrained to this specific range, on pain of death in many cases.

If individuations are constrained in various ways, then, both in advance and during their individuation, this means that Simondon's conception harbours a hylomorphic element he does not recognise. Some might respond that the preindividual (a term far scarcer in *Individuation* than many of Simondon's readers imply) gets him out of this jam, in the way that Bergson's *élan vital* or Deleuze's conception of the virtual might. But even if Simondon does not thematise it fully, he is clear that transductive individuation is discontinuous, unlike the continuity of Bergson's *élan vital*. It is important for Bergson's position that living beings are all somehow continuous with the *élan vital*, for otherwise its creativity would be constrained by categories in advance, its creative energy would be forced into closed systems without remainder. But whilst the preindividual is an indeterminate energy like the *élan vital*, it is a source to which individuations relate, not a continuous whole including all individuals. The problem, then, is that since the preindividual is not continuous with individuations (like the *élan vital*), but rather *relative* to each individuation, it appears like a principle that adds a dash of indeterminacy to a specific being or operation. A freshwater hydra – a species – would thus be made individual by its genesis or individuation, the indeterminacy of which is driven by the preindividual. Another way to express this is that indeterminate preindividual energy relates to material species – of both being and operation – as Bergson's *élan vital* relates to matter in general, which is undivided into vital categories. The *élan vital* is constrained by matter, the preindividual is constrained by natural kinds. Whatever one's position on this, Simondon's argument in *Individuation* relies on the materiality of species whilst at the same time claiming that he articulates individuation without any resort to genera and species.

Another blind spot in *Individuation* derives from the failure to thematise science, ultimately leading to a position whereby the veracity of the theories and examples on which the argument depends is taken for granted. Simondon's engagement with natural scientific theories and examples is close and rich, functioning as a condition for the possibility and plausibility of his argument for transductive individuation. But whilst natural science offers extensive theoretical and exemplary resources, and affords a counter-position between the cutting-edge of science and ancient ontology, he does not confront the historical nature of the scientific truth – beset by errors and rectifications – that he relies on. This is odd for a thinker so close to pivotal figures of French historical philosophy of science – Simondon was supervised by Canguilhem, as we have mentioned, and he worked with Gaston Bachelard in the late forties, maintaining correspondence with him at least until the early fifties. The lessons of Simondon's teachers are all but absent in his primary thesis. As such, his engagement might be described as an ontological snapshot of scientific history, pitched to the extreme of the synchronic, though without acknowledging this.

A related issue arises in the third and final section of the text, when Simondon comes to discuss psychic individuations. The problem is that there is no explanation given as to the role that psychic individuation plays for those apparently non-psychic individuations that concern the first half of the text. In keeping with Simondon's contention that any individuation is transductive, whether physical, vital, psychic or social (distinctions which provide the structure of the text), the section on psychic individuation amounts to an attempt to defend this claim in a new domain. In this regard, an interesting (albeit often elliptical and sometimes confusing) case is made for the genetic relativity of the individuation of affects, emotions and psychic unities. Crucially, however, Simondon does not properly confront the problem of whether or not those individuations previously dubbed 'physical' and 'vital' are really psychic individuations in naturalistic disguise. Indeed, whilst he makes an analogy here between the 'physical' example of crystallisation and psychic individuations in general, he does not explore whether a crystallisation may be both a physical and a psychic individuation. It seems plain that in order to know anything about crystallisations, they must be experienced (as 'psychic unities', Simondon would argue). The issue is whether or how we might know and say anything about the physical individuation of a crystal beyond this psychic individuation. Are physical and vital individuations made possible by psychic abilities? Or, do they also exist independent of them, and if so, what can we know about their independent existence?

The sense in which a cognitive faculty or knowledge might make possible and also limit what we might know or say about beings is a familiar problem for philosophy, especially since the eighteenth century. Since *Individuation* depends on the veracity of natural scientific descriptions and since both psychic and non-psychic or independent individuations are a part of its remit, it would seem a crucial problem to address. It is almost entirely absent here, however. When Simondon does very briefly reflect on this, he argues that individuation is a condition of possibility for the transcendental subject, suggesting a genetic and materialist rejoinder to Kant's transcendental philosophy. He fails to contend, however, with the critical rejoinder to his attempt to produce a 'pre-critical ontology that is an ontogenesis'; namely, that a transcendental unity of experience might be the condition of possibility for what appears a purely physical or natural crystallisation. Even if we might like to accept some part of Simondon's materialism – that the transcendental, like seemingly everything else, requires a energetic / material genesis – if the transcendental is the condition of access to everything, genesis included, then anything supposedly pre-transcendental will bear its indelible mark.

When one finally arrives at collective and transindividuation – after reading sections on physical, vital and psychic individuation – examples are almost entirely absent and the discussion is largely untethered from actuality. The thrust of the section is to argue that individuals are not isolated and substantial beings for which society is accidental, whilst neither are they merely functions or instances of the social – two positions described as psychological and sociological, though without any further specification. Rather, there is a reserve of preindividuality or indeterminacy which allows individuals to produce a new collective or trans-individuation, that is, without substantialising either individuals or the social.

The significant issue is that if the source of the collective is indeterminacy, then the difference and disagreement – in short, the politics – of social life is effectively obscured. This means that actual determinations, such as shared material or social conditions, or those of a future collective are not properly considered, either as obstacles or grounds for the formation of a collective. Membership of a class, or very general determinations such as humanity, or animality, are simply out of the question. Part of this difficulty stems from Simondon's failure to recognise the move from the naturalism earlier in the text to the social and political problems raised with regards to transindividuality. The collective seems to be generated with the same necessity as a crystallisation, without the problems associated with the social. Exclusion from a collective, oppression and struggle or war within or between collectives go unmentioned, for example, as does the question of policing, regulation or a state.

It is also unclear as to why the collective is only thought after the psychic (and the vital) in *Individuation*, and given less than half the space. Whilst the two appear to be in a dialectical unity of sorts at the end of the text – '[t]he social soul and the individual soul operate in inverse directions and individuate opposite from one another' – the social makes little prior appearance. If the individual and the social form a unified or inseparable opposition, they ought to be thought as co-conditioning. This and the potential of the predominance of the psychic for physical and vital examples mentioned above, seem symptomatic of the arrangement of the text from the simple to the complex – physical, vital, psychic, social. Ultimately, one wonders whether *Individuation* might have been better structured otherwise, beginning with the social and the psychic before turning to the vital and the physical, or otherwise attending more carefully to the ways in which each aspect might condition the other.

These criticisms aside, Simondon's expression of the near-universality of transductive genesis, his raising the question of individuation once again, and his careful engagement with cybernetics and the science of energy are reason enough to read this fascinating and difficult book with care and attention. It is about time that both of Simondon's major texts were available in English, and this translation has now fulfilled that demand. Discussions of Simondon's work to date have tended to remain somewhat reverent of their author. The widening of access that these volumes offer will hopefully enable closer and more critical appraisals of *Individuation*, which is, after all, what significant books deserve.

Gus Hewlett

Between context and transcendence

Martin Jay, *Genesis and Validity: The Theory and Practice of Intellectual History* (Philadelphia: University of Pennsylvania Press, 2022). 280pp., £26.99 hb., 978 0 81225 340 5

Can ideas transcend the context of their appearance? Can concepts depose the particularity of their origin to achieve validity? In the opening pages to a new collection of essays on the theory and practice of intellectual history, Martin Jay argues that such questions have been around 'at least' since the dawn of writing systems. They emerged, he claims, when different cultures came into contact with one another and realised the unhappy fact that their truths might be contingent. The questions Jay wants to ask are as such ancient, 'perennial' and valid – worthy of study because of the essentially extensive nature of the problems posed: about the possibility of harmony between cultures, of agreeing upon universal truths, and of a dialogical 'learning process' that might be contained therein.

It is a strikingly sweeping claim with which to begin a book on intellectual history, especially given that intellectual historical trends of the past decades have departed from grand, quasi-anthropological gestures towards the enduring or even ancient nature of 'big ideas' in favour of the more modest task of parsing a term or text in its context. Jay's insistence on the forever character of questions concerning genesis and validity acts, however, as preparatory motif to his commitment throughout the course of the book to resurrect validity itself as an important pillar (and perhaps lodestar) of intellectual historical work, despite the rise of contextualist preference for 'genesis' and its attendant forgetting of meaningful universals. We should not shy away, he contends, from recognising the transcendent *experiential* structure that contains historical work in the first place; and with it, the prospect of imbuing philosophical questions with appropriate grandeur.

There are ostensibly political reasons to want to hold onto validity. Following the lead of a slew of recent books about 'decolonising' or otherwise rerouting critical theory, the introduction pays lip-service to now familiar hand-wringing about 'relativism', or the weakening of broad-base political and social concepts, like human rights, that has accompanied critiques of Eurocentrism's false claims to universality. Jay also worries that 'identity politics' has trapped us into a relativism of 'situatedness' whereby we must always 'say where we're coming from' (or be forced to repeat our 'genesis'). On the flipside, too much validity can also be a dangerous thing. Naively advocating for the universal applicability of ideas might lead one to become much like 'American neoconservatives during the administration of George W. Bush' who wanted to export capitalist democracy abroad. The book ultimately provides a diplomatic attempt to dialectically reconcile these two schools or approaches to intellectual history – the genetic and the valid, contextualist and warily universalist, relativist and imperialist, 'the Cambridge School' and the Frankfurt School (or at least its American proponents) – arguing that the 'relationship between genesis and validity is not necessarily adversarial.' Yet, the delamination of the very terms of his title from their context sometimes betrays a preference for the valid that confuses the possibility of achieving a happy medium.

Rather than going back to writing systems at the dawn of time, nineteenth-century German philosophy might be one place to return to in order to understand the present tensions between different methodological approaches in contemporary intellectual history. Or, to call upon the language of 'genesis', a healthy dose of context can help us to denaturalise what Jay takes to be perennial. In the 1820s, historicism – a much-contested term applied to rag-tag intellectual movements broadly committed to making history scientific – was on the rise. While many agreed upon the general principles of historicism, a slew of different camps emerged with competing ideas about its scope and method. As intellectual historians Herbert Schnädelbach, Frederick Beiser and others have detailed, these camps were often cut along the lines of Hegelian idealist-historicists, who believed that historicism could be compatible with speculative philosophy, and historicists who rejected the intrusion of metaphysics into empirical source-based work, notably Friedrich Carl von Savigny and Leopold von Ranke.

While philosophical historicists claimed that historicism was about discovering the general rules of world history and development of ideas over time, the empiricists argued for the cultural specificity or contingency of historical phenomena. These debates produced a few different competing tendencies that would extend into the twentieth century. Friedrich Meinecke's *Entstehungsgeschichte* and its emphasis on 'genesis' became closely intertwined with liberal nationalism in Germany and the theory of the state. Around the same time, neo-Kantianism became concerned with rescuing historicism from relativism by injecting it with a bit of transcendence. Neo-Kantians, reworking the paradigmatic Kantian distinction between *quaestio quid facti*, regarding the origins or 'genesis' of knowledge, and the *quaestio quid juris*, regarding the validity of knowledge, argued that establishing the validity (*Geltung*) – or objectivity – of historical judgments would show that they are not merely relativist or subjective, but structured by an internal relationship to universality.

These different emphases – on a historicism that is in touch with the transcendent and one in which it is cordoned-off – have ricocheted throughout the past centuries in rotating shapes. By giving his book the title *Genesis and Validity*, it seems, on the one hand, that Jay is suggestively extending the vocabularies of these older historicism debates, showing us how intellectual history itself is formed through them. Indeed, there might be much to be gained from understanding contextualism, and its deep-seated focus on state theory and political thought, as a distant relative of the 'genetic' empirical-historicist perspective; and from understanding critical theory's insistence on validity as an unwitting extension of neo-Kantian frameworks (as Gillian Rose has argued). On the other hand, Jay takes for granted the reader's familiarity with this terminology, and never makes explicit why it is he uses this pairing in the first place. What does he think is to be gained by framing these conflicts in terms of validity and genesis? It is something that readers have to sort out for themselves over the course of thirteen wide-ranging chapters that contribute to articulating the state of the present stand-off, and possibly resolving it.

Each chapter of the book is a republished essay or article from the past decade, with contributions on free speech debates and photography somewhat shoehorned in. Nearly half of them are dedicated to tackling the Cambridge School, and Quentin Skinner's contextualist approach to intellectual history, head on. Like the empirical historicists of yesteryear, for Jay, contextualists have made a devil's bargain in which more historical rationality is exchanged for a loss of meaning or philosophical horizon-line. He argues that 'contextualization and value relativism are often cozy bedfellows', which is a problem in part because it absolves a thinker of responsibility – their work becomes 'symptomatic' of a larger context.

It is true that contextualism can quickly turn into clerical work, and that contextualists can be disinterested in deeper philosophical readings. In methods' classes at the University of Cambridge, we were encouraged to look for smoking guns amid archival detritus (if we can finally show that Hobbes read X, then we can make the claim that Y). The search for smoking guns also means the closure of arguments one is able to make as an intellectual historian; in the absence of indelible proof, one cobbles together a series of contexts for understanding a given text, with the possible effect of underplaying its philosophical dimensions.

In riposte, Jay echoes Randall Collins's claim that intellectuals are precisely the people 'who produce de-contextualized ideas.' To ignore this is to denude ideas of their ability to 'transcend our parochial horizons' and shock us with 'the audacity of their insolent ambition' – which is to say, perhaps, the capacity of ideas to change and shape reality. On such a rosy view of the potential of what he calls 'big ideas', it makes sense that for Jay 'contextual explanation, however we construe it, is never sufficient.' Still, staying true to his aim in the introduction, Jay also recognises that there are problems with the 'opposite impulse' of valorising 'the transcendental implications of ideas.' Seeing the present as more capable than the past of 'learning moral lessons', or as in a better position for judging ideas of the past, can entail the 'loss of false hopes and the rejection of utopian dreams.'

Jay seems to be operating in the land of lost hopes and dreams himself. In a chapter on Lukács, he confesses that reading *History and Class Consciousness* in the present political landscape is an 'unbearable experience'. It is unbearable, he contends, because there are presently no other books at such a high theoretical level that are 'written by someone engaged in life-or-death political activity.' The decadence of the contemporary political landscape is backed up by a showstopping claim that youth today, unlike their predecessors who fought in the Spanish Civil War, are 'more likely to join a jihadist movement to restore a religious theocracy that would have seemed repugnant' to Lukács and his generation. Is Jay not here tumbling into precisely the pitfalls of a transcendental presentism he has tried to avoid? It's a difficult comment to shake off, a 'big idea' floating freely from any historical reality, which is a shame because such moments distract from the book's more immanent goal:

to find a way to integrate the escape of meaning into intellectual historical practice itself; and to make historians recognise the fact that 'there is meaning without context'.

To aid him in this task, Jay frequently calls upon historian Frank Ankersmit's idea of 'sublime historical experience' and philosopher Claude Romano's idea of the 'event'. Both concepts point out the way that we are always 'apprehending [historical events] on a horizon of meaning that they have opened themselves.' Phenomenological attentiveness can mediate between context and transcendence by showing that the past 'defies both reassuring contextualization' as well as 'the current standards of truth or value' that we might apply in an ameliorative critical reading. There is an analogue, Jay argues, to this kind of mediation in the field of art. Art proves that there is a 'recursivity between context and transcendence' that is invoked by terms like 'autonomy' and 'aura' (Adorno's and Benjamin's respectively). Art contains an 'inexhaustible surplus', much as the historical past, but also often depends on judgement of its 'genetic pedigree', or an evaluation of the context in which it was produced. It is this analogy that also, presumably, welds a joint between the book's essays on photography to its larger story about genesis and validity.

In further attempting to mediate between context and transcendence, Jay claims we would do well to follow in Jürgen Habermas' footsteps. We can draw up a 'post-facto model of development based on the latent rules underlying the evolution of a tradition of thought' that can be 'used as a normative standard' that measures past and present contradictions within thought against each other. As an example of a thinker who does just this, Jay cites Althusser's conception of the history of political thought as a series of 'aporias that propel later theorists to try to solve on a higher level.' In a footnote to this section, Jay seems unsure if all of this might be the task of social critic rather than of an intellectual historian proper. Certainly, Habermas and Althusser are not intellectual historians in any sense that history departments in Cambridge or Berkeley would recognise. Moreover, is not solving a series of interlocked aporias one characterisation of the task of philosophy?

This buried comment enhances the impression that the stand-off between genesis and validity is rather a proxy battle regarding the role of social criticism within intellectual history, and intellectual history's conspicuously indeterminate relation to the production of philosophical ideas. The boundaries have always been a bit porous for Jay, who began his career as one of the first historians of the Frankfurt School's critical theory; the exposition of critical theory, and its attendant if sometimes opaque tendency towards 'emancipation', have shaped the parameters of his intellectual historical project. Sometimes this involves seeing the ways in which such tendencies are blocked. After all, much like Jay, the current generation of Frankfurt School critical theorists are ensnared in a stalemate over intruding Eurocentrism, relativism and context, arguing that such forces undermine the capacity for social criticism in the first place. In writing a book that attempts to reconcile and deal with the same set of problems, Jay shows that one of intellectual history's most formidable if implicit goals has been to save philosophy from itself, and to set it back on its path.

Mimi Howard

Back from the future

Keti Chukhrov, *Practicing the Good: Desire and Boredom in Soviet Socialism* (Minneapolis: eflux/University of Minnesota Press, 2020). 336pp., £22.99 pb., 978 1 51790 955 0

Spinoza's dictum that we ought to understand first – not ridicule, not cry, nor detest – is ignored surprisingly often, even in philosophical scholarship, when it comes to revising and appropriating intellectual labour from the context of 'real existing socialism' (RES). Such dismissal is usually not based on any kind of engagement with the contents and contexts of that project and thus ironically affirms what it pretends to criticise: since the intellectual labour and culture of RES, so it is said, were completely dependent on ideological pregivens, it may not be taken seriously, except perhaps in its early phases or dissident aspects. This view, apart from being historically inadequate, begs the question of its own ideological dependence and amounts to a taboo, cutting off past experiences, achievements and failures, debates and struggles from contemporary appropriation, which could help us to understand our own times better. In fact, the communist heritage of RES continues to pose a challenge not only in 'post-communist' contexts but globally.

Keti Chukhrov's recent book *Practicing the Good: Desire and Boredom in Soviet Socialism* can be best evaluated as an intervention in contemporary theoretical and cultural debates. It presents a perspective that uses cultural production in 'historical socialism', as she calls it, as a model to rethink the connection of political economy and cultural production in terms of alternatives to contemporary art and critical theory.

In its own way, the book thus relates to the question of 'capitalist realism' (Fisher, Jameson et al.) without discussing it explicitly. Chukhrov does not refute that analysis of the internalisation of neoliberal capitalism, but from the outset widens its scope, historically and methodologically. If capitalist mechanisms of extraction have infiltrated our minds so pervasively that they manage our desires, what about desire in socialism? Against the naturalisation of libidinal economy (an argument often used to explain the demise of RES), she argues that in a different society with a different political economy the emergence, meaning and expression of desire changes along with other 'ontics'. In this sense, cultural production in RES seems somewhat futuristic today.

This bold claim probably encompasses more than a single book can account for. Accordingly, Chukhrov aims at giving hints in this direction rather than trying to prove the hypothesis. With its four loosely interwoven parts – Political Economy, Sexuality, Aesthetics, and Philosophic Ontics of Communism – the book is best read as partly exploring and partly experimenting with communist thought embodied in late Soviet works, ranging from philosophical to artistic projects, to this end. What Chukhrov aims to unveil in these works is the actual experience of being part of a project towards the common good, reflecting the cultural implications of a non-surplus-value-economy on different levels.

The book allows us to get to grips, first, with the continuing Cold War schema in the 'West' that presents its own norms as the only possible universals, with all its stereotypes, contradictions and projections; and, second, with the capitalist unconscious of post-'68 'critical theories' and art. As Chukhrov argues, the dismissal of intellectual labour in RES, even within openly anti-capitalist projects since the 1960s, as in 'Western (post-)Marxism' and later poststructuralist continuations, leads to an impasse when attempting to think about the overcoming of capitalist conditions. Chukhrov argues that most of these projects do not really engage in changing what they criticise; they reflect rather than overturn capitalist social relations. In such projects, the desire to overcome capitalism is often not as strong as the desire to unbound desire. But as Spinoza said, 'a passion can only be overcome by a stronger passion'. The rebuke of socialist culture in terms of its dependence on historical societal constraints and prescriptive ideology is thus turned around by Chukhrov: what kind of ideology and which concrete socio-economic constellations shape the cultural production and mental labour of 'western modern-

ity', a modernity we 'capitalist subjects', somehow share, and which after 1989 presented itself as the only realistic socio-economic and political formation (an ideology presented as non-ideology, parading as pure neutrality)?

When the western left, in particular artists and critical theorists (in the broad sense), dismissed socialist culture in RES, Chukhrov argues, it followed assumptions (in particular about hedonism) formed by a capitalist reality, or implicitly hypostatised them. Unable to integrate the experience of what it actually means to develop communism and socialist culture under the abhorred conditions of RES, there was only one choice – the apology of the classic practice of avant-garde art: subversion.

For Chukhrov, this was (and still is) a necessary effect of the inability to actually have the slightest chance of changing societal conditions. But this has a psychological twist: the inability to think alternative realities to capitalism leads to a fascination *with* it and hence to its disavowed affirmation. In this way, the complicity of those forms of culture and reflection which are meant to criticise capitalism's practices in fact reproduce it theoretically, producing either hopelessness or auto-aggression.

Chukhrov follows here a basic idea of Soviet thinker Mikhail Lifshitz, who in discussions of the philosophy of avant-garde and modernist art called this predicament the 'herostratus complex' of (post-)modern culture, and already pointed to its inherent anti-enlightenment stance, with auto-aggressive tendencies and a zeal for destruction of humanist ideals. Chukhrov takes up Lifshitz's critique and concretises it with respect to contemporary art and theory in particular. Since subversion mostly remains on the level of negation, the actual question then becomes how 'the negation of negation' turns out.

This topic is particularly present in the first part of the book, where Chukhrov engages in an explicit critique of thinkers including Butler, Castoriadis, Deleuze, Guattari and Lyotard, among others. By trying to ground political action in subversion, they follow the modernist strategy in art: only a 'break' with, or a going 'beyond' of, all kinds of cultural and symbolic forms makes an overcoming of the existing modes of perception and social ontology conceivable. Any kind of generality or universal must be attacked. Nowadays, it may be obvious that this kind of apology of counterculture did not lead much further. For Chukhrov, it amounts to fighting alienation with more alienation.

After a transitional chapter on 'the poor object of the Soviet Commonwealth', drawing on Groys, Kolganov and artists of Moscow conceptualism, the last – very interesting – chapter of the first part on 'Political Economy' is dedicated to an analysis of Soviet films of the 1960s and 1970s. For Chukhrov, late Soviet fdrive is, from today's viewpoint, a 'non-cinema', not only because it did not work in terms of a capitalist cultural industry, but because of the framework intricately connecting the individual to their social conditions. Although western observers might assume that after the thaw period, socialist realism in film was abandoned (think, for example, of Tarkovsky), it in fact lived on. With discussions of selected works by filmmakers such as Larisa Shepitko and Vadim Zobin, Chukhrov illustrates a kind of socialist subjectivity present in these works, where protagonists had to face the tedious realities of everyday life under post-Stalinist socialist conditions – leading to a stance of resignation, while at the same time holding tight to the communist ideal. In this context, Chukhrov argues that desire changed form: 'in a constant conflict between individual desire and the necessity of the commons.' Thus Chukhrov argues that an inherent problem of RES was 'too much socialism', in which developing a socialist subjectivity was hindered by the actual contradictions of relations and forces of production, on the one hand, and on those between ideology, not least as associated with the commodity fetish, and the plain reality of use-value production, on the other. Nevertheless, Chukhrov reminds us that these 'realia' show what it means to practice the good, since they show that at the centre of these films is the urge to de-alienate.

This question is also discussed in the book's next section, 'Sexuality', which delves into Soviet theatre and literature, especially the work of Andrei Platonov, in comparison to the works of, for example, Pier Paolo Pasolini, while also referring to Alexandra Kollontai and György Lukács. The topic of desire is presented in the framework of the critique of psychoanalysis in Voloshinov and Vygotsky and again draws on the concept of 'anti-libidinal self-resignation'. One of Chukhrov's more controversial claims is her insistence on defending a conception of resignation, which does not refer to a death drive or self-annihilation, but relates to care for the commons.

The third part of the book on 'Aesthetics' mainly discusses the work of Lifshitz, a friend of both Platonov and Lukács. Chukhrov defends the realist conception of aesthetics in Lifshitz, emphasising its universal (non-prescriptive) normative claims. Lifshitz envisioned a Grand Aesthetic analogous to Spinoza's *Ethics* and defended a classicist conception of art because, as Chukhrov puts it poignantly, classical art actually is the most communist. In the same vein she discusses 'The Philosophic Ontics of Communism' in relation to the philosophy of Evald Ilyenkov. In siding with the Soviet Hegelo-Marxism of Lifshitz and Ilyenkov, understood as a form of 'cosmological humanism', it becomes clear why Chukhrov emphasises concepts like the universal (*vseobshee*), metanoia, human resignation, the ideal, the classical and realism as indispensable for rethinking critical theory. It is only through the transformation that these concepts underwent in the Soviet context (by including them in a truly materialist dialectic) that the significance of their absence or rather abolishment in the Western context becomes conceivable.

It is at this point that the possible limits of her argument about political economy and its influence on cultural production, social ontology and ontics become apparent. If capitalist conditions led to an abolishment of basic ideals of emancipation in capitalist contexts from the 1960s onwards because of the inability to overcome capitalism, how can the emergence of these ideals be explained? As is well-known, the communist ideal from Marx to Lenin and Ilyenkov is in explicit continuity with emancipatory projects which emerged in quite different conditions (like the French Enlightenment or German Idealism). Furthermore, criticising the synthesis of (post-)modernism and critical theory, Chukhrov often subsumes various thinkers under one category (e.g. 'Western Marxism'). But the incompatibility in terms of, say, a fascination with libidinal economy or even an internalised lust for capitalist liquidations can hardly be equated to the critique of the historical realities of RES for meeting neither the standards of Marxist insights nor the horizon of trans-capitalist prospects.

Chukhrov concedes from the start that she uses her claim about the frame of political economy as a 'logical tool' rather than for historical analysis. This defines the limits of her argument in historical terms. Since there is no consistent genealogical account, the argument is purely structural and works mainly as a foil for the present. Since the contrast does not work well before World War II, the book concentrates on the situation from the 1960s onwards, since by then the geopolitical stalemate seemed cemented and the forms of socialist culture concretised.

But another question remains: if Soviet culture was somehow *practically* in continuity with the Enlightenment project in terms of *Bildung* (also the word in Russian), while the West *practically* and (in the seemingly most advanced forms of art and critical theories) *theoretically* gave up on basic conceptual premises of emancipation and liberation, wouldn't it be more obvious to concentrate more concretely on what Lifshitz called 'the capitalist training of the people', that is, on the effects and possible real life contradictions in the concepts of education and psychology? To be sure, Chukhrov gives hints in this direction, as for example in her discussion of Vygotsky and the activity theory of Leontiev and in particular Ilyenkov's emphasis on educational and psychological conceptions from a Marxist point of view, which he developed further in engaging with the once famous Zagorsk school for blind-deaf children.

In a daring project like this, open questions remain. Chukhrov seems to oscillate between an explorative presentation and experimental provocations. The products of intellectual labour she focuses on, which reflect the conditions of life in socialism and embody the spirit of the common cause, can of course not be taken *pars pro toto* for conditions under RES. And how far did these conditions already represent actually dealienated conditions? Her suggestions, when taken generally, sometimes remain at the level of a provocative travesty of the western story and may be read as a parody of today's ideology. If the Soviet Union allegedly was not part of a 'common modernity' but was the 'absolute other' of modernity's legitimate representatives, it may follow that we can use its (counter-) image in a productive way. However, it is a merit of the ways in which Chukhrov's book tries to productively relate different levels that it goes beyond such mirroring. In this respect, Chukhrov insists, it needs to be asked why the Soviet experience was not taken into account in critical theories of the West? Why did that historical 'experiment' not become common knowledge, improving democratic conditions in the East and the West after 1989?

Her basic assumption throughout is that a society which abolished private property and surplus value along with the libidinal economy did actually exist. We therefore have to concede that despite all its failures and shortcomings, RES has to be seen as the most advanced societal experiment to date.

The book is engaged not so much with the past as with the present and the future: it is a counterhegemonic undertaking reclaiming something like radical leftism from the false appropriations of anti-communist postmodernisms. It provides an insightful, estranging perspective that shifts the settled horizon beyond its given normality in order to appropriate experiences from an at least partly more 'advanced' societal formation. In this way, a new panorama opens up in whose light a whole set of realities appear that have been hidden from view. Indeed, this ideology-critical shift is the most important move that *Practicing the Good* practices: a debunking heuristic tool. To reject implicit Cold War settings also *within* Western (post-)Marxism, Chukhrov makes clear that dialectical universalism is a more promising way to think towards a communist ideal on a global level. Since her book delivers a basic deconstruction of the capitalist re-conditioning of critical theories along the lines of the postmodern, it is to be counted as one of the most important publications for leftist self-criticism in recent years.

Sascha Freyberg and Lukas Meisner

Theoretical practices

Natalia Romé, *For Theory: Althusser and the Politics of Time* (Lanham, Boulder, NY: Rowman & Littlefield, 2021). 206pp., £81.00 hb., 978 1 53814 764 1

Although Natalia Romé's book *For Theory: Althusser and the Politics of Time* comes in the disguise of humble secondary literature, it is not just an account of Althusser's theory of temporality but also makes a claim for the power of theory in political struggle. She insists on the precise relation of theory and practice as central to Marxism. The book reengages with Althusser's most important question: how does theory accomplish the differentiation and demarcation that unites it with practice? In attempting to find an answer, Romé's book deals with what Warren Montag calls in his introduction Althusser's 'impatient' concepts: concepts, suddenly appearing only to disappear again, concepts that are used as vehicles to get him through certain kinds of terrain. On this ground, Romé presents a detailed account of Althusserian theory, that flourishes in close readings of the Althusserian classics, as well as providing an account of texts that were only recently edited.

Romé introduces us into her reading of Althusser through the political experience of her home country of Argentina. This project is connected with a certain theoretical tradition of reading Althusser, but it also uncovers a field of political struggle, first against the dictatorship and then against the 'democratic' variation of neoliberalism, especially the feminist struggles that broke out all over Latin America during the last decades. Romé describes her project as engaging with: 'Not only Althusser's writings, but also a wider Althusserian problematic that goes beyond Althusser himself and involves many names contradictorily connected and many "Marxist" fragments of still well-known "non-marxist" philosophies, returned as a sort of compass.' To describe this conjuncture at the core of her book, Romé reminds us that the 'historical block' of neoliberalism was forged in the military juntas of Argentina and Chile, which were backed by the traditional ruling classes as well as US and European capital. These juntas did not just imprison, torture and kill thousands of leftists, but also pushed huge parts of their population into misery through the reduction of real wages, the dismantling of welfare-programs and the privatisation of huge parts of the society. The technique was not just the crushing of workers' power through direct terror, but also the dismantling of working-class politics as an ideological wager, leaving the post-junta era as a deeply apolitical space. Romé states:

> The condition was this: that no one would talk about class struggle anymore and, especially, that the civic-military dictatorship could no longer be thought of as the dictatorship of capital. The modality would no longer be censorship but, rather, over-information, the infinite pluralization of discourses.

For Romé, Althusser represents a remainder that could not be appropriated by this new form of post-dictatorship discourse: 'his political prose and theoretical conceptualization did not lend itself to the processes of indoctrination, museumization, or aestheticization to which many others thinkers were subjected'. As she paraphrases Althusser: the very idea of 'applying' a theory to the 'visible concrete' cannot offer as a result any analysis of the concrete situation, but an 'absolute philosophy' that is supposed to already contain the truth of any conjuncture. She sees this tendency as both empiricist and historicist because it does not problematise its own concept of historical time (and therefore, of historical totality), and this impacts the way of 'conceiving the relation between theory and strategy.' Finding and marking this line of demarcation of theory and politics through Althusser's complex concept of time itself becomes a political project:

> It happens that, searching for the concept of time, capable of suiting Marxist dialectical materialism, Althusser's anachronic theoreticism can expose one of today's weakest flanks of critical theory facing neoliberal ideology's force: the lack of a political desire for the true.

The book is composed of two parts. The first part, 'Conjuncture', is occupied with Althusser's reading of Machiavelli and the problem of humanism. It sets as its goal the articulation of a plural temporality out of the concept of overdetermination. According to Romé, this is especially important in his analysis of state power, which Romé dissects carefully by navigating the complex interference between Althusser's readings of Hegel through Marx and Freud, his readings of Machiavelli as theoretician of political practice in the matrix of historical time, and his heterodox Spinozism.

In the second part, 'For Theory', Romé unfolds her account of the complex conjuncture of theory and practice, that shapes Althusser's thinking at its core. According to her, Althusser holds a materialist position *in* philosophy rather than pursuing materialist philosophy. His notion of overdetermination marks the paradoxical relationship between theory and practice, history and politics. The dual disposition of theory (aligned with the name of Marx) and practice (aligned with Lenin and Mao) does not function as a dualism but instead represents an effort to hold the space between two planes and make it consistent as problematic disjoint union. The struggle in theory is always already a struggle for practice; it is not a search for the one true truth, but for our position in the field of history and politics and therefore for our means to change it. Or as Romé puts it:

> This reading is not the reading of a manifest discourse, the pursuit of a voice, but a reading of readings, the pursuit of symptoms and misadjustments: it is the reading of a topique, because starting with Marxist theory, the text of history is not a text where a voice speaks (the Logos); it is instead the 'inaudible and illegible notation of the effects of a structure of structures'.

In these complex conjunctures Romé rediscovers the 'political' Althusser, an Althusser radically different from the 'apolitical', academic Althusser that is reduced to his ideas of reading, his stance against humanism or his concept of overdetermination. Against this kind of isolationist reading of single concepts, Romé favours a holistic approach to Althusser, an approach that thinks in conjunctures and currents, an approach that stays faithful to Althussers 'impatient' thought: a thought that gains its strength (but also its weakness) from concepts, that are never finished and absolute but temporal and fleeting, in order to structure a terrain that is itself only visible in its shifts and breaking points.

In this context, Romé's intellectual stance on the question of how to read Althusser is of a piece with her political stance on how to engage with politics through theory: it is not through the fixing of a static system of concepts but through fostering a radical openness of thought that we can engage in the political struggle for emancipation. An openness that is not relativist, but – on the contrary – bears witness to the complex network of modes and practices of reproduction that shape the capitalist social formation, which we strive to overthrow.

Here it is the radical politics of feminism, that Romé has in mind: 'Feminism can be in this sense as one of the most powerful weapons to fight against the forms of neoliberalization of the leftist intellectual field'. Seemingly at odds with Althusser himself, who can hardly be regarded as a feminist, Romé argues that within feminism as a historical plurality of interlinked struggles, we can find practices that combine revolutionary practice and theoretical analysis of the movement and the conditions it tries to overthrow in an exemplary manner: 'the long-term history of feminist movements and positions is in itself a permanent part of feminist research, critical analysis, and debates'. For Romé, the feminist struggles that have erupted with new force and ferocity all over Latin America during the last decade, are exemplary for this Althusserian approach: the struggles in themselves are often heterogeneous, sometimes even antithetical, but, through their interconnectedness with other struggles (like the struggle for the rights of indigenous people or the disenfranchised working-poor of the 'poblaciones') they become a vehicle for true social change – something that radically distinguishes this revolutionary feminism from the neoliberal brand of '#girlboss-feminism'.

All this means that Romé has written a highly complex book, and one can easily get lost in the richness and vastness of the terrain covered. It is therefore recommended to read the parts as essays in themselves and only afterwards discover the monograph, the thread that unites them as a whole. In this sense, the Althusserian gesture of thinking is repeated in the book itself: rather than writing a monograph on 'Althusser's politics of time', at the end of which we would find a definition of this concept, we find a complex network of approaches to a certain problem: the *problem* of a politics of time; politics of time as time of reproduction, of time as historical time and of time as means of categorical epistemology.

In this approach through problematisation, rather then through definition, we find Romé's true faithfulness to Althusser (a faithfulness that is radically different from an empty indebtedness). She invites us to reengage with Althussers writings, because she reminds us that, far from being just another toothless dead white man that litters the European canon, reading him can be a dangerous endeavour that calls into question not just how we think the conjuncture of politics and theory, but our very position as political beings inside a complex structure of reproduction; reproduction of subjectivity, of knowledge, of power and – first and foremost – the reproduction of temporality itself.

Till Hahn

Estranging capitalist estrangement

Mattin, *Social Dissonance* (Falmouth: Urbanomic/Mono, 2022). 256pp., £14.99 hb., 978 1 91302 981 4

Both a reconstruction of the notion of alienation and a partisan reflection on the relationship between experimental art and a social world, *Social Dissonance* could be considered the first work of 'Brassierian Marxism'. If the study of Wilfrid Sellars led Ray Brassier to a profound engagement with Marx's revolutionary contribution to thought, Mattin builds on his work, along with Thomas Metzinger's, to enrich traditional Marxian theories of alienation, complementing the 'alienation from above' instituted by the 'spectral objectivity' of value with a highly original rendering of the 'alienation from below' that constitutes the self as a sort of necessary appearance.

Much ink has been spilled discussing the proper role of the concept of alienation in Marx's work. Soldered, according to some, to a metaphysical notion of 'human essence' soon abandoned; crucial, according to others, as a reminder of Marx's deep humanist commitments. The entwinement of the debate with practical political problems has often served to occlude what was theoretically at stake in the first place.

What is perhaps most valuable about Mattin's contribution is his ability to vindicate both the cogency and enduring importance of the concept of alienation whilst circumventing most of the problems traditionally associated with Marxist humanism, be it its troubling nostalgia for a pre-alienated wholeness or its various appeals to an unhistorical 'essence' that contradicts Marx's own flattening of the latter into the 'ensemble of social relations'. Although he draws on Lukács's *History and Class Consciousness*, Mattin avoids some of that text's most flagrant flaws, such as the invocation of the 'soul of the proletariat' as an unmediated source of resistance against generalised reification. He instead resorts to Brassier's rendering of 'essence' as self-relating negativity. This interpretation salvages the notion whilst shattering any articulation of the latter as a substantial identity.

Mattin's appeal to the *externalisation* of alienation combines a farewell to any illusion of an estranged immediacy, either predating capitalism or coming after its demise, with a call for the supersession of its *specifically capitalist* forms. Communism, in short, is not a 'reappropriation' of any kind, but the *estrangement* of capitalist estrangement. Moreover, his rigorous – and equally Brassierian – deployment of the dialectic of immediacy and mediation circumvents a further contentious point of Lukács's work: his tendency to depict *praxis* as an essentially *free* activity lurking behind the reified immediacy of capitalist social forms. This interpretation fatally severs the link between social practice and social forms as the necessary mode of existence of the former. Unlike Lukács, Mattin correctly asserts that alienation, properly understood, is not a mere mystification but the truth of our social being under capitalism.

However, a third complication haunts Lukács's critique of reification, one which Mattin's work does not avoid entirely. It concerns the proper role of labour in a theory of alienation. The latter point is crucial because for Marx, and even for the young Marx, alienation is first and foremost *the alienation of labour*. This is what makes his theory both socially critical and historically specific. Alienation does not stem from our 'thrownness', the pervasiveness of the 'they' or the role of the signifier: it is socially grounded in a dynamic of expropriation and accumulation, wherein our social powers (the productive powers of humanity) take a quasi-objective existence in the form of commodities, money and capital. Crucially, those collective powers are not something inherent in 'human sociality' or any other mystified abstraction: they are a product of capital, yet could point beyond its rule. Thus, the overcoming of alienation is not, for Marx, a re-encounter with a lost immediacy, but the collective appropriation, through the revolutionary action of the working class, of the social powers alienated in the forms of the commodity, capital and the state.

In *History and Class Consciousness,* Lukács operated under an inversion whereby the alienation of labour appeared as a by-product of a generalised and all-encompassing reifying trend arising out of the commodity-form, a Weberian body in Marxian clothes that necessarily leads to a mystified conception of politics. In truth, however, the products of labour only take the commodity-form as a consequence of the former's alienation, which creates a society built around the double split between (1) classes and (2) private and independent units of production. Mattin rightly asserts that alienation is 'a process founded on the fundamental asymmetry between workers who lack the means to convert their material energy into social wealth and a production process that converts this potential material wealth into the actuality of wealth: capital'. However, his quick move to the general ramifications of this original alienation obscure one important political point: how workers' struggle 'in-and-against' the wage-relation and the concomitant dictatorship of the capitalist in the working place is *already* a struggle against alienation. Capitalist alienation is the mode of existence of a contradiction, a reality internally split by struggle. When the struggle *for* the wage develops into a struggle against the wage-*form,* class struggle – the mode of existence of capitalism – takes a revolutionary shape. And insofar as the former is grounded in the daily experiences and collective practices of the working class, the wage-form might well constitute the weakest link of fetishism. As Mattin repeatedly points out, seeing through its mystified appearance requires a theoretical effort, but this effort is fuelled by the impositions made by the valorisation process on the working class.

This latter point should not be mistaken for a call for a workerist politics (a demand of 'fair redistribution' confined to represent the interests of the working class as variable capital): it is just an attempt to highlight the identity of the self-abolition of the proletariat and the abolition of the wage-relation as the central determination of a *communist* politics. Only the fusion of theory and struggle in a revolutionary organisation could demystify capitalist mediations, pointing to their immanent overcoming.

After analysing the 'spectral objectivity' of value and its mediations, Mattin moves to the 'phantom subjectivity' (re)produced by capitalist relations, where the private individual confined within the self confronts the social world as something purely external. In the best Marxian fashion, he demonstrates how the critique of political economy is not an analysis of an inert objectivity somehow lying 'out there', but an immanent unfolding of the form-determinations of both objectivity and subjectivity. Social practice mediates between the two, producing a reified objectivity and the private 'abstractly free' consciousness of the commodity-producer as two sides of the same alienated coin. This rigorous materialist standpoint allows Mattin to denounce Reza Negarestani´s one-sided identification of social praxis with *conceptual* practice for remaining idealist, trumping its emancipatory intentions.

Mattin's audacious innovation, however, lies in showing that there is a deeper layer of alienation that has not been thematised in the Marxist tradition, yet is by no means incompatible with it. It concerns the production of selfhood in a *neurobiological* sense, a topic he explores through the works of Thomas Metzinger. According to the latter, 'biological systems produce self-models in order to cope with the exorbitant costs of processing in-

formation in their environment'. Selfhood is a product, yet it appears as something *given*. As an immediate appearance that conceals the (neurobiological) mediations that give rise to it, the logic underlying the production of selfhood is closely linked to Marx's concept of *fetishism*.

Mattin pushes Metzinger's contribution towards Marxism because the actuality of selfhood cannot be detached from the social forms that mediate it. Selfhood as a neurological phenomenon intersects with the capitalist (re)production of the private individual (grounded in the indirectly social nature of commodity production and sanctioned by the state). The exaltation of experience as self-possession dovetails with the logic of ownership. It reifies experience as a form of immediacy, perpetuating the (liberal) myth of the sovereign subject.

The explicitly political dimension of Brassier and Mattin's attempt to disentangle selfhood – i.e., phenomenological immediacy – and subjectivity – i.e., rule-governed agency – derives from this entwinement. Experience is neither transparent to itself nor self-validating, but socially (Marx) and conceptually (Sellars) mediated through and through. Although 'phantom subjectivity' has neurobiological foundations, it is ultimately instituted by the 'social actuality of abstraction'. Thus, the creation of a *communist* subjectivity would have to pass through the destitution of the self in a process whereby capitalist real abstractions are abolished and the relationship between the social recogniser and the recognised individual takes a radically different shape.

Mattin's analysis of the unity-in-difference of subjective and objective alienation from the perspective of its potential overcoming furnishes his vindication of an aesthetic of noise. Noise is a peculiar phenomenon that seems to elude both cognitive apprehension (conceptual mediation) and commodification (social validation). It is disturbing, baffling, *alienating*. However, positing noise as the *other* of mediation would turn it into another form of immediacy. Mattin's project goes in the opposite direction: a radical aesthetic of noise, he asserts, ought to inscribe the latter (which is precisely that which cannot be smoothly inscribed, i.e., represented) *within* our social and conceptual practices, using its estranging powers to explore *social dissonance*, the estrangement of our social being. By estranging us from ourselves and our environment, noise sheds light on the estranged nature of our *selves* and our social world, both on the subjective and objective sides of alienation.

In Mattin's account, the practice of noise is neither a puerile exaltation of senselessness nor an abstract expression of discontent, but a radical and theoretically grounded exploration of negativity. Noise is negativity-in-act, and its practice aims to expose the negativity of our social world. By disrupting immediacy, it breaks its semblance of givenness, exposing the latter as the product of a complex net of mediations. It estranges us from the reality of our estrangement.

Despite the cogency and indubitable appeal of Mattin's argument, a few objections come to mind. First, the estranging powers of noise are arguably more ambiguous than Mattin suggests. It might well be that encountering noise when harmony was expected would simply end up fuelling feelings of anger and aggressivity. Second, and most importantly, the senselessness of noise could reinforce the feeling of powerlessness among the oppressed rather than, as Adorno would put it, 'break the spell' of alienation. Thus, despite Mattin's insightful criticism of the entwinement of avant-garde art and certain romantic tropes, his aesthetic of noise is not entirely alien to one of the most troubling problems of the former in its relation to emancipatory politics: elitism.

More generally, in the absence of a link between the practice of noise and a broader, more explicitly political struggle against alienation, the disentanglement of the latter from the insidious *noise* that is part of the fabric of our everyday life (a profoundly disempowering exposure to an endless stream of information, stimuli, etc., streaming from opaque social mediations) might prove a Herculean task.

These problematic issues notwithstanding, *Social Dissonance* more than meets the most important requisite of any contribution to Marxian theory: reminding us that there is much to think, and much to be done, whilst providing some precious tools to face this challenge.

Mario Aguiriano

Allegorical mappings

Fredric Jameson, *Allegory and Ideology* (London and New York: Verso, 2019). 432pp., £19.99 pb., 978 1 78873 043 3

A concern with allegory as a mode of interpretation rather than as a literary historical description of a moribund genre has been a leitmotif in Fredric Jameson's thought from *Fables of Aggression* (1979) and *The Political Unconscious* (1981) to *Brecht and Method* (1998) and *A Singular Modernity* (2002). In *Allegory and Ideology* – announced as the second volume of the 'Poetics of Social Forms' series – Jameson returns to concepts and arguments that will be familiar to many of his readers. There are the Greimas-inspired diagrams; the discussions of totality, cognitive mapping, Brecht, Walter Benjamin, Paul De Man and science fiction; and the defence of Marxist criticism as an expansive approach that makes of the literary work an act in history rather than reducing texts to an expression of economic relations. This latter claim recalls Jameson's Althusserian suggestion in *The Political Unconscious* that history is understood as an 'absent cause' in literary texts, and that it can only be apprehended through effects which set 'inexorable limits to individual as well as collective praxis'. Yet Jameson's latest account of allegory as a dynamic and multidimensional system of reference and signification also allows for rich and varied reflections on the ways in which the construction of the modern subject entails the transformation of 'named emotions into feelings that challenge language itself'.

Likening his dialectical materialist approach to that of a scientist in a laboratory, Jameson also reframes some of these ideas through new readings of Dante, Spencer, Shakespeare and Goethe, and a rethinking of his controversial 1986 essay on Third World Literature. To develop these readings, Jameson takes the three-level model of allegory that he adopts from mediaeval philosophy via Northrop Frye, recasting it as a dynamic and transversal mode of historical interpretation. This approach is distinct from the argument he makes in *The Political Unconscious*, where Frye's allegorical method is reframed in terms of three horizons of interpretations, and the collective and the subject/body swap places, so that 'the imagery of libidinal revolution and of bodily transfiguration once again becomes a figure for the perfected community'. Drawing together this previous work on Frye and the Greimas square with Félix Guattari's concept of transversality, Jameson argues that the fourfold scheme of allegorical reading involves 'perpetual dissolution and recombination' in a way that also 'scrambles the levels' of allegorical analysis.

If this approach seems rather too poststructuralist for a Marxist thinker such as Jameson, it is perhaps worth considering some of the examples he invokes. At one point during the response to critics of his Third World Literature essay ('Third-World Literature in the Era of Multinational Capitalism' (1986)), Jameson turns to the globalisation of men's professional football, both in respect of the transfer of players and of capital between top league clubs in Europe and Latin America, and in the take-over of such clubs by oil tycoons and oligarchs. For Jameson, it is the circulation of foreign national football players that characterises 'the mapping problem of the world system today'; this football player, he adds, 'caught between his [sic] origins, his home team, and his national representation, is only the most dramatic figure for the multidimensionality of globalisation evoked and presupposed in the essay on national allegory'. One might well take exception to the exclusion of women's professional football from Jameson's analysis, the perfunctory account of football club ownership and sports washing, and the exclusion of fan's voices from the way that many elite clubs are run. Yet this allegorical football player does, in a certain way, help to clarify, if not personify, some of the key points that Jameson's critics missed in their response to his essay on national allegory: that the nation refers to a national bourgeoisie that mediates between multinational corporations and local extraction industries; and that allegory is a much more complex and multidimensional form of reading than Jameson's critics have allowed.

Critics of Jameson's Third World literature essay have tended to focus on his 'sweeping hypothesis' that 'all Third World texts are to be read as national allegories' – a hypothesis that seems both reductive and generalising. For Aijaz Ahmad, the difficulty with Jameson's theory is that it 'is inseparable from the larger Three Worlds Theory which permeates the whole of Jameson's own text'. Such strident critiques tend to overlook the precise way in which Jameson understands allegory and allegoresis. As Imre Szeman argues in a careful re-assessment of 'Third World Literature' published in *South Atlantic Quarterly* in 2001, Jameson offers a dialectical approach to 'third world' literary texts as complex objects that imagine the nation as a utopian horizon for political change. By tracing the conceptual trajectory of 'national allegory' in Jameson's work from an earlier reading of Wyndham Lewis through to his more recent critical reflections on globalisation, Szeman challenges what he calls the wilful misreadings of Jameson's essay. As he puts it:

> ... the claim that Jameson makes about third world texts ('by way of a sweeping hypothesis') cannot help but distract from his broader aim, which is not to pass aesthetic judgment on third world texts, but to develop a system by which it might be possible to consider these texts within the global economic and political system that produces the third world as the third world.

Szeman's re-assessment is indispensable for clarifying the ways in which 'Third World' texts are indeed 'complex objects'. Yet it is important to emphasise as well that Jameson does not explicitly reference the fourfold model of allegory that he formulates in *The Political Unconscious* when he is discussing Third World literature. Had he done so, Jameson might have been able to clarify how these 'complex objects' are also often anti-systemic, in the sense that they variously mobilise the political energies of decolonisation and the dynamic resources of anti-colonial thought in order to imagine a concrete utopian idea of an alternative world. The revolutionary optimism of much postcolonial thought in the 1950s and early 1960s, and the utopian idea of a 'Third World' alternative to capitalism and Soviet communism, may now seem like a distant memory. As Jameson acknowledges in a recent response to Ahmad, 'the concept of a Third World can no longer have the same currency today in a world in which some of the countries in question have evolved into industrial and manufacturing centers, China become the second-greatest world power, the former Second or socialist World has disintegrated, most of it enjoying a dubious "transition to capitalism".' And yet the remnants of pre-capitalist cultures in contemporary postcolonial literary and visual artworks stand as a powerful reminder that the spectre of decolonisation has not been completely subsumed by the logic of commodity fetishism, and may yet return in another form. As Neil Lazarus puts it in a bold critical assessment of Fanon's thought, 'throughout Africa and elsewhere in the colonial world, precolonial social, cultural and ideological forms survived the colonial era meaningfully. Indeed, they continue to survive meaningfully today, in the "postcolonial" present'.

Such concerns lie beyond the purview of Jameson's analysis. Instead, Jameson's transversal rethinking of allegory is developed further through readings of *Hamlet*, Mahler's Sixth, Spencer's *Faerie Queen*, Dante's epic poetry, Goethe's *Faust II*, and the fiction of Lu Xun, Ousmane Sembene, David Mitchell and Tom McCarthy. What emerges through these readings is an account of how classical allegory is replaced by allegoresis, which entails a rethinking of how personification is transformed into reification; and an understanding of how a collective sense of affect (or disaffection with the contemporary world economic system), which Jameson compares to Lévi-Strauss' idea of *pensée sauvage*, may also provide the utopian resources for changing the world in the wake of anthropogenic climate change. This concern with affect is developed in a Lacanian reading of *Hamlet*, where Jameson traces how different moods or affects – such as 'melancholia, euphoria, eagerness, fury, indolence, disdain' – 'course through the senses' in ways that exceed any one particular character. The playing out of these affects serves to highlight both the allegorical and the pedagogical significance of *Hamlet*, which uses the representation of a father 'who does not know he is dead' as a vehicle to dramatise the inability of an 'old order' to acknowledge 'their obsolescence' and realise 'that they are dead'. 'Perhaps', Jameson adds in a tantalising aside, 'our own moment of late capitalism is in a similar situation, of denial and rebirth'.

Aside from the somewhat perfunctory readings of Lu Xun and Sembene, one might well object that most of the texts Jameson selects for these allegorical readings are taken from a rather narrow European and American literary canon that offers little sustained account of the multidimensional allegorical significance of literary texts from the global South. And yet, Jameson's re-assessment of Lévi-Strauss' account of *pensée sauvage* offers a thought-provoking account of the allegorical structures of indigenous thought that are germane to the decolonisation of allegory. In a move that both recalls and extends his commentary in *The Political Unconscious* on Lévi-Strauss' analysis of Caduveo face painting in *Structural Anthropology*, Jameson argues that *pensée sauvage* is 'something like a perceptual science', 'a set which is part of itself, the name of a specific leaf doing double duty as the name of leaves in general'. Jameson's clarifying note that the English translation of *pensée sauvage* as savage mind 'fails to render the adjective with its natural and spontaneous overtones, as in *grève sauvage*, or *wildcat strike*' makes clear how this term is a constitutive part of modern radical political thought. This intriguing observation implies something radical about indigenous thought as a dynamic allegorical system of knowledge that is also immanent to the modern capitalist world-system. In Dene stories about tar sands extraction in Athabasca or West African narratives of fossil oil imperialism, for instance, allegorical figures from indigenous thought are mobilised to question the devastation of indigenous ecologies and societies. Jameson does not pursue this line of inquiry. Instead, by subordinating the rethinking of Lévi-Strauss to an allegorical reading of canonical western literature, Jameson misses the opportunity to develop the more detailed and sophisticated rethinking of allegory and indigenous thought in 'Third World literature' that his work enables.

The distinctive contribution of *Allegory and Ideology* lies not merely in its account of how allegoresis allows for a multidimensional mapping of the totality of the world economic system, but also in its painstaking and rigorous reconstruction of the Utopian truth content of modern allegory. Jameson's concluding gesture to the reinvention of the terraform after the anthropocene certainly reframes some of the concerns he raised about the salutary value of failed utopias in *Archaeologies of the Future*; but it also prompts further questions about how allegoresis can shed further light on the ways in which cultural narratives from the global South both register and contest the uneven ecological devastation that capitalist modernity has left in its wake.

Stephen Morton

Intersectional humanism

Kevin B. Anderson, Kieran Durkin and Heather A. Brown eds., *Raya Dunayevskaya's Intersectional Marxism: Race, Class, Gender, and the Dialectics of Liberation* (London: Palgrave Macmillan, 2021). 350pp., £99.99 hb., 978 3 03053 716 6

Raya Dunayevskaya (1910-1987) was a Marxist, humanist, feminist and revolutionary thinker, neglected in both Marxist and feminist traditions. This collection presents Dunayevskaya as a strong Hegelian-Marxist philosopher, focusing on her novel interpretations of Hegel on absolute negativity as emphasising the positive that is contained in the negative, which, for Dunayevskaya, is a path to an absolute humanism. She reads Hegel's absolutes as new beginnings, as a new form of liberation for today's freedom struggles. Hegel's absolutes, on her reading, constitute no closed ontology. For instance, Dunayevskaya argues that Marx's engagement with the working class and their struggles led to the creation of an entirely new intellectual dimension and new philosophy of labour. The book discusses Dunayevskaya's total opposition to existing society, one which does not stop at a first or bare negation, but which moves on to a second negation, to the positive within the negative, to express philosophically the longing of humans to be whole. The humanism that characterises Dunayevskaya's account of the dialectics of liberation is her central contribution to Marxism: a unique form of humanism that speaks to the movement from practice to theory (and from theory to practice) in the processes of realising the whole human dimension.

In their contribution, Anderson and Hudis set out Dunayevskaya's dual movement from theory to practice and from practice to theory. They mark an important shift found in Dunayevskaya's work: that spontaneous revolts in social movements raise and develop *theoretical* questions in struggles against oppression, but that a philosophically grounded alternative to capitalism is needed to give action to their direction. The book successfully opens and defends the notion that the philosophy of liberation is indispensable, since the movement from practice is *a* form of theory, not *the* form of theory. Dunayevskaya takes from Marx his resistance to all static, stagnant ways of being, the deep apprehension of motion and transformation as principles of thought and of human process, and the mind-weaving dialectic as the flying shuttle in the loom of human activity (as shown in Monzo's essay in this volume). The collection develops the engagement of Dunayevskaya's *Marxism and Freedom* with the dialectical relation between theory and practice and between organisation and spontaneity that, she claims, will prove necessary to bring down capital. This dialectical relationship is crucial for creating opportunities for change and for reorganising social relations under capitalism. Dunayevskaya's insights into these dialectical relations propose ways of imagining how current social movements can become better organised for challenging capital and its many antagonisms.

The collection focuses on Dunayevskaya's 'intersectional' Marxist feminism. Dunayevskaya did not use this term herself, but she nonetheless engaged with intersectional questions and dialectics of history throughout her lifetime. The collection develops specific aspects of her work that explore intersectional feminism under the influence of Black struggles in the US and Africa, the revolutionary humanism of Frantz Fanon, and philosophies of revolution and revolutionary subjects. They also explore the unity of idealism and materialism and the dialectical relationship between practice and theory (influenced by Rosa Luxemburg and Gloria E. Anzaldúa), discussing women in movements for change (such as Black Lives Matter, the Zapatistas, Rojava, Idle No More). Ndina Kitonga's essay discusses revolutionary politics beyond class reductionism and directed towards the creation of human society. The collection shows that Dunayevskaya's tendency towards intersectionality and her philosophy of freedom was developed in her dialogues with C.L.R. James and Grace Lee Boggs, through her philosophical correspondence with Herbert Marcuse about Hegel, Marx and dialectics, in her interest in socialist humanist tendencies in Eastern Europe and Africa, and in her correspondence with Erich Fromm on his *Marx's Concept of Man*, where Dunayevskaya set out her Marxist-humanist understanding of Maoism and Guevarism.

Heather A. Brown's essay explores gender politics in relation to historical events and the dialectics of history. She discusses instances in which women have taken leading roles against oppressive aspects of patriarchal capitalism, building non-racist, non-sexist societies with gender equality. Durkin, along the same lines, treats Dunayevskaya's intersectional Marxism as a form of 'absolute humanism', which is nothing other than the articulation needed to sum up a classless, non-racist, non-sexist society, where truly new human relations self-develop. Relatedly, Kevin B. Anderson discusses Dunayevskaya's distinction between two kinds of subjectivity: 'revolutionary will' (a form of subjectivity that has no regard for objective conditions) and an 'alienated form of subjectivity' (rooted in the dialectical development of the ground for revolution). The collection's section on intersectionality shows that Dunayevskaya consistently focused on how the revolt of one oppressed group enables others to see their own oppressed state.

This collection also considers Dunayevskaya's new interpretation of the dialectic against totalitarian communism. Her Marxist humanist reading of Hegel is presented as one of the most innovative aspects of her analysis of the USSR. This is directly linked to her break with Trotsky, reclaiming the concept of the politicisation of philosophy against authoritarianism and state repression. The collection successfully presents this in relation to black, brown and other race-based movements, pointing out that Dunayevskaya remained committed to understanding structural racism and its relationship to capital.

The contextualisation of Dunayevskaya's work provided by these collective insights shows how she envisaged movements towards a better world to come, placing feminist concerns at the centre of her life and work. It covers the late 1970s work where she was turning increasingly toward a critical analysis of revolutionary feminism in the US and her new treatment of Rosa Luxemburg. Dunayevskaya was not Luxemburgian and criticised her failure to support anti-imperialist movements, but she extolled Luxemburg's attacks on reformism, her concept of spontaneity, her refusal to separate feminism from revolutionary Marxism, and her commitment to revolutionary democracy, as seen in her critique of the one-party regime of Lenin and Trotsky. The collection insists on Dunayevskaya's systematic approach to theory that reaches beyond economic analyses to new forces and passion in the dialectical movement of society. I find this aspect of her work the most generative for the future life of radical feminist social philosophy today. These collected essays show that Dunayevskaya proceeded to discuss Marx's reconstruction of economic science, offering an interpretation of Marx's critique of political economy: that original economic categories were so philosophically rooted that a new unity was created out of economics, philosophy, revolution. Dunayevskaya's economic issues are 'dissolved' into philosophic ones in the collection, as Dunayevskaya strongly criticises Luxemburg's lack of engagement with the dialectic. Dunayevskaya developed a post-Marx Marxism instead, targeted at not only Engels but also Lenin, Trotsky and Luxemburg, noting that none of them developed a fully dialectical version of Marxism and humanism.

The philosophical turn in this impressive collection comes in dreaming of building a new real-world alternative to capitalism across nation, gender, race. In these days of apocalyptic nuclear rhetoric, there has never been a more important time for Dunayevskaya's intersectional Marxist feminism, her radical feminist social philosophy, articulated now through scenes of Eastern European migrations, anti-imperialist and anti-war movements of our times, and a longing for a new radical humanity based on solidarity to come.

Senka Anastasova

Crisis within crisis

Dario Gentili, *The Age of Precarity: Endless Crisis as an Art of Government*, trans. Stefania Porcelli in collaboration with Clara Pope (London and New York: Verso, 2021). 136pp., £12.99 pb., 978 1 78873 380 9

This is the new English translation of a book first published in Italian in 2018. In a world that is still struggling with the crisis of the pandemic and its aftershocks, the 2018 Italian edition feels prescient and the English edition timely, explaining the role of crisis in the contemporary world and giving some clarity to understanding why governments acted in the manner that they did in the face of the Covid-19 crisis.

Gentili identifies precarious living as a direct consequence of the role of crisis as a form of governmentality. He argues that under conditions of constant crisis and neoliberal forms of governance, precarity becomes a form of life defining every aspect of our lives. This implies a crisis within a crisis: the critical conditions enacted by governments as a response to collective forms of crisis place individual lives in a state of constant uncertainty and ruptures. This process transforms existence itself into a crisis.

The book is divided into three parts: Krisis, Modern Age, and Forms of Life. Gentili engages in a genealogical exercise to explore and uncover the origins and development of the meaning of crisis, showing that this meaning has changed from antiquity through modernity to the present. Etymologically 'crisis' is presented as meaning judgment, election or choice but also separation or division. Thus for the Ancient Greeks, crisis is related to two types of decision-making processes and judgements: a juridical type and a medical type. Placed together these two dimensions uncover the contemporary formulation crisis, which is a biopolitical one, whereby medical discourse becomes a political discourse.

From the outset, Gentili shows the originality and poignancy of his reading of crisis. He states that we should be looking at crisis not as a concept but as a function, a *dispositif*. He argues that crisis functions as a means to govern by the established order of power to respond to an urgent or present need. Thus, the genealogical project undertaken by Gentili is not simply about the meaning of crisis, but is instead an uncovering of the notion of *dispositif* as developed by authors like Foucault, Deleuze and Agamben, leading towards a reading and understanding of crisis as a *dispositif*. Crisis has a governing function that allows the order of power to maintain its standing and to curtail any threats against it. This quality of crisis supports Gentili's claim that crisis is a form of *dispositif* that plays a dominant role in contemporary society.

The major significance of Gentili's argument lies in how he reveals the proximity between the medical role of crisis and its function as a tool to govern, thus showing that, in its contemporary iteration, crisis is a *biopolitical dispositif* that is enforced by the dominant force of the contemporary world, neoliberalism. In this way, the book is also a critical analysis of how neoliberalism has an ability to govern, and maintain its primacy, by controlling life itself. The book applies a radical rhetoric that reveals the ability of neoliberalism to control human life through various measures, and more unnervingly its potential for creating new forms of life, which serve to maintain and reinforce its stranglehold over society and its institutions. In this context, precarity is not just understood as a type of labour or industrial relation but is shown to be a state of being that defines the value and potential of those who fall within its bounds.

There are many works and authors that tackle the issues raised by neoliberal policies. What Gentili presents, though, is a more profound reading of neoliberalism and its effects through critically engaging with its ideological and theoretical foundations. By looking back at Margaret Thatcher's famous claim that 'There is No Alternative', Gentili shows how neoliberalism has created a system in which crisis loses its function as an engine of change and instead becomes a means of reproducing and reaffirming the neoliberal agenda. The various cycles of economic crisis are not a way of rethinking our economies and politics, but a means of governmentality by which people are forced to change to suit the needs of those in power. This is why Gentili defines neoliberal crisis as a biopolitical crisis, because it opens up opportunities to regulate and mould people's conduct and way of life.

During the 2008 financial crisis, there were extensive calls for a complete overhaul of the financial sector and a rethinking of the economic model. There was a widespread consensus on the need to regulate the financial market and the way that banks conducted their business. Although these sectors were the guilty party who caused the crisis and upheaval, ultimately it was the people who had to withstand the worst of the consequences and foot the bill. Apart from losing their savings, their jobs and sometimes their homes, whole segments of the population were coerced into giving up their rights and their quality of life in the name of austerity. Austerity was the *pharmakon*, the medicine needed to cure the illness. New policies regulated the way that people had to behave, and in the meantime, eliminated the prospects and opportunities that people came to rely on, like a pension that guarantees a good quality of life. A similar scenario is also unfolding in the post-Covid world. All these events illustrate how neoliberal biopolitics functions.

Gentili's work also offers a critical evaluation of Hayek's politico-economic theories to show why precarity is the logical and unavoidable consequence of Hayek's theoretical framework. For Hayek, the market is not a human institution but a cosmic order. The free market does not follow the principles of an economic order, which can be rationalised and is humanly driven, but instead it follows the structures of a cosmos. For Hayek, the universe is designed as a competitive order with embedded principles and laws that are unavoidable because they are reality itself. Living in a constant state of competition is thus the only way of living because this is how the universe we inhabit functions.

The enterprise of the self is not about free enterprise anymore. If one is forced into self-enterprise, then that is no longer a free enterprise. This analysis emphatically explains the false myth of the gig economy as a disruptive and liberating mode of work. Because of economic hardships or loss of employment, many find themselves having to take up roles as 'associates' or 'partners' to business platforms. These working conditions force those who enter into them to constantly compete with other individuals who are offering the same service and thus into inhumane working hours and conditions to make money. As Gentili observes, in a world in which everyone is your competition and work is an individualised and solitary activity, the possibility of class consciousness and class unity is drastically diminished, leading to an erosion of labour conditions and precarity becoming the norm.

The Age of Precarity offers an insightful reading of our human condition under the rule of neoliberalism. Gentili's work offers compelling reasons why, if we want to find ways of improving the conditions of the people, we need to think outside of the neoliberal framework and cannot satisfy ourselves with merely reforming it.

Francois Zammit

Dan Graham, 1942–2022.
Partially reflective mirror-writing

Jeff Wall

Dan Graham, mid 1970s, photographer unknown. Courtesy of Studio Dan Graham and Marian Goodman Gallery, Paris. Copyright: Dan Graham.

Dan Graham and I were friends for about 50 years. We began a correspondence in the late 1960s and met for the first time in London in 1972, when he had his first exhibition at the Lisson Gallery, which had opened five years earlier. In his later years Dan became increasingly forthright about the psychological problems he experienced for most of his life. But for the first 20 years or so, I knew him as an energetic, brilliant, generous and untroubled person, enthusiastic about the work of other artists and writers, who he constantly tried to connect with each other and with people who could appreciate and support their work. Dan was one of those anomalous talents who found an identity and a metier in the expanded field of art that opened during the 1960s. He never completely identified himself as an 'artist' because he was always very clear about the character of the new field and what was at stake in exploring it. As time passed, he was very aware of the processes of acceptance and canonisation of the art that began as a challenge and even an affront to the very notion of the 'canon' and, for the most part, accepted and comprehended the inevitably marginal position he had earned for himself. So, he never attempted to redesign his work to find a niche in the leader-board version of artistic supremacy that has emerged since around 1980. But he found one anyway, not because his work mutated to resemble more obviously conventional forms but because his singular genius for perceiving and broadcasting affinities, reinventions, likenesses and echoes between aspects of mass culture, critical histories, aesthetic involutions and intellectual manners won him an audience with three or four generations of younger artists, writers and museum people who kept finding new ways of thinking and seeing from his work, his writing and the great stand-up comedy routines of his public talks. Underlying this is the fact that he managed to keep the dissensus invented by the art of the 1960s on younger people's agendas through an era where those values have been dismissed, reinvigorated, diluted and reshaped, seemingly in a single culture-war process. Dan was devoted to the stakes he and his colleagues played for in 1965. The fact that he kept redefining them over the years is part of their nature – they couldn't be static.

I wrote 'Partially reflective mirror-writing' in 1999, at Alex Alberro's invitation, for a collection of Dan's writing, *Two-Way Mirror Power*. (Jeff Wall, 'Introduction: Partially reflective mirror-writing', in *Two-Way Mirror Power: Selected Writings by Dan Graham on his Art*, ed. Alexander Alberro (Cambridge, Massachusetts: MIT Press, 1999), x–xvii.) I did it almost 20 years after having managed to finish 'Dan Graham's Kammerspiel'. That essay was written in a tense, lofty style marked by my admiration for Adorno's prose (in translation) which was the only way I could express those thoughts in 1980. 'Partially reflective mirror-writing' treats what I consider the fundamental problem and achievement of Conceptual Art in a comic mode, one shaped by me hearing Dan's voice in my mind, maybe reciting 'Dean Martin/entertainment as theater' or 'Eisenhower and the Hippies'. I believe Dan lost interest in me as an artist as the years passed and I think I understand why. But I kept his esteem because he knew I appreciated his devotion to the decisions he made about what to do in art right from the beginning of his career. Reading 'Partially reflective mirror-writing' again in the shadow of his passing, I felt that it sounded the way he would like that devotion talked about.

Partially reflective mirror-writing

In the early 1960s, Dan Graham, who then thought of himself as a writer, fell in with a group of young literary-artistic types who were interested in making some new alliances between word and image, word and thing, people like Sol LeWitt, Lawrence Weiner and Robert Smithson, among others. He began writing things and taking photographs and, in the spirit of then-emergent Conceptual Art, proposed that at least some of the things he made from writing be considered as works of art. He has never gone all the way to claiming that his photographs are works of art, calling them a 'hobby'.

The idea that a written essay or commentary could be validly considered as an art object the way a painting or a sculpture had been is now part of the lore of the 1960s. It has been ignored, dismissed, studied and researched, and has become a kind of falsehood that will not disappear. The claim thus constitutes a moment of unknowability, in which the logic of what we call 'art' appears to re-invent itself. We think we know, without really having to prove it, that an written essay cannot, as Art & Language termed it, 'come up for the count' as a work of art, even a work of art like a Readymade. Essays are about art objects, therefore they cannot be art objects. But an art object can be 'about' its own status as an art object, so why can we not accept the fact that the written text as art object just makes all that perfectly explicit? And so the argument goes on. The experimental claim made in Conceptual Art can neither be proven nor disproved. Rather, it has the status of a vanishing point in the logic of aesthetics, a vanishing point which may have in fact vanished, since it is hardly taken seriously any more, but which nevertheless informs the whole spectrum of contemporary practices in which virtually anything, any thing, gesture, event or action, can be and is considered to be an art object, for example Vanessa Beecroft's performances or Damien Hirst's shark in a tank of formaldehyde.

There is a relationship between the conceptual 'degree zero' of the essay-about-its-own-status-as-an-art-object-as-art-object and the juggernaut of total artistic liberty that has characterised the past thirty years. Duchamp invented this liberty of course, but, because he did not care to explain himself, left implicit the logical problem he raised. The movement from implicitness to explicitness was therefore placed on the historical agenda, and the generation that made Conceptual Art addressed itself to the question, giving it what seems to be a definitive answer. The content of that answer, that there is no logical or theoretical barrier to making the claim that a written text on the subject here at hand can and even must be considered an art object, showed that Duchamp's Readymades were not special Readymades and that, indeed, in the words of the French artist-group, 'Readymades belong to all', they could be made and remade by any artist because there was no means to invalidate the repetition of the practice of making something that evoked, more or less explicitly, art's dubious, unproveable logical status. This 'could', this implicit liberty, of course, has tended to become a 'should', a 'must', a kind of categorical imperative, one that it seems less and less easy for any artist to avoid.

In the 30 years since Donald Judd championed art which had the 'look of non-art', almost all new art has taken on that appearance, so much so that the 'look of art' – lushly made oil paintings or bronze sculptures – now almost has the look of non-art. Dan Graham is one of those who took most seriously the look-of-non-art approach. This was, in part, natural for him, since what he was making was, in the terms of the time, not art, but journalism, poetry, criticism or photography. He was therefore one of those who abandoned the older aesthetics of representation or the slightly less older one of expression. Along with Nauman, Matta-Clark, Weiner, Smithson, Bochner, Kosuth and others, he experienced and helped to instigate the freedom from the aesthetic which opened so many doors in the 1960s.

This freedom – to make things as art which did not resemble art – was animated by the desire to have art draw itself closer to everyday experience. The contradiction here was that everyday experience had, for centuries, included the experience of works of art as they had been. The young artists of the 1960s protested that too few people in modern societies were able to have that experience, being barred from it by social and political factors, and so art as it had been was irrelevant to those people, and, if that was the case, it was irrelevant to the artists too. It had been for some time, they – or we – argued, but now it was being recognised and radical action was being taken, and so, in the wake of Pop Art, the new experimental art moved towards its engagement with new cultural forms.

Although some of the new forms were in fact familiar from their history in popular culture, they were unfamiliar in the guise of works of art. This unfamiliarity was interpreted, correctly, as a new version of the 'defamiliarization' process to which the earlier avant-garde movements, like Constructivism and Surrealism, were so committed. The look of non-art was the new version of modernist 'difficulty'. A difficult work is one which cannot be experienced as a work without some insight into the historical conditions to which it is responding and which, in that sense, have brought it into being. The new look-of-non-art art succeeded in forcing new patterns of perception, but these were not spontaneously available. Explication was required. Such works, not being familiar, demanded a new social role for commentary, primarily written commentary.

The legitimation of an art requiring, and therefore including, a moment or process of explication was one of the achievements of 1960s–70s art. It might be a dubious achievement. The idea that a work of art required some kind of explanation – as part of the experience of the work – was and remains hotly contested, since it appears to violate one of the canonical aesthetic rules: that a work of art is self-sufficient and need be experienced, not necessarily understood. The fact that it can be experienced successfully without really being understood has always been considered a mark of its self-sufficiency, its distinctness from other kinds of practice, like science or philosophy. The new art, deriving as it did from an intellectual apprehension of the historical, logical and structural problems of the notion of art – the Duchampian strain – was driven to challenge this criterion.

The new argument, derived from aspects of structuralist and post-structuralist theory, claimed that all works exist in a constant atmosphere of commentary and evaluation, and indeed would have no meaning outside that. The meanings we appreciate in art appear to us in the necessary form of commentary. Necessity becomes a virtue, no apology is made for the commentary required to legitimate the new forms. Instead, the new idea of commentary is woven into a concept of the socially-necessary process of experiencing art .The commentaries which were always outside the experience of the work were, after and with Derrida, recognised as an interior, and even an anterior, condition of experience and perception. The idea that an unfamiliar experience included the commentary that it would provoke a viewer to call for, emerges from the same dynamic in which an essay could itself be seen as an art object.

Over the past 20 or 25 years, Graham, of all his generation, has been perhaps the most consistently involved with this problematic of the commentary. Although during the 1960s and early 1970s he made a number of significant purely conceptual works in language-form, his writing soon moved in a different, even opposite direction, into the genre of the commentary.

The transition from linguistic conceptual work to the commentary form was rather gradual, emerging from both pragmatic production conditions and philosophical questions about the autonomy of the work of art – the ways in which its content could be experienced in the absence of a commitment to representation or expression. Graham's commentaries were written during and then after the establishment of the legitimacy of the essay-as-a-work-of-art, and they continually respond to that problematic legitimacy. Once a written text could be accepted, or rendered acceptable, in these terms, a new question emerged, one which, again, could probably not be answered: under what conditions, now, could an essay *not* be considered a work of art or an art object?

This question seems absurd, since almost no essays achieved such status, but the absurdity doesn't really affect the fact that, for an artist like Graham, there had to be a means to either establish definitively the identity of every text as now an artwork akin to a drawing, or to withdraw a text, a group of texts or even a class of texts, from that condition without necessarily returning them to the identity they held previously – that is, as writings simply outside the work of art. Since most of the world never accepted, or even took seriously, the inclusion of a text as an artwork, there was no problem in continuing with an external relationship. But, for those whose artistic direction had been, at least to a degree, defined by experiments of this kind, a return to the social or cultural status quo was not an acceptable option. For Graham, as for the others, there was never any question of being a writer. What artists wrote was not literature, not even art criticism; somehow it was art, or at least it had an internal, and maybe a historically new, relation to art.

Graham was not the only artist who understood that a text could be an artwork only under certain very specific conditions, conditions he helped to define with early pieces like *Schema (March 1966)*. The first condition was, as we have noted, that the text refer exclusively to its own status both as text and as proposal for an art object. Only if this condition was met was it possible for the text to take its place in a historical development which originated with the Readymade, and included the other extremist formulations of art's boundaries – the monochrome and the unrealised work which may not aim to be realised, like Tatlin's tower. Kosuth or Art & Language wrote this kind of text, published it and attempted to think through the ways in which the ideas presented in these texts-as-art-objects could be developed in other texts, and whether the subsequent texts would also be art objects, or have to be art objects.

A new situation emerged, in which it was conceivable that texts could be written which could not be withdrawn from the condition of being art objects. To follow the argument, if an essay on the conditions under which an essay could be legitimated as an art object should actually achieve such status – to the extent not only of being presented as such, but actually accepted as such, by being exhibited by reputable institutions and acquired in art collections – then could another essay on the same topic, even if written from a somewhat different point of view, be excluded from such status? Several possibilities appeared, each comparable to other accepted artistic practices. For example, could the same artist rewrite essentially the same text, with maybe a few minor textual variations, and present it as another work of art, related to but distinct from the first essay? At the same time, On Kawara was making paintings bearing only the date on which they were painted, after having made other, very similar, paintings on previous dates. Each of these paintings was accepted as a discrete work, related to but independent of each other regardless of the repetition involved. In this context, how could a slightly different essay be ruled out if a previous one was accepted? There are obviously other possibilities, each as dizzying as the previous; all of them resemble the model of the extremist, experimental art object or gesture which, once established as an expression of the boundaries of art, can and even must be repeated in order for the seriousness of the reflection on the logical problem of art to be conveyed. Buren's stripes, Kawara's, Opalka's, Charlton's canvases, or Toroni's brush marks, gain rather than lose aesthetic lustre by their having been repeated over what are now long periods of time. Nothing like this has ever happened, explicitly at least, in art before now. I say 'explicitly' because repetition has always been present in art, but not as a mark of art's legitimacy. The repetition of stereotypical formulae by mediocre artists is just as consistent and relentless as Buren's repetition of his motif, but Buren has taken on that negative energy in art and worked dialectically with it, turning it into something else. In the post-Buren, post-Kawara, post-Ryman, post-Toroni, post-Art & Language period, repetition tends towards the inescapable, and most artists have included it in their practice in one way or another.

The critical literature on Graham has clearly established the fact that his work is ambivalent about these strategies of repetition in an important, exemplary way. As time has passed and we can experience the continuation of projects like Buren's or Toroni's, we understand that, regardless of the apparently unbreakable legitimacy they have achieved, they are nonetheless limited. After some decades it is now the insistent, even the resigned, theatre of repetition which we accept in these works. The fact that they have abjured, apparently for good, any involvement with the world outside the methodological possibilities established 30 years ago, is both a mark of achievement and a reason for now looking elsewhere for seriousness in art. Graham articulated this kind of discontent at the very beginning of the process, in the 1960s and 1970s. Yet, unlike most critics and opponents of Conceptual Art, he did so from a position almost indistinguishable from those from which he was seemingly taking his leave.

Graham's aim was to remain involved with the wider world as a subject and occasion for art, but to structure that involvement in the rigorously self-reflexive terms made mandatory by the intellectual achievements of Conceptual Art. *Schema* was made at the same time he was writing articles for art magazines on his own and other artists' work, as well as what used in the magazine world to be called 'think pieces' – discursive essays on phenomena or epiphenomena of culture – pieces like the famous 'Eisenhower and the Hippies' (1968), 'Dean Martin/Entertainment as Theater' (1969) and 'Homes for America' (1966–7). The think pieces were both actual essays on actual topics and at the same time glosses on the artworks or photographs Graham was then making or preparing to make. He has consistently referred to these writings as 'journalism'. And they are journalism, except they are also not quite journalism, in the sense that, with them, the category 'journalism' is re-articulated and re-legitimated in terms established by the self-reflexivity of the category essay-as-a-work-of-art. This implies that a work of art is to be made through the principle of 'the look of non-art' in the sphere of the written. Just as Flavin made sculptures by repositioning common lighting equipment, Graham moved towards making textual artworks or 'magazine pieces', as he calls them, by writing about various subjects as if he were writing the essay about its possible status as a work of art. This process of mimesis, of constructing journalism in the 'as if' mode, was a way of testing the new category of the essay-as-a-work-of-art. It is clear, maybe only in hindsight, that the outcome of the test was known in advance. That is, to reiterate, the essay-as-a-work-of-art can only be an essay about the proposal of that essay as a work of art; it can't be about any other subject. Nevertheless, Graham seems to have thought, if an artist could write an essay about another subject, but write it 'as if' it were an essay about the proposal of itself as a work of art, would the resulting essay then be able to be experienced as a work of art the way the accepted essay-as-a-work-of-art is experienced? The answer seems clearly to be 'no', but it is a complex 'no' nevertheless, especially if we imagine the resonance of that 'no' around 1969 or 1970.

Let us follow this unlikely argument one step further. Graham might have thought that, OK, the essay-as-a-work-of-art is definitely limited to the one subject. He might then have thought about the possibility of writing a second such essay, with a few minor textual changes, as mentioned above, and he would have concluded that that essay, too, would obviously be an essay-as-a-work-of-art, for the reasons we have already outlined. A certain perspective and logic necessarily appears to the mind at this point. It would be clear that what has been created is a unique and transformed version of the methodology of artists like Buren or Toroni, but in written form, that is, in a form that will always remain liminal and problematic as visual art or as an art object.

Graham might have thought that this liminal space was both absolutely determined in the terms we have established, but that, at the same time, by being a liminal and problematic category, it contained unknown possibilities. The most immediate way to experiment with those possibilities was to breach the apparently fundamental rule by introducing another subject matter while still attempting to write, or make, a 'magazine piece' rather than a magazine article, strictly speaking. It is clear that this was a failure, and that the essays have become magazine articles or critical essays, and, generally speaking, this has been the case with Graham's writings. Previous collections, like *Articles* (1978), *Video-Architecture-Television* (1979) and *Rock My Religion* (1993), have treated them that way. We can make no argument against this categorisation, except one.

Graham, like a few other artists of his generation, has appeared to accept the idea that he could do more than one thing, and that he could be an artist and an essayist or journalist or critic. The world has also accepted this, as they have done with Don Judd, Robert Smithson or, more recently, Peter Halley. Nevertheless, we understand that none of these essays would be written, no critiques would have been composed, unless somehow the content of the essay was connected to the inner aspects of the artist's work. This is what distinguishes these artists from others, who have often had far more public and distinguished careers as art critics – artists like Patrick Ireland, Peter Plagens, Thomas Lawson or, among the younger generation, Collier Schorr. Their critical writing must have some relation to their artistic work, but it has been occasioned by the institution of criticism and essayism in a way that Graham's have never been. With Graham, as with Smithson and one or two others, there has always been a resistance against writing on any occasion except one provided by the evolution of their artistic work as a whole. Although we can find that Graham's essays emerge from various specific contexts, we can see that they are not created in response to a summons from the institution of criticism. They may function as criticism, even cultural criticism, but this function can be compared to the function of a work by Buren as criticism. That work might be critical of something – for example, the institution in which it is found – but that criticism is not made directly, as actual criticism, that is, as writing within the institution of criticism. It is made incidentally, in the process of making a certain kind of work of art, and that art is made within the institution of art. This work of art might be called 'functionalist', or post-autonomous, as it has been. What that means is that it achieves its functional purposes by means of being a work of art, and taking on the form of a work of art, albeit an experimental form. Post-autonomous art achieves its functional aims through the process of nevertheless being created within the framework of autonomous art; that is, it responds to no external functional or practical command, it is freely chosen and made by the artist. The artist chooses to make his or her work useful in some way, or even just to pretend it might be useful, to act 'as if' it could be useful. This pretence invents possible functions, and presents them to the public, which might not have otherwise ever thought of them. In this light, post-autonomous art is only a liminal type of autonomous art. In saying this, I mean no negative criticism of that art. The borderland of these categories generates experiments which might lead somewhere authentically new.

Graham's essays occupy this borderland. They achieve their discursive and critical aims not through the artist's acceptance of his identity or role as critical writer, but rather through his avoidance of it, his stance as a 'writer' in quotes, an artist impersonating a writer in order both to write, freely, and also to work as an artist in the expanded way 'artistic practice' got defined in the 1960s and 1970s. The critical essays and commentaries on his own work are in a permanent state of 'category-shift', in that they are simultaneously about their various subjects and are yet formulations which emerge from contemporaneous aspects of Graham's practice, whether it be in photography, his architectural-pavilion work, performance or video. Graham's writing is not writing about art or even 'art-writing'; rather, Graham's art is an art with writing in it, or, maybe more precisely, an art with the writing it contains glinting in the form of texts.

Jeff Wall is an artist and occasional writer. Anthologies of his texts include: Jeff Wall: Selected Essays and Interviews *(Museum of Modern Art, 2007) and* Jeff Wall: Works and Collected Writings *(Polígrafa, 2007).*

Sylvère Lotringer, 1937-2021

David Morris

Sylvère Lotringer's life been celebrated as a 'total work' – a lived embodiment of the radical theories he did so much work to disseminate and promote. His commitment to an art of living, his embodiment and dissemination of thought, and his cultural experimentation have been widely affirmed – with the 'primary text' of his life often eclipsing his published work; as Gayatri Spivak put it: 'an example of how this kind of philosophy is also an act of the mind, of life, of how to actually live philosophically rather than simply think in a certain way'.[1] Semiotext(e) press is also celebrated as his great life's work – although the singular approach and sensibility that he instilled in it makes it impossible to understand as an individual creation. Like so much of his work, Semiotext(e) is a shared project, as Sylvère would often insist. This situation also allowed him to perform a kind of disappearing act on himself. The many tributes that have appeared following his death have shown his multiplicity, but his 'personal' writings and projects (about which he would no doubt have said that there is nothing 'personal') have to some extent disappeared from view. The 'total' lifework can obscure the work in which he was energetically engaged throughout his life.

The range and quantity of that which he authored and co-authored under his own name is extraordinary – despite occasional self-deprecations as lazy or unproductive – especially so, given the parallel work of editing, travel, teaching, etc. His writings and projects are many and scattered, spanning fictions, interviews, critical and historical essays and films, reworking themes and ideas through different moments in time – recurrent questions approached from different angles – a nomadic creative practice, without pause or end. *Mad Like Artaud* is one document of such an approach – Sylvère playing out a delirium of his own to produce a collage work that was published multiple times, in different forms, languages and situations – each version a variation on the last.[2] So it may be understandable that his published works have not received the attention they deserve. There is a refusal of fixity that runs through them, a deferral of any final form or version, an ongoing reinvention, revision, rehearsal. To note this is not to try to pull the many lines of his life into a narrative, or worse yet, an individual biography – Sylvère already did a good job of evading this. But it is an attempt to find an alternative opening into his multiple life; to ask, in a different way, *what happened?*[3]

His early biography holds some clues as to the directions his life would take: born in Paris to Polish-Jewish migrants in 1938; his early life as a 'hidden child' during the Nazi occupation of France; his coming-of-age in the Marxist-Zionist youth movement Hashomer-Hatzair; his self-mimeographed magazines of writings and drawings that he would give to his comrades; his time as Sorbonne student president, producing literary publications, organising and demonstrating for Algerian independence; his work interviewing modernist writers in Britain and Ireland as English correspondent for *Les Lettres françaises* (edited by Louis Aragon); his work in French television; his doctoral thesis on Virginia Woolf, supervised by Roland Barthes and Lucien Goldmann.

While researching the 'Schizo-Culture' conference of 1975 and the beginnings of Semiotext(e), I wrote to him out of the blue. He replied that the conference's audio recordings had just been rediscovered, later inviting me to join him to realise what would become the *Schizo-Culture* publication, published in 2013. It continues to feel to me unfamiliar and unresolved. Gilles Deleuze, Félix Guattari, Michel Foucault and Jean François Lyotard spoke there, as did William Burroughs, John Cage, Judith Clark, Ti-Grace Atkinson, R.D. Laing and others. Marcuse was invited but declined. It drew from the aesthetic foment of its time. The archive swirls with connections to Loft Jazz, No Wave, Patti Smith, the Last Poets, the Ontological-Hysteric Theater, Lincoln Detox and Martine Barrat's films in the Bronx. As a combination of disparate forces, it was bound to collapse, and the book explores the 'breakdown' that the event enacted. What might now be understood as a symptom of broader crises – a breakdown at the limits of white Western (un)reason – was also a moment of personal crisis for Sylvère; although, as he described it, this breakdown was also a breakthrough. His name sounded like *l'etranger* and at this point he was becoming that. Semiotext(e) journal became increasingly singular and adventurous, bringing an aesthetic sensibility that shifted across each edition (schizo-culture, polysexuality, Italian autonomism…).

Photo: Iris Klein

If Sylvère's writings and projects had a tendency to disappear, the reasons are various, a mixture of happenstance and intentionality. At some stage he was working on a collection – *Extrapolations* – but he cared deeply about his own writing, and could express reticence about publishing it. He published in a piecemeal way, sometimes in obscure places. His generosity of spirit, self-deprecating nature and disinterest in career-building all characterised how he approached his work. There is also the acutely uncomfortable, uncompromising, confrontational character that his own writing could take – in sharp contrast to his gentleness and good humour in person. It is as if his work was always moving deliberately towards the most unspeakable, unthinkable areas – his ongoing concern was with the 'enterprise of systematic dehumanization that is affecting the entire planet',[4] and he sought theoretical and aesthetic means to understand and intervene on appalling and catastrophic conditions.

Sylvère's works – his books, writing, performances and films – may be understood as a series of practices that developed through different phases.

The interview, for example, is central and consistent: his recording of interactions goes back to the literary interviews he conducted in the 1960s. This was a tool he would use to gain access to something – a concept, a historical moment, an atmosphere. It became his way of relating to New York when he arrived in the 1970s; it was the basis of his collaborations with Paul Virilio and Jean Baudrillard. Much of his later work shared this framework, from the interviews with Artaud's doctors in 1983-85 out of which emerged *Mad Like Artaud*, the film *Voyage to Rodez* and the performance 'I Talked about God with Antonin Artaud' (both in collaboration with Chris Kraus); his mid-80s performance work where he interviewed himself; his book *Overexposed*; the book on David Wojnarowicz; many other published interviews in various Semiotext(e) publications; the interviews with his mother that informed his late autobiographical essays; and the many interviews he gave to others. Interviews were what he did, over and over again, into an art. These interviews fed different phases of his work, they entered into different aspects of it in different ways. They were one of several tools for combining things that don't go together.

Another consistent practice was *theory*. 'Doing theory' was how he described the active practice of *thought* that, for him, produced the most compelling moments in intellectual life, as contrasted with its deadening effects, particularly as it became institutionalised through the 1980s and 1990s. More particularly, literary theory was a consistent concern, from the structuralism that provided the focus of the earliest Semiotext(e) activities, including their first conference (on Saussure) and first journal editions. His doctoral thesis was a structural analysis of Virginia Woolf, with an initial part on the Fabians 'to please Lucien Goldmann': 'Virginia Woolf: de la mort des valeurs aux valeurs de la mort' ('From the death of values to the values of death').[5] Woolf was not well known in France at the time, he told me, and it was through Nathalie Sarraute that he became aware of her work. His first publication was on La Princesse de Clèves, and he was hired at Columbia as a specialist in seventeenth-century French Literature.[6] He also prepared a book-length 'Théorie du Roman', after Lukács and Barthes – a structural analysis of various writers, from Homer to Alain Robbe-Grillet, with chapters on Chrestien de Troys, La Princesse de Cleves, Sade, Manon Lescaut, Balzac, Proust, and others. 'This is a sunken world and no one has opened it yet. Rrose...'[7] The book was finished, but only published in pieces.[8]

Sylvère was already somewhere else and the sequence of Semiotext(e) journal editions gives a sense of the trajectory – 'Alternatives in Semiotics' and 'The Two Saussures' (1974); 'Ego Traps' and 'Saussure's Anagrams' (1975); 'George Bataille' (1976); 'Anti-Oedipus' (1977); 'Nietzsche's Return' and 'Schizo-Culture' (1978).[9] It is interesting to read Sylvère's own writings around this time – you can almost feel the structuralism loosening up, deterritorialising, becoming stranger. There is indeed something strange about these writings, which becomes more pronounced, especially in the texts he published in the pages of the Semiotext(e) journal (he was also publishing regularly in other journals such as *boundary 2* and *Diacritics* in the US, and *Critique*, *Literature* and *Poétique* in France). The intellectual orientations shift and the writing style itself becomes more compressed, telegraphic, enigmatic. Sylvère undertook another study 'Analytical Fiction, Fiction of Analysis'.[10] The study is introduced as an attempt to 'turn literature against psychoanalytic interpretation' – a counteranalysis, informed by Nietzsche, of Freud's 'Delusion and Dream in Jensen's Gradiva'. The first part, 'The Fiction of Analysis', sets up the project – effectively an extrapolation of a brief remark in *Anti-Oedipus* that approvingly affirms the Freud of 'Delusion and Dream' and *Gradiva*, the Freud that went 'too far'.[11] In 'The Dance of Signs' (1978), the second part of the study that was published, he continues along this line before abruptly embarking on a kind of experiment in reading:

> I will, here and now, stop wanting the story to go somewhere. I will forget what I know feebly, in advance, in order to gather the whole complexity of forces at play in a text. I will learn to resist the melody of causal relations and the torpor of narrative accumulations in order to reinvent the intensity of risks, ceaselessly menacing and forever being reborn'.[12]

He undertakes a re-reading of the *Gradiva* story without interpretation or narrative. This feels like an intensification or perversion of his role as a literary theorist; we watch as he drifts from the norms of his academic training, breaks the fourth wall to destabilise his own position and the frameworks he relied upon until now. Cage, Merce Cunningham, Burroughs and Robert Wilson appear as guides to this new territory, along with Nietzsche and Deleuze and Guattari. The text concludes: 'Why then should one insist on forcing dreams, texts, words, and actions to signify? Keep the dream-bursts apart; let them resound together without filling the intervals that allow them to coexist in all their richness within dissonance ... Forget meaning and with it the subject. Repression cannot resist the folly of winds. Beauty will be amnesiac or it will not be at all.'[13]

'Schizo-Culture' marks one or several breaks for Sylvère. The *Schizo-Culture* conference, and the edition of Semiotext(e) journal bearing the same name, were three years apart, and a lot happened during that time. The conference was untimely, and it took the journal a few years to catch up – you see it on the page, the *Schizo* edition introducing cartoon punk nihilism, No Wave aesthetics and cut-ups – and you see it in Sylvère's shift into interviews, and the milieu he connects to, since it is here that his interviews first appear. Interviews were also, for him, a way to displace himself or to think with or through other people. At this point the typical activities of an academic literary theorist dissolve into all manner of speculative projects, connecting philosophy, art, film, performance and literature. It is as if he had absorbed the lessons of the artists he spoke to through the 1970s. He would often reference the 'philosopher-artist' invoked by Nietzsche, and this was also part of the appeal for him of Baudrillard or Virilio, who embodied a certain attitude to thought that places high value on creative extrapolation. It was in 1978 that Sylvère would appear as a voiceover on Kathryn Bigelow's student film *The Set-Up*; Bigelow in turn was part of the group who produced the *Schizo-Culture* issue; and it is in that issue that Sylvère's interview with Jack Smith appears – an interview that has echoed through subsequent activities.[14] Smith introduced him to the New York art world at that time – 'a mixture of craziness and creativity, anarchism, paranoia, immediacy, flashing insights' – and also warned him off a fixation on language as a barrier to thinking-doing: '"If I could think of a thought that has never been thought of before, the language will fall into place in the most fantastic way, but the thought is what's going to do it." For a semiotician, it was a rough lesson, but it worked.'[15]

It wasn't long before the compulsion to record expanded to video. This was in some respects a return to his work in television during the 1960s, producing programmes on literature and politics. The 1980s was a generative time, resulting in a number of films, such as: *Too Sensitive to Touch* (1981) with Michael Oblowitz; *How to Shoot a Crime* (1985) and *Voyage to Rodez* (1986) – and the performance 'I Talked about God with Antonin Artaud' (1985); and *Violent Femmes* (1998). Although he would habitually shoot video footage of interviews and events throughout his life, the 1980s would account for the majority of his published work in film, until *The Man Who Disappeared* in 2015.[16] The way he approached working with film is hard to describe. Consider this reflection on the making of his unfinished film project *Second Hand Hitler* in Berlin in the mid-1980s: 'It wasn't planned, just happened, and then it snowballed into something that strived to be a film, and remains at least a strange and muddled experience. … The emotional "torpor" that made it possible didn't belong to anyone, not even me. The nightmare of history was still alive. And there was nothing one could do with it.'[17] Rather than dictate or concern himself too much with 'correct' film-making – even though he had studied film-making, scriptwriting and acting – Sylvère seemed to follow an instinctive and improvisatory path that ignored the rules in pursuit of the line between chaos and complexity. His concerns were not those of a typical film-maker, and he did not make typical films; the works are committed to an experiment, in the sense of a question for which one does not have the answer.

1981 offers another snapshot of several lives. This year saw a culmination of Sylvère's academic work in semiotics with the publication of *Polyphonic Linguistics: the Many Voices of Emile Benveniste*, which Sylvère edited with Thomas Gora, published by specialist journal *Semiotica*. A different territory is mapped in 'Defunkt Sex', the text he published as part of the 1981 Semiotext(e) 'Polysexuality' issue, exploring sex as a sign in the United States – pointing towards his 1988 book *Overexposed* – the launch of which, at the Kitchen, caused a small scandal. It also saw the completion of *Too Sensitive to Touch*, a film collage he made with Michael Oblowitz, overlaying a discussion of sexual offenses with 1980s graphics, video effects and music (soundtrack by Human Sexual Response). The *Foreign Agents* book series was also in development at this moment.

It was around this time that 'Shooting Death' emerged, another of his unrealised projects. Death was a space of ongoing enquiry since at least his doctoral work on Woolf. There is footage from around this time of when Sylvère invited a crime scene photographer, George Diaz, to document him in his apartment, as if it were a crime scene. The camera pans slowly across the bookcase, a whole shelf of books about death – *Death: The Final Stage of Growth*, *Tibetan Book of the Dead*, *Psychosomatique et Cancer*, *Anthropologie de la Mort*, *Psychology of Funeral Service*, *The Denial of Death*, *On Death and Dying*, *Morgue* – before coming to Sylvère, motionless, face down on the bed. Following an Artaudian line that art produces death, the 'Shooting Death' project addressed 'the current "return" of death in our society', where 'death is a fiction that has to be produced as a reality, invented anew through an artistic experience in order to become available again in its full emotional and cultural dimensions.'[18] The archive from the project contains interviews with Diaz alongside the cast and crew of Wim Wenders' *Lightning Over Water* (documenting the death of Nicholas Ray, a film which Virilio described as 'the very first post-modern tragedy'). Death was a running concern of his work as part of a fierce commitment to the *live* – for him, thought is something that happens 'live', something that is lived, something that is itself alive.

This work would modulate into an increasingly complex exploration of modernity and the Holocaust, which reappeared in various registers throughout his work. As he wrote in 'The Art of Evil' (a contribution to a student project in the mid-90s):

> When such writers as Antonin Artaud, Georges Bataille, Céline, and Simone Weil embodied 'the passions and contradictions of European society', they imbibed the madness, violence, hatred and humiliation which were about to rock Western civilization, unleashing atrocities on an unprecedented scale.
>
> None of these writers were even aware of the Nazi genocide. Yet from the mid 1920's until well into the war their work seems to anticipate the Holocaust, responding to it from a distance, 'like victims signaling through the flames.' (Artaud)[19]

Sylvère was drawn to those who made the unimaginable their subject matter, as 'modernist "vaccines" meant to build the immunities of the social body against the incoming threat.' Such vaccines could also be poisons, which he explored through various currents of nihilism, racism, fascism or anti-Semitism that run through these modernist figures (Cioran was another figure he hoped to finish a book on, later in his life). This phase inaugurated some of Sylvère's most powerful and affecting writing – one is drawn to imagine the book that might have been, and to consider how it couldn't be. 'The Anthropology of Unhappiness', an essay that was never published, engages with Antelme's *L'espèce humaine* and Duras's *La Douleur*,[20] in which he makes an argument for the 'fictionalisation' of Duras's account over the 'authentic' monumentalisation of Antelme's personal testimony: 'suffering, for her, just like writing or desire, wasn't something personal, something you could lock away or treat like a private possession, to the point of becoming its self-styled custodian. It was a force that invaded you from the outside, shaking your mind loose from all previous attachments, bringing chaos and disorder into your life, but also an acute sense of momentum to everything you did.'

As Sylvère reached the end of his life he increasingly returned to the beginning. In his writings from the 1990s onwards, he begins to explore and reconstruct aspects of his early life – biographical elements having remained largely absent from his interviews and work up to this time. He would appear as an interviewer, his way of becoming other people, or otherwise as a corpse (in *How to Shoot a Crime*). This began to change with texts such as 'Never Any Ever After' (1994), an auto-fiction published as a small edition by Pataphysics Press in Melbourne, 'unraveling memories of his childhood as a hidden child during the Nazi occupation, a trip to Germany visiting a concentration camp with his clueless friends, weaving it to the present in New York';[21] 'Pavilion in Time' (2003), a reflection on a photograph of his mother taken during the German occupation; or 'Étant Donnés' (2014), which recounts the story of his being given the identity of another schoolboy, as a strategy to evade the Nazis, and his attempt to find this person. He also emerged as a generous and prolific interviewee, and these have produced some fascinating documents of his life-work.[22]

Like so much of Sylvère's work, his autobiographical writings were published piecemeal, without a plan for their future – a breadcrumb trail for only the most dedicated to follow and/or a move towards obscurity and oblivion. They expand the work on modernity and the Holocaust – some version of the imaginary opus *The Anthropology of Unhappiness*, described by Kraus in her novel *Torpor*, would incorporate them all together. One of the last things he was working on, 'The Man Who Slips', was a memoir of his time in the Jewish youth movement. These writings evoke a profound coming-to-terms with the unthinkable – and this was his way to come closer to it, and guard against it. Speaking in 2016, he observed: 'We've been told for a long time that fascism didn't have a chance, especially in America. Now, suddenly, fascism comes back fresh as a rose. It's at the door and knocking at six o'clock in the morning.'

In my notes for this obituary I copied out the following line at the top of the page: '*Giving one's own life away is the only present that cannot be reciprocated.*' I can't now find the reference – I don't know if Sylvère said it, or if someone else did, and I don't think it matters. His life was a point of connection across continents of thought. It was something he constantly gave away, as he kept moving – he was always looking for escape routes and flight lines. His work was usually developed in relation – connecting, interviewing, editing, publishing. During his final days I had been listening to a recording of him speaking as part of a panel discussion, paying particular attention to the way his thought moved. I heard him oscillate between opposing positions – it was a group discussion, and he seemed to move in counterpoint to those around him – his style of thought was anarchic and his positions could often move in ways that destabilised those around him. He was extremely agreeable but rarely in agreement, usually looking for points to which to apply pressure. (He described Baudrillard in this way, as someone who looks for a rickety idea-structure in order to give it a good shake.) In his writings, a favourite formulation was 'more than'. Bataille was more Nietzchean than Nietzche; Artaud was more Jewish than the Jews; Simone Weil, more Christian than the Christians. And himself, more American than the Americans. This 'more than' might be a way to understand him. Sylvère was always more than himself. Sylvère was a multiplicity, unique and dear to an enormous number of people. He set changes in motion that continue into the present, and that may take a lifetime or more to work themselves out.

David Morris is a research fellow and editor at Afterall Research Centre, and co-leads the Exhibition Studies MRes at University of the Arts London. Together with Sylvère Lotringer he edited Schizo-Culture *(Semiotext(e)/MIT, 2013).*

Notes

1. Carolina A. Miranda and Dorany Pineda, 'Sylvere Lotringer, intellectual who infused U.S. art circles with French theory, dies at 83', *Los Angeles Times*, 11 November 2021. Other notable tributes include: 'Hedi El Kholti and Chris Kraus on Sylvère Lotringer', *Artforum*, February 2022; McKenzie Wark, 'Theory Daddy', *NLR Sidecar*, 16 November 2021.
2. See Lotringer, *Mad Like Artaud* (Minneapolis: Univocal, 2015). Earlier versions of the book, with different contents, were published in French and Italian, and its materials formed the basis of a number of other creative projects.
3. Sylvère liked to reference F. Scott Fitzgerald's short story 'The Crack-Up', as analysed by Deleuze and Guattari: 'Different kinds of lines cross people's lives, often unrecognised for what they are, capable of triggering irrevocable ruptures and transformations. Something happened that was never forgotten afterward, but what? Or whom? All we can ask is: *Whatever could have happened for things to come to this?*' Sylvère Lotringer, 'Forget Foucault', *October* 126 (Fall 2008), 22.
4. Sylvère Lotringer, *The Miserables* (Los Angeles: Semiotext(e), 2014).
5. Correspondence with the author, 29 April 2018.
6. 'La Structuration Romanesque', *Critique* 26, 177 (1970), 498–529.
7. Correspondence with the author, 29 April 2018.
8. Sylvère Lotringer, 'Le Roman Impossible', *Poétique* 3 (1970), 297–321; 'Vice de Forme', *Critique* 27 (1971), 195–209; 'Mesure de la démesure', *Poétique* 12 (1972), 486-94; 'Artaud, Bataille, et le Matérialisme Dialectique', *SubStance* 2:5/6, (1972-73), 207–225; 'The Game of the Name', *Diacritics*, 3:2 (1973), 2–9; 'Argo-Notes: Roland Barthes Textual Trip', *boundary 2* 2:3 (1974), 562–572; 'Sade Incesticide', *Literature* 30 (1978), 67–78; 'Proust polymorphe', *Poétique* 42 (1980), 170–176.
9. The journal continued into the 1980s with 'Autonomia' and 'Loving Boys' (1980); 'Polysexuality' (1981); 'The German Issue' (1982); 'Oasis: Fourth World' (1984).
10. I am unsure whether this was ever completed, but excerpts appear across a couple of issues. See 'The Fiction of Analysis', *Semiotext(e)* 2:3 (1977), 172–189; and 'The Dance of Signs', *Semiotext(e)* 3:1 (1978), 54–67.
11. Departing from Deleuze-Guattari's remark that, 'Never was Freud more adventurous than in *Gradiva*', he develops the image of 'a Freud who is fairly unexpected inasmuch as he is made in their image: bearded socio-libidinal philosopher, hirsute schizo-revolutionary militant merrily liberating–hallucinating continents and cultures.' 'The Fiction of Analysis', 173.
12. 'The Dance of Signs', 58.
13. Ibid., 188.
14. This conversation with Smith echoes through the later milestones of Semiotext(e), providing the title to the 2002 anthology *Hatred of Capitalism* – Smith's alternative proposal for the title of Semiotext(e) journal – and reproduced as a vinyl 7-inch picture disk as part of the featuring of Semiotext(e) at the Whitney Biennale in 2014.
15. 'Interview with Sylvère Lotringer', *Log* 15 (2002), https://physicsroom.org.nz/archive/log/archive/15/lotringer/ .
16. The project was part of a series of events organised by Katherine Waugh (who co-produced the film) and a collaboration with three locally-based artist/filmmakers, Tom Flanagan, Maximilian Le Cain and Vivienne Dick. Artaud was played by Jeremy Hardingham. (I was fortunate to join for the trip – Sylvère had invited me along as an additional camera).
17. 'The Making Of A Monster: Summertime For Hitler & Conversation With Cult German Actress Lotti Huber (Berlin, July 20, 1985)', *Pataphysics Magazine* (2006), 113.
18. 'Shooting Death' outline document, 'Sylvère Lotringer Papers and Semiotext(e) Archive, 1960-2004 (Bulk 1973-2000)', Fales Library & Special Collections, NYU.
19. 'The Art of Evil', *FAT Magazine* 1:1 (2004), https://www.thing.net/~fat/vol1no1/sylvere.htm.
20. 'Anthropology of Unhappiness', unpublished manuscript, Fales Library and Special Collections, NYU; 'The Person Who Tortures Is Me: Violence and the Sacred in the Work of Margurite Duras', *Paroles gelées* 18:2 (2000); *The Miserables* (Los Angeles: Semiotext(e), 2014).
21. Brigitte Engler, in 'In Memoriam: A Tribute to Sylvère Lotringer', ed. Donatien Grau, *The Brooklyn Rail* (March 2022).
22. Two book-length interviews have recently been published: *I Was More American than the Americans: Sylvère Lotringer in conversation with Donatien Grau* (Zürich: diaphenes, 2021); *Ce que Sylvère Lotringer n'écrivait pas*, ed. François Aubart and François Piron (Paris: Paraguay Press, 2022). See also the multi-part interview by Jonathan Thomas, https://caligaripress.com/Part-1.

The myth of *Aufheben*
A comment on Matthieu Renault's Hegelian myth of counter-violence

Nigel Tubbs

Matthieu Renault argues in a recent issue of *Radical Philosophy* (*RP* 2.10, Summer 2021) that justifications for the counter-violence of the oppressed which draw on Hegel's master-slave relation are based on a myth originating from Kojève's Paris lectures (1933-9). The Kojève myth is that history begins with the violence of the master over the slave in the life-and-death struggle and ends with the counter-violence of the slave over the master, in a reverse of that original struggle. Kojève's emphasis on this reversibility, Renault argues, lends 'an intrinsic value to revolutionary violence.'* Renault sees a similar reversibility in Frantz Fanon and Angela Davis, among others, but finds it 'untraceable in Hegel's account' (22). There is nothing in Hegel's *Phenomenology of Spirit* that suggests the life-and-death struggle which creates the master-slave relation must itself be repeated in order to undo that relation. Instead, Hegel's silence on the slave's emancipation leaves it open to 'multiple and competing interpretations' (23).

I propose we add three further myths to the myth of reversibility or counter-violence: the myth of the struggle for recognition, the myth of the cowardice of the slave, and, more significantly, the myth of *Aufheben* itself as an essentially absolutist and imperial form of mastery, or of overcoming, resolution and completion. This latter myth, explained below, continues to frame our most familiar readings of Hegel. Less discussed is how this myth and these readings carry the continued domination of property relations deep into radical philosophy. According to Hegel, the life-and-death struggle takes shape as the culture of property. Property preserves life as the master by keeping death alive in the form of the slave. Property then defines truth and logic in its own image. Truth masters error, and logic masters contradiction. When philosophy conforms to this culture, it reproduces this propertied truth and logic of mastery. When radical philosophy critiques such mastery or absolutism, it often does so in a reversal that tries to master or overcome property's – and, by implication, Hegel's – absolutism. But life and death have a necessity and a logic that preserves and negates them differently than within the logic of property. Against the myth of *Aufheben* as mastery I suggest that in Hegel radical *Aufheben* is this different logic of living and dying[1] and that it has significant implications for the way Renault 'completes' his article as 'myth'.

The myth of the struggle for recognition

The relevant sections of Hegel's *Phenomenology* can be divided into three parts: paragraphs 177-184 on the myth of recognition; paragraphs 185-189 on the experience of life and death; and paragraphs 190-196 on the master-slave relation.

Hyppolite states unequivocally that the life-and-death struggle is waged for recognition.[2] But as staged in Hegel's text, the encounter does not actually involve two self-consciousnesses meeting each other with such intentions. Self-consciousness emerges *from* the struggle. What participates in the struggle is desire wherein, by

---

* Matthieu Renault, 'Counter-violence, a "Hegelian" myth: Minor variations on the master-slave dialectic', *Radical Philosophy* 2.10 (Summer, 2021), 29. Further page numbers are given in parentheses in the text.

the satisfaction of its physical needs, life preserves itself against negation or death. This living desire is indifferent to its objects. It is not in search of political or social recognition. The myth of recognition emerges, rather, from the passages on mutual recognition. When presented as 'the "I" that is "We" and the "We" that is "I"',[3] mutuality is abstracted from the experience of life and death, and therefore from work and property relations.

To counter this abstraction Hegel demonstrates in paragraphs 185-9 how desire experiences life and death as self-consciousness – or how pure recognition 'appears to self-consciousness'[4] – and then, in paragraphs 190-6, he shows how the now self-conscious life-and-death relation takes embodied form as master and slave, or as property. The drama is of two desires meeting in a world of limited resources. They approach each other with the same indifference they have for the object they desire. They are not set on fighting for recognition or indeed on killing each other. Recognition is not the motivation for the struggle. That would put the cart before the horse, presupposing that recognition already exists before the struggle, whereas recognition only becomes an issue as a result of the struggle. They meet as desire in pursuit of desire, and they learn of their mortality in the experience – which is not planned – of risk. Risk is the negative experience that is carried in fear, and fear arises in response to the prospect of death, i.e. fear is prompted by the death of *this* life. *This* life is now a new awareness, a self-consciousness of life and death, or the I-life-and-death that is self-consciousness.[5]

The myth that this is a struggle for recognition gives rise to a further myth, found in Kojève and Hyppolite, that one of these desires refuses to risk its life and becomes slave to the master. For Kojève the slave 'did not want to risk his life'[6] and for Hyppolite the slave 'has retreated in the face of death, preferring servitude to liberty in death.'[7] Such views are part of the myth of counter-violence that Renault identifies, for it is this original defeat, due to cowardice, that the slave in the future must then reverse for its liberation. These charges of cowardice are unwarranted. The slave is the person who, in risking the life-and-death encounter, and in becoming I-life-and-death, becomes aware that living, not dying, is the truth of *this* life, even if not under conditions of its own choosing. The slave courageously preserves I-life-and-death while the master avoids it through property.

The myth of *Aufheben*

Familiar readings of the third section (paragraphs 190-6) are themselves further determined by these myths of a struggle for recognition, and of cowardice in the face of danger. But the truth of master and slave in this section unfolds not just against immediate propertied violence, but also by way of a less familiar logic – one that expresses the necessity (evoked above) of life and death that is not the culture of mastery and property. This less familiar logic is that of life and death experienced as *learning* and expressed as *Aufheben*. In the familiar logic of (Aristotelian) non-contradiction and identity the master's independence is self-contradictory, for mastery is dependent upon the work of its enslaved. By contrast, the strange logic of the slave's 'mind of his own'[8] is that its lack of identity is some kind of truth, though not one that makes sense from within the logic of mastery that defines truth as independence or identity in-itself. The enslaved experiences the illogicality of being nothing in-itself as fear in the 'absolute melting away of everything stable.'[9] But it also lives true to this illogicality in its work, where it is actually nothing in-itself because it is wholly for-another. When mastery is for-itself it is so as an in-itself that is unsustainable. When enslavement is for-itself it is so as a sustainable, albeit unfamiliar, mind of its own.

What is modern thinking to make of this strange non-masterful sense of self? The key to this again lies in the most important of Hegelian myths, the myth of *Aufheben* defined according to the propertied logic of mastery. In this myth the result of the *Aufheben* is an in-itself, a mastery, that overcomes previous negations or oppositions or contradictions. It is within this same myth that the slave is believed to achieve a mind of its own *in-itself* which overcomes the master's self-contradiction and becomes the truth in-itself of a universal class. This myth of *Aufheben* is the logic and metaphysics of the myth of counter-violence that Renault highlights. But when life and death are not totally defined within this myth of *Aufheben* a different, un-propertied picture of humanity commends itself. I rehearse this now.

Life and death posit themselves in cultures of preservation and negation. But one such culture of the relation of life and death dominates all others, and that is life and death preserved and negated as private property. Hegel's account demonstrates how life learns of singular death and singular self-consciousness in the risk necessitated by being for-another. But such self-consciousness is dependent for that self-consciousness upon its relation to death. How then, is this self-conscious life to preserve the relation to death that it needs for its experience of mortality, but without actually risking death in every encounter? How can it overcome death yet also preserve death? How can it live as preservation in-itself? The solution is to keep death alive and at a safe distance as the nothing in-itself of *property* which can live the master's vulnerability on his behalf. The slave, as property, is the living death that preserves life in a relation to death, but one that is removed, as Hegel says, from the risk that freedom requires.

Property creates and defines the myth of *Aufheben* in its own image. Negation is overcome, and preservation in-itself triumphs. Freedom is then defined in this logic of mastery as independence, just as enlightenment or myth-busting is defined as knowledge in-itself. Such propertied freedom and enlightenment are then reproduced in the cultures that base themselves on the myths of violence and counter-violence. Property determines the opposition to property in its own image and to its own advantage. Hence recent accusations that the tradition is exhausted and hence, too, the recent attraction of something messianic to break its hold.

But the propertied solution to mastery's contradictions is self-defeating. The necessity of this negation and its preservation has its truth not in having death again lived by a surrogate, but by living its own death. And it does this by means of an unfamiliar logic of education, one that is different from the masterful notion of enlightenment that enjoys victory over that which it defeats. Learning has its own logic or its own necessity in that learning must negate itself in order to preserve itself. Learning, here, is the risk that freedom requires and takes. It has 'the mind of its own' of the slave. Enlightenment is only propertied learning. But the Hegelian *Aufhebung* works not to a logic of mastery, not to a logic that overcomes what it negates, but to a logic of life and death that lives and dies, negates and preserves, as learning. Property will tempt this *Aufheben* back to the myth of counter-violence and challenge it to overcome property. If accepted, regardless of the outcome of such a challenge, mastery will win. If refused, mastery issues a renewed challenge: how will education get rid of property once

117

and for all? Education replies that when surrogates for negation and death, and for the risk of freedom, are no longer required, then property will have lost its *raison d'être*.[10]

The myth of myth

One final remark. Renault ends his piece by acknowledging the openness of learning in trying to avoid the mastery of myth-busting. He knows that he and we have learned something about Hegelian myths. And he is rightly concerned that if this is seen as myth-busting, it will only repeat a logic of mastery in the form of enlightenment triumphing over myth. Myth will have 'revealed to itself' or 'made explicit' something previously unknown to it and will have overcome its negative condition (30). To avoid such enlightened counter-violence Renault prefers to call his meta-myth a continuing variation on a theme, or a 'new chapter in the history it tells' (30). But if this is to avoid the mastery of being seen to offer a 'conclusion' (30) or completion then it is only a counter-*Aufheben* that in effect reverses the mastery of the myth of *Aufheben*. The relativity of Levi-Strauss's variations on a myth reverses the closure of any final conclusion by overcoming closure *per se*. In this familiar theatre of dogmatism and scepticism, once again life and death are known only in their propertied form.

If closure in-itself is not also to be closed in-itself by the mastery of something like contingency in-itself, then something new has to be learned here about the logic of this propertied aporia of life and death. When what is newly learned is made counter-*Aufheben* by Renault then the negation and preservation of learning figure once again as master and counter-master. Alternatively, when what is newly learned is that learning is not learning and counter-learning, but learning living its own life and death, then it is open to a logic and necessity different to that of property, of mastery, and of myth-busting.

Nigel Tubbs teaches at the University of Winchester. His books include Education in Hegel *(2008) and* Socrates on Trial *(2021).*

Notes

1. See Nigel Tubbs, *Socrates on Trial* (London: Bloomsbury, 2021), books 8–11.
2. See Jean Hyppolite, *Genesis and Structure of Hegel's Phenomenology of Spirit*, trans. Samuel Cherniak and John Heckman (Evanston: Northwestern University Press, 1974), 173.
3. Georg W.F. Hegel, *Phenomenology of Spirit*, trans. A.V. Miller (Oxford: Oxford University Press, 1977), §177.
4. Hegel, *Phenomenology*, §185.
5. This phrase is used in Tubbs, *Socrates*, book 8.
6. Alexandre Kojève, *Introduction to the Reading of Hegel*, trans. James H. Nichols Jr. (Ithaca: Cornell University Press, 1980), 22.
7. Hyppolite, *Genesis and Structure*, 173.
8. Hegel, *Phenomenology*, §196.
9. Hegel, *Phenomenology*, §194.
10. For a vision of such a city or a new Republic in which property becomes otiose, see Tubbs, *Socrates*, book 17.

www.ingramcontent.com/pod-product-compliance
Lightning Source LLC
Chambersburg PA
CBHW050716090526
44588CB00015B/2340